T0350175

Intelligent Big
Multimedia Databases

Intelligent Big
Multimedia Databases

Andreas Wichert

INESC-ID/ Instituto Superior Técnico -
Universidade de Lisboa, Portugal

 **World Scientific**

NEW JERSEY · LONDON · SINGAPORE · BEIJING · SHANGHAI · HONG KONG · TAIPEI · CHENNAI

Published by

World Scientific Publishing Co. Pte. Ltd.

5 Toh Tuck Link, Singapore 596224

USA office: 27 Warren Street, Suite 401-402, Hackensack, NJ 07601

UK office: 57 Shelton Street, Covent Garden, London WC2H 9HE

British Library Cataloguing-in-Publication Data
A catalogue record for this book is available from the British Library.

INTELLIGENT BIG MULTIMEDIA DATABASES

ISBN 978-981-4696-64-7

Printed in Singapore

for Manuela

Preface

Multimedia databases address a growing number of commercially important applications such as media on demand, surveillance systems and medical systems. The book will present essential and relevant techniques and algorithms for the development and implementation of large multimedia database systems.

The traditional relational database model is based on a relational algebra that is an offshoot of first-order logic and of the algebra of sets. The simple relational model is not powerful enough to address multimedia data. Because of this, multimedia databases are categorized into many major areas. Each of these areas are now so extensive that a major understanding of the mathematical core concepts requires the study of different fields such as information retrieval, digital image processing, fractals, machine learning, neuronal networks and high-dimensional indexing. This book unifies the essential concepts and recent algorithms into a single volume.

Overview of the book

The book is divided into ten chapters. We start with some examples and a description of multimedia databases. In addressing multimedia information, we are addressing digital data representations and how these data can be stored and manipulated. Multimedia data provide additional functionality than would be available in traditional forms of data. It allows new data access methods such as query by images in which the most similar image to the presented image is determined.

In the third chapter, we address the basic transform functions that are required when addressing multimedia databases, such as Fourier and cosine transforms as well as the wavelet transform, which is the most popular.

Starting from continuous wavelet transforms, we investigate the discrete fast wavelet transform for images, which is the basis for many compression algorithms. It is also related to the image pyramid, which will play an important role when addressing indexing techniques. We conclude the chapter with a description of the Karhunen-Loève transform, which is the basis of principal component analysis (PCA) and the k-means algorithm.

The size of a multimedia object may be huge. For the efficient storage and retrieval of large amounts of data, a clever method of encoding the information using fewer bits than the original representation is essential. This is the topic of the fourth chapter, which addresses compression algorithms. In addition to lossless compression, where no loss of information is present, lossy compression based on human perceptual features is essential for humans, and in this form of compression, we only represent the part of information that we experience.

Lossy compression is related to feature extraction, which will be described in the fifth chapter. We introduce the basic image features and outgoing from the image pyramid, and for the scale space, we describe the scale-invariant feature transform (SIFT). Next, we turn to speech and explain the speech formant frequencies. A feature vector represents the extracted features that describe multimedia objects. We introduce the distinction between the nearest neighbor similarity and the epsilon similarity for vectors in a database. When the features are represented by sequences of varying length, time wrapping is used to determine the similarity between them.

For the fast access of large data, divide and conquer methods are used, which are based on hierarchical structures, and this is discussed in the sixth chapter. For numbers, a tree can be used to prune branches in the processing queries. The access is fast: it is logarithmic in relation to the size of the database representing the numbers. Usually, the multimedia objects are described by vectors rather than by numbers. For low-dimensional vectors, metric index trees such as kd-trees and R-trees can be used. Alternatively, an index structure based on space-filling curves can be constructed.

The metric index trees operate efficiently when the number of dimensions is small. The growth of the number of dimensions has negative implications for the performance of multidimensional index trees; these negative effects are called the "curse of dimensionality." The "curse of dimensionality", which states that for an exact nearest neighbor, any algorithm for high dimension d and n objects must either use an n^d-dimension space or have a query time of $n \times d$ [Böhm *et al.* (2001)], [Pestov (2012)]. In approximate indexing, the data points that may be lost at some distances are distorted. Approximate indexing seems to be, in some sense, free from the curse of dimensionality. We describe the popular locality-sensitive hashing (LSH) algorithm in the seventh chapter.

An alternative method, which is based on exact indexing, is the generic multimedia indexing (GEMINI) and is introduced in the eighth chapter. The idea is to determine a feature extraction function that maps the high-dimensional objects into a low-dimensional space. In this low-dimensional space, a so-called "quick-and-dirty" test can discard the non-qualifying objects. Based on the ideas of the image pyramid and the scale space, this approach can be extended to the subspace tree. The search in such a structure starts at the subspace with the lowest dimension. In this subspace, the set of all possible similar objects is determined. The algorithm can be easily parallelized for large data. Chunks divide the database; each chunk may be processed individually by ten to thousands of servers.

In the following chapter, we address information retrieval for text databases. Documents are represented as sparse vectors. In sparse vectors, most components are zero. To address this, alternative indexing techniques based on random projections are described.

The tenth chapter addresses an alternative approach in feature extraction based on statistical supervised machine learning. Based on perceptrons, we introduce the back-propagation algorithm and the radial-basis function networks, where both may be constructed by the support-vector-learning algorithm. We conclude the book with a chapter about applications in which we highlight some architecture issues and present multimedia database applications in medicine.

The book is written for general readers and information professionals as well as students and professors that are interested in the topics of large multimedia databases and want to acquire the required essential knowledge. In addition, readers interested in general pattern recognition engineering can profit from the book. It is based on a lecture that was given for several years at the Universidade de Lisboa.

My research in recent years has benefited from many discussions with Ângelo Cardoso, Catarina Moreira and João Sacramento. I like to acknowledge financial support from Fundação para a Ciência e Tecnologia (Portugal) through the programme PTDC/EIA-CCO/119722/2010.

Finally, I would like to thank my son *André* and my loving wife *Manuela*, without their encouragement the book would be never finished.

Andreas Wichert

Contents

Preface   vii

1. Introduction   1

    1.1   Intelligent Multimedia Database   1
    1.2   Motivation and Goals   5
    1.3   Guide to the Reader   6
    1.4   Content   7

2. Multimedia Databases   13

    2.1   Relational Databases   13
          2.1.1   Structured Query Language SQL   15
          2.1.2   Symbolical artificial intelligence and relational
                  databases   16
    2.2   Media Data   19
          2.2.1   Text   19
          2.2.2   Graphics and digital images   21
          2.2.3   Digital audio and video   23
          2.2.4   SQL and multimedia   27
          2.2.5   Multimedia extender   27
    2.3   Content-Based Multimedia Retrieval   28
          2.3.1   Semantic gap and metadata   31

3. Transform Functions   35

    3.1   Fourier Transform   35
          3.1.1   Continuous Fourier transform   35
          3.1.2   Discrete Fourier transform   37

3.1.3   Fast Fourier transform   40

3.1.4   Discrete cosine transform   43

3.1.5   Two dimensional transform   45

3.2   Wavelet Transform   53

3.2.1   Short-term Fourier transform   53

3.2.2   Continuous wavelet transform   57

3.2.3   Discrete wavelet transform   61

3.2.4   Fast wavelet transform   70

3.2.5   Discrete wavelet transform and images   76

3.3   The Karhunen-Loève Transform   78

3.3.1   The covariance matrix   79

3.3.2   The Karhunen-Loève transform   83

3.3.3   Principal component analysis   84

3.4   Clustering   87

3.4.1   *k*-means   88

4.   Compression   91

4.1   Lossless Compression   91

4.1.1   Transform encoding   91

4.1.2   Lempel-Ziv   93

4.1.3   Statistical encoding   93

4.2   Lossy Compression   96

4.2.1   Digital images   96

4.2.2   Digital audio signal   99

4.2.3   Digital video 101

5.   Feature Extraction   105

5.1   Basic Image Features 105

5.1.1   Color histogram 105

5.1.2   Texture 108

5.1.3   Edge detection 109

5.1.4   Measurement of angle 111

5.1.5   Information and contour 112

5.2   Image Pyramid 113

5.2.1   Scale space 116

5.3   SIFT 116

5.4   GIST 123

5.5   Recognition by Components 123

5.6 Speech 124
   5.6.1 Formant frequencies 125
   5.6.2 Phonemes 125
5.7 Feature Vector 127
   5.7.1 Contours 127
   5.7.2 Norm 128
   5.7.3 Distance function 128
   5.7.4 Data scaling 129
   5.7.5 Similarity 130
5.8 Time Series 131
   5.8.1 Dynamic time warping 131
   5.8.2 Dynamic programming 132

6. Low Dimensional Indexing 133

6.1 Hierarchical Structures 133
   6.1.1 Example of a taxonomy 133
   6.1.2 Origins of hierarchical structures 134
6.2 Tree 138
   6.2.1 Search tree 138
   6.2.2 Decoupled search tree 139
   6.2.3 B-tree 140
   6.2.4 kd-tree 141
6.3 Metric Tree 147
   6.3.1 R-tree 147
   6.3.2 Construction 152
   6.3.3 Variations 152
   6.3.4 High-dimensional space 153
6.4 Space Filling Curves 156
   6.4.1 Z-ordering 156
   6.4.2 Hilbert curve 161
   6.4.3 Fractals and the Hausdorff dimension 167
6.5 Conclusion 169

7. Approximative Indexing 171

7.1 Curse of Dimensionality 171
7.2 Approximate Nearest Neighbor 173
7.3 Locality-Sensitive Hashing 173
   7.3.1 Binary Locality-sensitive hashing 174

            7.3.2   Projection-based LSH   176
            7.3.3   Query complexity LSH   176
      7.4   Johnson-Lindenstrauss Lemma   177
      7.5   Product Quantization   178
      7.6   Conclusion   180

8. High Dimensional Indexing   181

      8.1   Exact Search   181
      8.2   GEMINI   182
            8.2.1   1-Lipschitz property   183
            8.2.2   Lower bounding approach   185
            8.2.3   Projection operators   188
            8.2.4   Projection onto one-dimensional subspace   189
            8.2.5 l_p norm dependency   194
            8.2.6   Limitations   197
      8.3   Subspace Tree   198
            8.3.1   Subspaces   198
            8.3.2   Content-based image retrieval by image pyramid .   200
            8.3.3   The first principal component   203
            8.3.4   Examples   205
            8.3.5   Hierarchies   207
            8.3.6   Tree isomorphy   208
            8.3.7   Requirements   210
      8.4   Conclusion   211

9. Dealing with Text Databases   215

      9.1   Boolean Queries   215
      9.2   Tokenization   217
            9.2.1   Low-level tokenization   217
            9.2.2   High-level tokenization   218
      9.3   Vector Model   218
            9.3.1   Term frequency   218
            9.3.2   Information   219
            9.3.3   Vector representation   220
            9.3.4   Random projection   220
      9.4   Probabilistic Model   222
            9.4.1   Probability theory   222
            9.4.2   Bayes's rule   223

9.4.3   Joint distribution 224

9.4.4   Probability ranking principle 226

9.4.5   Binary independence model 226

9.4.6   Stochastic language models 230

9.5   Associative Memory 231

9.5.1   Learning and forgetting 232

9.5.2   Retrieval 233

9.5.3   Analysis 234

9.5.4   Implementation 235

9.6   Applications 236

9.6.1   Inverted index 236

9.6.2   Spell checker 237

10.   Statistical Supervised Machine Learning   239

10.1   Statistical Machine Learning 239

10.1.1   Supervised learning 239

10.1.2   Overfitting 240

10.2   Artificial Neuron 241

10.3   Perceptron 243

10.3.1   Gradient descent 245

10.3.2   Stochastic gradient descent 248

10.3.3   Continuous activation functions 248

10.4   Networks with Hidden Nonlinear Layers 249

10.4.1   Backpropagation 250

10.4.2   Radial basis function network 252

10.4.3   Why does a feed-forward networks with hidden nonlinear units work? 254

10.5   Cross-Validation 255

10.6   Support Vector Machine 256

10.6.1   Linear support vector machine 256

10.6.2   Soft margin 257

10.6.3   Kernel machine 257

10.7   Deep Learning 258

10.7.1   Map transformation cascade 258

10.7.2   Relation between deep learning and subspace tree 263

11.   Multimodal Fusion   269

11.1   Constrained Hierarchies 269

11.2   Early Fusion 270
11.3   Late Fusion 270
    11.3.1   Multimodal fusion and images 271
    11.3.2   Stochastic language model approach 271
    11.3.3   Dempster-Shafer theory 272

12. Software Architecture   275

12.1   Database Architecture 275
    12.1.1   Client-server system 275
    12.1.2   A peer-to-peer 276
12.2   Big Data 276
    12.2.1   Divide and conquer 276
    12.2.2   MapReduce 276
12.3   Evaluation 278
    12.3.1   Precision and recall 279

13. Multimedia Databases in Medicine   281

13.1   Medical Standards 281
    13.1.1   Health Level Seven 281
    13.1.2   DICOM 282
    13.1.3   PACS 282
13.2   Electronic Health Record 282
    13.2.1   Panoramix 283
13.3   Conclusion 289

Bibliography   291

Index   301

Chapter 1

Introduction

Multimedia databases are employed in an increasing number of commercially important applications, such as media-on-demand, surveillance systems and medical systems. Multimedia databases divide a subject into numerous major areas. Because each area is extensive, a major understanding of the mathematical core concepts requires an investigation of the different areas. In this book, we attempt to unify the essential concepts and recent algorithms.

1.1 Intelligent Multimedia Database

During prehistoric times and prior to the availability of written records, humans created images using cave paintings that were frequently located in areas of caves that were not easily accessible, as shown in Figure 1.1. These paintings were assumed to serve a religious or ceremonial purpose or to represent a method of communication with other members of the group [Curtis (2006); Dale (2006)]. As human societies emerged, the development of writing was primarily driven by administrative and accounting purposes. Approximately six thousand years ago, the complexity of trade and administration in Mesopotamia outgrew human memory. Writing became a necessity for recording transactions and administrative tasks [Wells (1922); Rudgley (2000)]. The earliest writing was based on pictograms; it was subsequently replaced by letters that represented linguistic utterances [Robinson (2000)]. Figure 1.2 displays a Sumerian clay tablet from 4200 years ago; it documents barley rations issued monthly to adults and children [Edzard (1997)]. Approximately 4000 years ago, the "Epic of Gilgamesh", which was one of the first great works of literature, appeared. It is a Mesopotamian poem about the life of the king of Uruk [Sandars (Pen-

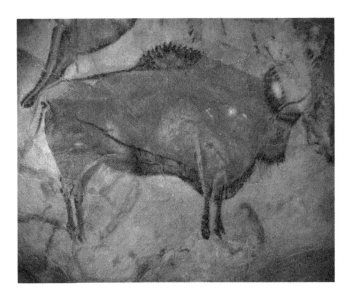

Fig. 1.1   Reproduction of a prehistoric painting that represents a bison of the cave of Altamira near Santander in Spain.

guin)]. The dominance of text endured in modern times until our century. Paper-based information processing was created. Letters advanced to symbols that no longer exist; they represent the constructs of a human society and simplify the process of representation. They are used to denote or refer to something other than themselves, namely, other things in the world (according to the pioneering work of Tarski [Tarski (1944, 1956, 1995)]). The first computers were primarily used for numerical and textual representation, as shown in Figure 1.3. Paper-based information processing was replaced by computer-based processing, and administrative tasks prompted the development of the original databases. Databases organized collections of symbolical and numerical data. The relational database model is based on relational algebra, which is related to first-order logic and the algebra of sets. The relational model is powerful enough to describe most organizational and administrative tasks of modern society. Figure 1.4 shows an interface of a relational database. In our century, the nature of documents and information is changing; more information is represented by images, films and unstructured text, as shown in Figure 1.5. This form of information is referred to as multimedia; it increasingly influences the way we compute, as shown in Figure 1.6. Multimedia representation frequently

Fig. 1.2   Sumerian clay tablet from 4200 years ago that documents barley rations issued monthly to adults and children. From Girsu, Iraq. British Museum, London.

corresponds to a pattern that mirrors the manner in which our biological sense organs describe the world [Wichert (2013b)]. This form of representation is frequently defined as vector-based representation or subsymbolical representation [Wichert (2009b)]. Databases that are based on multimedia representation are employed in entertainment, scientific and medical tasks and engineering applications, instead of administrative and organizational tasks. The elegant and simple relational model is not adequate for handling this form of representation and application.

Our human brain is more efficient in storing, processing and interpreting visual and audio information as represented by multimedia representation compared with symbolical representation. As a result, it is a source of inspiration for many AI algorithms that are employed in multimedia databases. We have a limited understanding of our human brain, see Figure 1.7. No elegant theory can describe the working principle of the human brain as simple as for example relational algebra.

When examining multimedia databases, we have to consider subsymbolical AI, algorithms from signal processing, image recognition, high-dimensional indexing and machine learning. The history of multimedia databases began

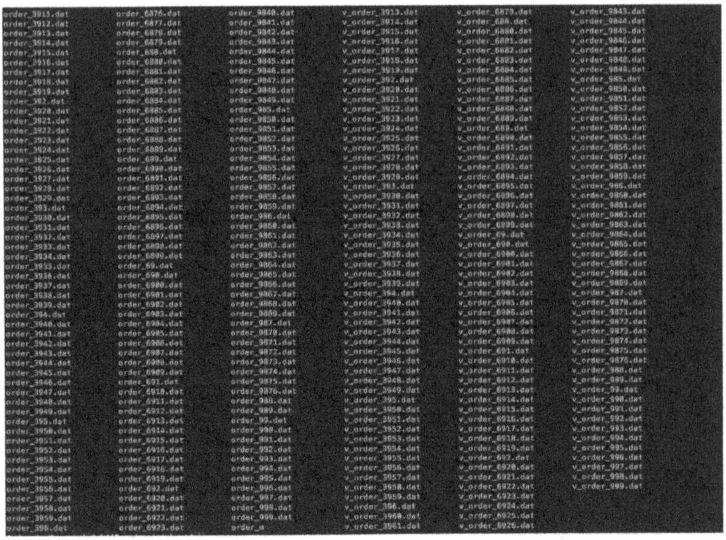

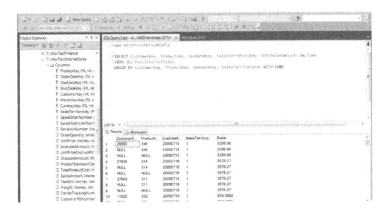

Fig. 1.3   Computer screen with textual representation of the information.

Fig. 1.4   Interface of a relational database.

with the use of photography to record known criminals as early as the 1840s
[Bate (2009)]. Early applications of multimedia database management systems only employed multimedia for presentational requirements: a sales
order processing system may include an online catalog that includes a picture of the offered product. The image can be retrieved by an application

Fig. 1.5 The nature of documents and information is changing; more information is represented by images, films and unstructured text.

process that referenced it using a traditional database record. However, this simple extension of the relational model is insufficient when handling multimedia information.

1.2 Motivation and Goals

When handling multimedia information, we have to consider digital data representations and explore questions regarding how these data can be stored and manipulated:

- How to pose a query?
- How to search?
- How can information be retrieved?

A multimedia database provides more functions than are available in the traditional form of data representation. One example of such a function is content-based image retrieval (CBIR). An image or drawn user input serves as a query example; as a result, all similar images should be retrieved. Feature extraction is a crucial step in content-based image retrieval. The extracted features of a CBIR system are mapped into points in a high-dimensional feature space, and the search is based on points that are close to a given query point in this space. For efficiency, these feature vectors

Fig. 1.6   Tablet computer and a smartphone.

are pre-computed and stored. The problem of a rapid exact search of large high-dimensional collections of objects is an important problem with applications in many different areas (multimedia, medicine, chemistry, and biology). This problem becomes even more urgent when handling large multimedia databases that cannot be processed by one server but require the processing power hundreds to thousands of servers.

1.3   Guide to the Reader

This book discusses some core ideas for the development and implementation of large multimedia database systems. The book is divided into thirteen chapters. We begin with some examples and a description of multimedia databases. We present basic and essential mathematical transform functions, such as the DFT and the wavelet transform. We present ideas of compression and the related feature extraction algorithms and explain how to build an indexing structure that can be employed in multimedia databases. We describe information retrieval techniques and essential statistical supervised machine learning algorithms. The book is based on the idea of hierarchical organization of information processing and representa-

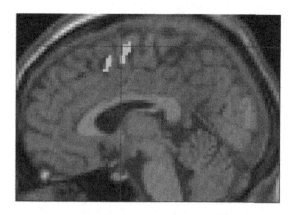

Fig. 1.7 We have a limited understanding of our human brain. An example of an fMRI image indicated row positions of changes of brain activity associated with various stimulus conditions. A cluster indicates a brain activity during an experiment [Wichert *et al.* (2002)].

tion, such as the wavelet transformation, the scale space, the subspace tree and deep learning.

1.4 Content

Multimedia Databases - Chapter 2 We begin with a short introduction to relational databases and introduce examples of popular multimedia information. Multimedia data enable new data access methods, such as query by images, in which the most similar image to the presented image is determined, which is also referred to as content-based image retrieval (CBIR).

Transform Functions - Chapter 3 Transform functions can be used for lossy and lossless compression; they form the basis of feature extraction and high-dimensional indexing techniques. We address a basic transform, such as Fourier and cosine transform, as well as the wavelet transform. Beginning with continuous wavelet transforms, we investigate the discrete fast wavelet transform for images, which is the basis for many compression algorithms. It is also related to the image pyramid, which will serve an important role when addressing indexing techniques. We conclude the chapter with a description of the Karhunen-Loève transform, which is the basis of principal component analysis (PCA) and the k-means algorithm.

Compression - Chapter 4　The size of a multimedia object may be immense. For the efficient storage and retrieval of large amounts of data, a clever method for encoding information using fewer bits than the original representation is essential. Two categories of compression exist: lossless compression and lossy compression. Both types of compression reduce the amount of the source information. No information is lost during lossless compression, which is not the case during lossy compression. When compressed information is decompressed in lossy compression, a minor loss of information and quality occurs. This is achieved by the identification of unnecessary or unimportant information that can be removed. Lossy compression is primarily based on human perceptual features.

Feature Extraction - Chapter 5　The extraction of primitive out of media data is referred to as feature extraction. The set of features represents relevant information about the input data in a certain context. The context is dependent on the desired task, which employs the reduced representation instead of the original input. The set of primitives is usually described by a feature vector. Feature extraction is related to compression algorithms and is frequently based on the transform function described in the previous chapter. During content-based media retrieval, the feature vectors are used to determine the similarity among the media objects. We introduce the basic image features and then describe the scale-invariant feature transform (SIFT). The GIST is a low-dimensional representation of a scene that does not require any segmentation. We highlight the concept of recognition by components (GEONS). Next, we explain the speech formant frequencies and phonemes. A feature vector represents the extracted features that describe multimedia objects. We introduce the distinction between the nearest neighbor similarity and the epsilon similarity. When the features are represented by sequences of varying length, time wrapping is employed to determine the similarity between these features.

Low Dimensional Indexing - Chapter 6　For fast access to large data sets, divide and conquer methods that are based on hierarchical structures are employed. For numbers, a tree can be used to prune branches in the processing queries. The access is fast: it is logarithmic in relation to the size of the database that represents the numbers. The multimedia objects are usually described by vectors instead of numbers. For low-dimensional vectors, metric index trees, such as kd-trees and R-trees, can be utilized. Alternatively, an index structure that is based on space-filling curves can be constructed. At the end of the chapter, we introduce fractals and the Hausdorff dimension.

Approximative Indexing - Chapter 7 The metric index trees efficiently operate with a small number of dimensions. An increase in the number of dimensions has negative implications for the performance of multidimensional index trees. These negative effects, which are referred to as the "curse of dimensionality", state that any algorithm for high dimension d and n objects for an exact nearest neighbor must either use an n^d-dimension space or have a query time of $n \times d$ [Böhm *et al.* (2001)], [Pestov (2012)]. In approximate indexing, data points that may be lost at certain distances are distorted. Approximate indexing seems to be free from the curse of dimensionality. We describe the popular locality-sensitive hashing (LSH) algorithm and its relation to Johnson-Lindenstrauss Lemma. We then present product quantization for the approximate nearest neighbor search.

High Dimensional Indexing - Chapter 8 Traditional indexing of multimedia data creates a dilemma. Either the number of features has to be reduced or the quality of the results in unsatisfactory or approximate query is preformed, which causes relative error during retrieval. The promise of the recently introduced subspace tree is the logarithmic retrieval complexity of extremely high-dimensional features. The subspace tree indicates that the conjecture "the curse of dimensionality" may be false. The search in this structure begins in the subspace with the lowest dimension. In this subspace, the set of all possible similar objects is determined. In the next subspace, additional metric information that corresponds to a higher dimension is used to reduce this set. This process is repeated. The theoretical estimation of temporal complexity of the subspace tree is logarithmic for the Gaussian (normal) distribution of the distances between the data points. The algorithm can be easily parallelized for large data. Chunks divide the database; each chunk may be individually processed by ten to thousands of servers.

Dealing with Text Databases - Chapter 9 The descriptor represents the relevant information about a text by a feature vector that indicates the presence or absence of terms. Terms are words with specific meanings in specific contexts; they may deviate from the meanings of the same words in other contexts. In addition, the frequency of the occurrence of each term in a document and the information content of the term according to the entire document collection can be employed. During information retrieval, the feature vectors are used to determine the similarity between text documents represented by the cosine of the angle between the vectors. Alternative indexing techniques based on random projections are described. We introduce an alternative biologically inspired mode "the associative memory" which is an ideal model for the information retrieval task. It is composed of a cluster of units that represent a simple model of a real biological.

Statistical Supervised Machine Learning - Chapter 10   Several parallels between human learning and machine learning exist. Various techniques are inspired from the efforts of psychologists and biologists to simulate human learning using computational models. Based on the Perceptron, we introduce the back-propagation algorithm and the radial-basis function network; both may be constructed by the support-vector learning algorithm. Deep learning models achieve high-level abstraction by architectures that are composed of multiple nonlinear transformations. They offer a natural progression from a low level structure to a high level structure as demonstrated by natural complexity. We describe the Map Transformation Cascade (MTC), in which the information is sequentially processed; each layer only processes information after the previous layer is completed. We show that deep learning is intimately related to the subspace tree and provide a possible explanation for the success of deep belief networks and its relation to the subspace tree,

Multimodal Fusion - Chapter 11   A multimodal search enables an information search using search queries in multiple data types, including text and other multimedia formats. The information is described by some feature vectors and categories that were determined by indexing structures or supervised learning algorithms. A feature vector or category can belong to different modalities, such as word, shape, or color. Either late or early fusion can be performed; however, our brain seems to perform a unimodal search with late fusion. Late fusion can be described by the stochastic language model approach and the Dempster-Shafer theory. In the Dempster-Shafer theory, measures of uncertainty can be associated with sets of hypotheses to distinguish between uncertainty and ignorance. The Dempster rule of combination derives common and shared beliefs between multiple sources and disregards all conflicting (nonshared) beliefs.

Software Architecture - Chapter 12   We highlight basic architecture issues related to the multimedia databases and big data. Big data is a large collection of unstructured data that cannot be processed with traditional methods, such as standard database management systems. It requires the processing power of hundreds to thousands of servers. To rapidly access big data, divide and conquer methods, which are based on hierarchical structures that can be parallelized, can be employed. Data can be distributed and processed by multiple processing units. Big data is usually processed by a distributed file-sharing framework for data storage and querying. MapReduce provides a parallel processing model and associated implementation to process a vast amount of data. Queries are split and distributed across parallel nodes (servers) and processed in parallel (the Map step).

Multimedia Databases in Medicine - Chapter 13   We present some examples of multimedia database applications in medicine. A clinical health record includes information that relates to current and historical health, medical conditions and medical imaging. Panoramix is an example of an electronic health record that incorporates a content-addressable multimedia database via a subspace tree. We introduce subpattern matching, which can be converted into entire multiple match queries of the same image. The idea is to compare the query image with an equally sized area of the database image. Using subpattern matching with a template that corresponds to a certain example, we can ask the question "How does my patient's tumor compare with similar cases?"

Chapter 2

Multimedia Databases

We begin with a short introduction to relational databases and introduce examples of popular multimedia information. Multimedia data enables new data access methods, such as query by images, in which the most similar image to the presented image is determined; it is also referred to as content based image retrieval (CBIR).

2.1 Relational Databases

The database evolved over many years from a simple data collection to multimedia databases:

- 1960: Data collections, database creation, information management systems (IMS) and database management systems (DBMS) were introduced. DBMS is the software that enables a computer to perform the database functions of storing, retrieving, adding, deleting and modifying data.
- 1970: The relational data model and relational database management systems were introduced by Tedd Codd (1923-2003). He also introduced a special-purpose programming language named Structured Query Language (SQL), which was designed for managing data held in a relational database management system. It is the most successful data model.
- 1980: The introduction of advanced data models were motivated by recent developments in artificial intelligence and programming languages: the object oriented model and the deductive model. Neither of these models gained popularity. They are difficult to model and are not flexible.

Table 2.1   Employee database with information about employees and
the department. Employee and department are entities represented by
symbols and the relationships are the links between these entities. A
relation is represented by a table of data.

employeeID	name	job	departmentID
9001	Claudia	DBA	99
8124	Ana	Programmer	101
8223	Antonio	Programmer	99
8051	Hans	System-Administrator	101

- 1990: Data mining and data warehousing were introduced.
- 2000: Stream data management, global information systems and
  multimedia databases become popular.

The relational database model is based on relational algebra that is an
offshoot of first-order logic and of algebra of sets. Logical representation is
motivated by philosophy and mathematics [Kurzweil (1990); Tarski (1995);
Luger and Stubblefield (1998)]. Predicates are functions that map objects'
arguments into true or false values. They describe the relation between
objects in a world which is represented by symbols. Symbols are used to
denote or refer to something other than themselves, namely other things
in the world (according to the, pioneering work of Tarski [Tarski (1944,
1956, 1995)]). They are defined by their occurrence in a relation. Symbols
are not present in the world; they are the constructs of a human society
and simplify the process of representation. Whenever a relation holds with
respect to some objects, the corresponding predicate is true when applied to
the corresponding objects. A relational database models entities by symbols
and relationships between them. Entities are the things in the real world
represented by symbols, like for example the information about employees
and the department they work for. Employee and department are entities
represented by symbols and the relationships are the links between these
entities. A relation is represented by a table, see Table 2.1.

Each column or attribute describes the data in each record in the table.
Each row in a table represents a record. If there is a functional dependency
between columns A and B in a given table,

$$A \to B,$$

then, the value of column A determines the value of column B. In the Table
2.1 *employeeID* determines the *name*

$$employeeID \to name.$$

A key is a column (or a set of columns) that can be used to identify a row in a table. Different possible keys exist; the primary key is used to identify a single row (record) and foreign keys represent links between tables. In the Table, 2.1 *employeeID* is a primary key and *departmentID* is a foreign key that indicates links to other tables. A database schema is the structure or design of the database without any data. The employee database schema of Table 2.1 is represented as

$$employee(employeeID, name, job, departmentID).$$

A database is usually represented by several tables. During the design of a database, the design flaws are removed by rules that describe what we should and should not do in our table structures. These rules are referred to as the normal forms. They break tables into smaller tables that form a better design. A better design prevents insert anomalies and deletion anomalies. For example, if we delete all employees of department 99, we no longer have any record that indicates that department 99 exists. If we insert data into a flawed table, the correct rows in the database are not distinct. The relational model has been very successful in handling structured data but has been less successful with media data.

2.1.1 Structured Query Language SQL

The role of the Structured Query Language SQL in a relational database is limited to checking the data types of values and comparing using the Boolean logic. The general form is

```
select a1, a2, ... an
  from r1, r2, ... rm
  where P
  [order by ....]
  [group by ...]
  [having ...]
```

For example

```
select name
  from student, takes
  where student.ssn = takes.ssn
  and takes.c-id = 15-826.
```

Numeric types are called numbers, mathematical operations on numbers are preformed by operators and scalar numerical functions in SQL. Scalar functions perform a calculation, usually based on input values that are provided as arguments, and return a numeric value. For example

```
select 9 mod 2
```

```
9 mod 2
1.
```

There are no numerical vectors, we can not define a distance function like

```
select * from image
where dist(image, given-image) <= 100
```

and preform similarity search. For example, it is not possible to find pairs of branches with similar sales patterns.

2.1.2 *Symbolical artificial intelligence and relational databases*

Knowledge representation in symbolical artificial intelligence tries to model the way we humans represent and process knowledge. Of course this representation is far more complex then the organisational and administrative knowledge representation by relational databases. The relational model could be seen as AI motivated since it is based on the first-order logic. Beside this, the influence of symbolical AI is mainly marginal and is related to the object-oriented representation and the rule based systems that will be introduced in the next sections. This is not the case with subsymbolical artificial intelligence, it plays an essential part in the domain of data mining and multimedia databases.

2.1.2.1 *Semantic nets and frames*

Frames describe individual objects and entire classes [Minsky (1975, 1986); Winston (1992)], they are composed of slots which can be either attributes, which describe the classes or object, or links to other frames. With the aid of links, a hierarchy can be represented in which classes or objects are parts of more general classes. In this taxonomic representation, frames inherit attributes of the more general classes (see Figure 2.1). Frames can be viewed as generalization of semantic nets. They are psychologically motivated and

were popularized in computer science by Marvin Minsky. One important
result of the frame theory is the object-oriented approach in programming
and the object-oriented extensions of SQL. The object-oriented extensions

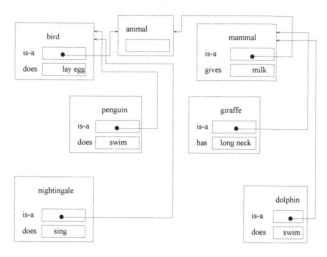

Fig. 2.1 Taxonomic frame representation of some animals.

of SQL:1999 (formerly SQL3) provides the primary basis for supporting
object-oriented structures and the definition of new primitive types, called
user-defined primitive types. Related to object-oriented programming language is the object database. An object database stores complex data
and relationships between data directly, the database is integrated with
the object-oriented programming language. The programmer can maintain
consistency within one environment, this makes it suitable for complex applications. A big disadvantage of this approach is lack of a clear division
between the database model and the application.

2.1.2.2 *Expert systems*

Expert systems are used in artificial intelligence systems to represent some
specific knowledge and to imitate the reasoning skills of a human expert
when some problems are solved [Jackson (1999)]. An expert system is composed of two separated parts, of the inference engine and the knowledge
base [Lucas and van der Gaag (1991); Jackson (1999)]. The knowledge
base contains essential information about the problem domain and is often
represented as facts and rules. A rule [Winston (1992); Russell and Norvig

(1995); Luger and Stubblefield (1998)] contains several "if" patterns and one or more "then" patterns. A pattern in the context of rules is an individual predicate which can be negated together with arguments. The rule can establish a new fact by the "then" part, the conclusion whenever the "if" part, the premise, is true. When variables become identified with values they are bound to these values. Whenever the variables in a pattern are replaced by values, the pattern is said to be instantiationed. Here is an example of rules with a variable x:

- If $\underbrace{\text{(flies(x)} \lor \text{feathes(x))} \land \text{lays eggs(x)}}_{premise}$ then $\underbrace{\text{bird(x)}}_{conclusion}$
- If bird(x) $\land$ swims(x) then penguin(x)
- If bird(x) $\land$ sings(x) then nightinagle(x)

The following fact are present:

- feathers(Pit)
- lays eggs(Pit)
- swims(Pit)
- flies(Airbus)

Pit is a bird because the premise of the first rule is true when x is bound to Pit. Because bird(Pit), the premise of the second rule is true and Pit is a penguin. The inference engine applies the rules to the known facts to deduce new facts. Inference engines can also perform an explanation, which justifies the new determined facts. By the separation of the represented knowledge and the inference mechanism a greater flexibility is achieved. In traditional computer program the knowledge and the inference logic is embedded in the code. The rules are represented in a simple and intuitive way so that they can be easily understood by a domain experts rather than IT experts. Expert systems are used in problem solving, like configuration of a system, hypothesis testing or in diagnostic systems. They can as well represent administrative and organisational knowledge, however the main goal is to simulate the reasoning skills of a human expert through knowledge (like for example a manager or a lawyer) rather then the representation of large collection of data. A knowledge base management system represents the integration of both modalities, of the relational database and an expert system. By the integration it is possible to develop software for applications that require knowledge oriented processing of distributed knowledge.

2.2 Media Data

When addressing multimedia in databases, we have to consider digital data representation. We will introduce examples of the most popular multimedia information, namely, text, graphics, digital images, digital audio and digital video.

2.2.1 *Text*

Text plays the main role in information retrieval (IR). There are four types of text that are used to produce pages of documents;

- unformatted text,
- formatted,
- hypertext,
- text with mark-up language.

Unformatted text is also known as plaintext enables pages to be created which compromise strings of fixed-sized characters from a limited character set. American Standard Code for Information Interchange, the ASCII character set, is the most popular code. It was developed based on the English alphabet around 1963. Each character is represented by 7 bits. There are $128 = 2^7$ alternative characters, see Figure 2.2. In addition to all normal alphabetic characters, numeric characters and printable characters, the set also includes a number of control characters. The character set was extended to 8 bits by adding additional character definitions after the first 128 characters. The limitation of the ASCII character set was overcome by Unicode [Consortium (2006)]. Unicode is an industry standard that is designed to enable text and symbols from all writing systems of the world to be consistently represented and manipulated by computers. The standard has been implemented in many recent technologies, including XML, the Java programming language, and modern operating systems. Unicode covers almost all current scripts (writing systems), including Arabic, Armenian, Thai and Tibetan, as shown in Figure 2.3. Most popular encodings include:

- UTF-8: an 8-bit, variable-width encoding that is compatible with ASCII.
- UTF-16: a 16-bit, variable-width encoding 16 is the native internal representation of text in many operating systems.

Intelligent Big Multimedia Databases

Char	Dec	Oct	Hex	Char	Dec	Oct	Hex	Char	Dec	Oct	Hex	Char	Dec	Oct	Hex
(nul)	0	0000	0x00	(sp)	32	0040	0x20	@	64	0100	0x40	`	96	0140	0x60
(soh)	1	0001	0x01	!	33	0041	0x21	A	65	0101	0x41	a	97	0141	0x61
(stx)	2	0002	0x02	"	34	0042	0x22	B	66	0102	0x42	b	98	0142	0x62
(etx)	3	0003	0x03	#	35	0043	0x23	C	67	0103	0x43	c	99	0143	0x63
(eot)	4	0004	0x04	$	36	0044	0x24	D	68	0104	0x44	d	100	0144	0x64
(enq)	5	0005	0x05	%	37	0045	0x25	E	69	0105	0x45	e	101	0145	0x65
(ack)	6	0006	0x06	&	38	0046	0x26	F	70	0106	0x46	f	102	0146	0x66
(bel)	7	0007	0x07	'	39	0047	0x27	G	71	0107	0x47	g	103	0147	0x67
(bs)	8	0010	0x08	(	40	0050	0x28	H	72	0110	0x48	h	104	0150	0x68
(ht)	9	0011	0x09	)	41	0051	0x29	I	73	0111	0x49	i	105	0151	0x69
(nl)	10	0012	0x0a	*	42	0052	0x2a	J	74	0112	0x4a	j	106	0152	0x6a
(vt)	11	0013	0x0b	+	43	0053	0x2b	K	75	0113	0x4b	k	107	0153	0x6b
(np)	12	0014	0x0c	,	44	0054	0x2c	L	76	0114	0x4c	l	108	0154	0x6c
(cr)	13	0015	0x0d	-	45	0055	0x2d	M	77	0115	0x4d	m	109	0155	0x6d
(so)	14	0016	0x0e	.	46	0056	0x2e	N	78	0116	0x4e	n	110	0156	0x6e
(si)	15	0017	0x0f	/	47	0057	0x2f	O	79	0117	0x4f	o	111	0157	0x6f
(dle)	16	0020	0x10	0	48	0060	0x30	P	80	0120	0x50	p	112	0160	0x70
(dc1)	17	0021	0x11	1	49	0061	0x31	Q	81	0121	0x51	q	113	0161	0x71
(dc2)	18	0022	0x12	2	50	0062	0x32	R	82	0122	0x52	r	114	0162	0x72
(dc3)	19	0023	0x13	3	51	0063	0x33	S	83	0123	0x53	s	115	0163	0x73
(dc4)	20	0024	0x14	4	52	0064	0x34	T	84	0124	0x54	t	116	0164	0x74
(nak)	21	0025	0x15	5	53	0065	0x35	U	85	0125	0x55	u	117	0165	0x75
(syn)	22	0026	0x16	6	54	0066	0x36	V	86	0126	0x56	v	118	0166	0x76
(etb)	23	0027	0x17	7	55	0067	0x37	W	87	0127	0x57	w	119	0167	0x77
(can)	24	0030	0x18	8	56	0070	0x38	X	88	0130	0x58	x	120	0170	0x78
(em)	25	0031	0x19	9	57	0071	0x39	Y	89	0131	0x59	y	121	0171	0x79
(sub)	26	0032	0x1a	:	58	0072	0x3a	Z	90	0132	0x5a	z	122	0172	0x7a
(esc)	27	0033	0x1b	;	59	0073	0x3b	[	91	0133	0x5b	{	123	0173	0x7b
(fs)	28	0034	0x1c	<	60	0074	0x3c	\	92	0134	0x5c	|	124	0174	0x7c
(gs)	29	0035	0x1d	=	61	0075	0x3d	]	93	0135	0x5d	}	125	0175	0x7d
(rs)	30	0036	0x1e	>	62	0076	0x3e	^	94	0136	0x5e	~	126	0176	0x7e
(us)	31	0037	0x1f	?	63	0077	0x3f	_	95	0137	0x5f	(del)	127	0177	0x7f

Fig. 2.2   ASCII table of the first 128 characters.

- 22 (hex 7A)   small Z (Latin)   007A   z
- 27700 (hex 6C34)   water (Chinese)   6C34   水

Fig. 2.3   Some example of the Unicode, Latin and Chinese.

Formatted text   is used by word processors. It enables pages and complete documents, which are composed of strings of characters of different styles, size and shapes with tables, graphics, and images inserted at appropriate points, to be created.

Hypertext   enables an integrated set of documents that each comprise formatted text, which have defined linkages created by hyperlinks. Hyper-Text Markup Language (HTML) is an example of a more general set of mark-up languages.

Mark-up languages   are used to describe how the content of a document is to be presented on a printer or a display. It comprises a language for annotating a document in a manner that is syntactically distinguishable from the text. Examples of mark-up languages include Postscript, TeX, LaTeX, and Standard Generalization Mark-Up Language (SGLM) on which Extensible Markup Language (XML) and HTML are based.

2.2.2 Graphics and digital images

2.2.2.1 Vector graphics

Vector graphics use geometrical primitives, such as points, lines, curves, and polygons, which are based on mathematical equations to represent images in computer graphics. Vector graphics are used in contrast to the term raster graphics (refer to Figure 2.4), which is the representation of images as a collection of pixels (dots) and is related to mark-up languages (refer to Figure 2.5). Consider a circle of radius r. The main pieces of information

Fig. 2.4   A simple raster graphic represented by binary pixels.

that a program needs to draw this circle are the radius r, the location of the center point of the circle, the stroke line style and color and the fill style and color (possibly transparent). The amount of information translates to a much smaller file size compared with large raster images (refer to Figure 2.6), and the size of representation does not depend on the dimensions of the object. A user can indefinitely zoom in on a circle arc and it remains smooth. In Figure 2.7, an image in a pixel-based representation is converted to a vector graphics representation. In Figure 2.8 (a), we zoom in on the pixel-based image (refer to Figure 2.7); we can recognize the pixels. In Figure 2.8 (b) we zoom in the same area this time in the vector based representation, the regions remains smooth.

2.2.2.2 Raster graphics

A raster graphics image is a data file or structure that represents a generally rectangular grid of pixels or points of color on a computer monitor, paper, or other display device. The VGA is an example of a video graphics array type of display that consists of a matrix of 640 horizontal pixels by 480 vertical pixels. Each pixel is represented by 8 bits, which yields $2^8 = 256$

Graphics3D[{Blue, Cylinder[], Yellow, Polygon[{{-3, -3, -2}, {-3, 3, -2}, {3, 3, -2}, {3, -3, -2}}], Green, Opacity[.3], Cuboid[{-2, -2, -2}, {2, 2, -1}]}]

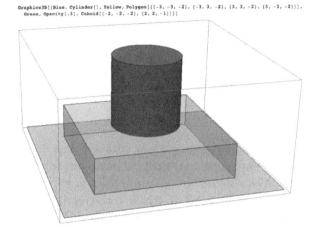

Fig. 2.5   Example of vector graphics.

different colors. The images in the red, green, and blue (RGB) color space consist of colored pixels that are defined by three numbers: one for red, one for green and one for blue (RGB image). The range of different colors that can be produced is dependent on the pixel depth. For a 12 bit pixel depth, four bits per primary color yields

$$2^4 \cdot 2^4 \cdot 2^4 = 4096$$

different colors. For a 24 bit pixel depth, 8 bits per primary color yields 16 million colors. The human eye cannot discriminate among this range of colors. Less colorful images require less information per pixel. An image with only black and white pixels requires only a single bit for each pixel. A black and white picture with 256 different grey values requires 8 bits per pixel. The mean value of the three RGB numbers represents approximately the grey value. A voxel (a portmanteau of the words volumetric and pixel) is a volume element that represents a value on a regular grid in three-dimensional space. Analogous to a pixel, which represents 2D image data, voxels are frequently employed in the visualization and analysis of medical and scientific 3D data (refer to Figure 2.9).

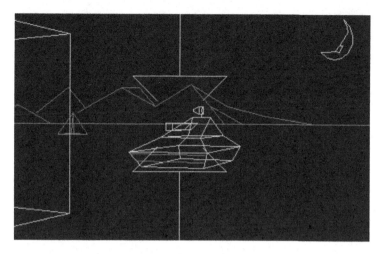

Fig. 2.6 Battlezone is an arcade game that was developed by Atari in 1980 using vector graphics. Vector graphics were used for some video games in 1980 due to limited computing resources.

2.2.3 Digital audio and video

2.2.3.1 Audio

In signal processing, sampling is the reduction of a continuous signal to a discrete signal. It is the conversion of a sound wave (a continuous time signal) to a sequence of samples (a discrete time signal; refer to Figure 2.10). The sampling frequency or sampling rate f_s is defined as the number of samples obtained in one second; for T seconds, f_s is

$$f_s = \frac{1}{T}$$

T is referred to as the sample period or sampling interval. The sampling rate is measured in hertz (symbol Hz). Prior to 1960, it was measured in cycles per second (cps). Since 1960, it was officially replaced by the hertz. The sampling or Nyquist theorem indicates a relation between continuous signals $x(t)$ in time and discrete signals $x[n]$, It states that if a function $x(t)$ in time t contains no frequencies higher than M hertz, it can be completely determined by its ordinates for a series of points spaced

$$\frac{1}{2 \cdot M}$$

seconds apart. With

$$T = \frac{1}{f_s}$$

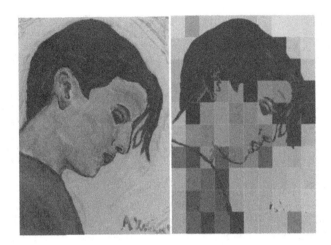

Fig. 2.7   An image of Sophie Scholl in a pixel-based representation is converted to a vector graphics representation.

T represents the interval between the samples, the samples of function $x(t)$ are represented as $x[n]$ with

$$x[n] = x(nT) \tag{2.1}$$

for all integers n. The double-rate requirement, as specified by the sampling theorem, is approximately used for signals that represent speech and music. For speech signals, the sampling rate is 50Hz - 10kHz; for stereo signals, this value is multiplied by two. For music-quality audio, the sampling rate is 15Hz - 20kHz; for stereo signals, $2 \cdot 20$ kHz, which is 40 kHz (samples per second). The number of bits per sample must be selected to ensure that the quantization noise generated by the sampling process remains at an acceptable level (reconstructing). In speech, 12 bits per sample are used; in music, 16 bits per sample are used. In most applications that involve music, stereo signals are required and two stereo signals need to be digitized. In practice, a lower sampling rate and fewer bits per sample are utilized.

2.2.3.2   *Video*

Video is referred to as moving pictures or frames. The problem of an illusion of motion when a series of video frames is displayed in rapid succession instead of the perception of individual frames has not been resolved. According to the theory of persistence of vision, a visual form of memory,

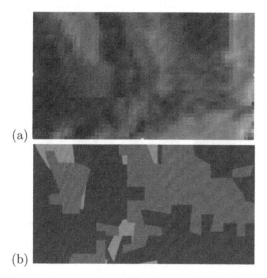

(a)

(b)

Fig. 2.8 (a) We zoom in on the a pixel-based image (refer to Figure 2.7); we can recognize the pixels. (b) We zoom in on the same area in the vector-based representation; the regions remain smooth.

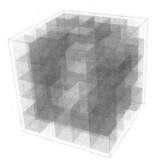

Fig. 2.9   3D Figure represented by voxels.

which is known as iconic memory, has been described as the cause of this phenomenon. The illusion is explained by the fact that the human eye briefly retains an image of a frame. However, this theory is rejected and considered to be a myth. A possible explanation is based on temporal integration, which consists of a temporal platform with a duration of 2 to 3 seconds, in which the signals from different sources are integrated [Pöppel (2009)].

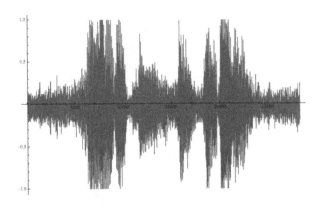

Fig. 2.10   The sound signal "You return safely" spoken during Apollo 13 mission.

In multimedia databases, video signals need to be in digital form to store them. A digital video film is composed of images and sound that are separately stored. We measure the rate at which frames are displayed in frames per second (FPS). For example, each second, 25 frames (25 FPS) represents an image with a size of 250 kb, which are represented by a bit rate (BR) of 6.25 Mb/sec. A frame represents a digital color image in a YCbCr color space [Halsall (2001)], which is extensively employed in video. The YCbCr color space is closer to the human perception than the RGB color space. The retina of the human eye is covered with light-sensitive receptors [Hubel (1988)]. Two types of receptors exists: rods and cons. Rods are primarily used for night vision and the detection of movements. They sense shades of grey and cannot discriminate among colors. Because more rods exist than cons, humans are more sensitive to greyscale information than color information. Cones are utilized to sense color. Three photopigments (blue, green, and red) are utilized to sense color; however, they are not evenly distributed. Few blue photopigments and numerous red photopigments exist. The YCbCr color space represents this uneven distribution compared with the RGB color space. In the YCbCr color space, Y represent the greyscale of the image, Cb represents the scaled difference between blue and Y and Cr represent the scaled difference between red and Y.

2.2.4 *SQL and multimedia*

SQL was extended to the use of multimedia for presentational requirements. A sales order processing system can include an online catalog that contains a picture of the offered product. The image can be retrieved via a traditional database record with a key. The extended SQL language is named SQL:1999 (formerly SQL3); it offers two new data types that can store media data [Dunckley (2003)].

- BLOB for binary large objects.
- CLOB for character large objects.

The types are restricted in terms of many SQL operations; for example, for use with comparisons instead of pure equality tests. The manner in which new data types are implemented varies. The media objects can be externally stored as operating system files or in the database.

- Binary large objects (BLOB) that are locally stored in the database and contain audio, image, or video data or other heterogeneous media data.
- File-based large objects (BFILE) that are locally stored in operating system-specific file systems and contain audio, image, or video data or other heterogeneous media data. A data link enables the SQL to provide a transparent interface for the data that is stored in both the database and the external files.

Because SQL editors cannot cope with the display or input of multimedia in a database, an additional multimedia extender outside the relational database framework is required. The multimedia extender supports popular formats (audio, image, and video data formats) and enables access via traditional and Web interfaces. They also enable querying using media content with optional specialized indexing methods.

2.2.5 *Multimedia extender*

A multimedia extender is a module outside the relational database model. It is frequently implemented in a programming language, such as Java or C#. The multimedia extender communicates with the relational database via an interface (for example, JDBC for Java). It extends the reliability, availability, and data management of the database as follows:

- Support for popular audio, image, and video data formats.

- Access via traditional and Web interfaces.
- Querying using associated relational data.
- Querying using extracted metadata.
- Querying using media content with optional specialized indexing methods. This type of querying is referred to as content-based multimedia retrieval.

2.3 Content-Based Multimedia Retrieval

Traditional text-based multimedia search engines use text-based retrieval methods, which frequently requires manual annotation of multimedia, such as images. An alternative approach is content-based multimedia retrieval. Content-based image retrieval (CBIR) is the most common content-based visual information retrieval application. Other examples include content-based music retrieval or content-based video retrieval. Different content-based query types, such as exact queries and approximative queries, exists. An exact query can be represented by a predicate that describes the image; for example, we are searching images in which more than half of the image represents the sky,

$$amount\ sky > 60\%.$$

An approximate query can be represented by an image example or a sketch. The retrieval can be performed by a query (example) image to determine the most similar images (refer to Figure 2.11). For music retrieval, an approximate query can be represented by singing or humming. For video retrieval, the video segment can be decomposed into shots; each shot is represented by a representative frame to enable a query to be performed by CBIR. Generating transcripts from spoken dialogs can also enable text-based retrieval methods. During content-based image retrieval (CBIR), the image is the only available independent information (low-level pixel data). It is a technique for retrieving images that are based on automatically derived features. An image or drawn user input serves as a query example, and all similar images should be retrieved as the result. An image query is performed by the generation of a weighted combination of features and its direct comparison with the features stored in the database. A similarity metric (e.g., the Euclidean distance) is applied to find the nearest neighbors of the query example in the feature vector space. Feature extraction is a crucial step in content-based image retrieval. In traditional content-based

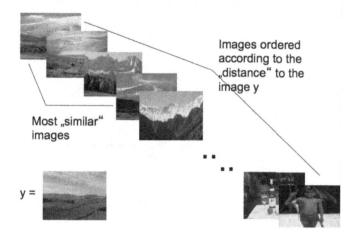

Images ordered according to the „distance" to the image y

Most „similar" images

y =

Fig. 2.11   The retrieval by a query (example) image.

image retrieval methods, features that describe important properties of images are employed, such as color, texture and shape [Flickner *et al.* (1995)], [Smeulders *et al.* (2000)], [Quack *et al.* (2004)], [Dunckley (2003)].

The impact of the features is dependent on the image domain, as demonstrated by two different domains of oil paintings (refer to Figure 2.12) and photos (refer to Figure 2.13).

The features that describe the properties of the image are referred to as the image signature. Any query operations solely address the image signature and do not address the image. Using the image signature, a significant compression is achieved. For a better performance with large image databases, an index for searching the image signatures is constructed. Every image inserted into the database is analyzed, a compact representation of its content is stored in the signature and the index structure is updated. Traditional data structures are insufficient. The feature extraction mechanism and the indexing structure are a part of the multimedia extender.

The best known content-based image retrieval system is the IBM query by image content (QBIC) search system [Niblack *et al.* (1993)], [Flickner *et al.* (1995)]. The IBM QBIC employs features for color, texture and shape, which are mapped into a feature vector. Similar features are employed by the Oracle Multimedia (former interMedia) extender, which extends a relational database to enable it to perform CBIR [Dunckley (2003)]. The VORTEX system [Hove (2004)] combines techniques from computer vision

Fig. 2.12   Oil paintings.

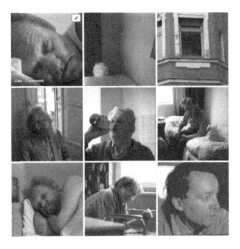

Fig. 2.13   Some photos.

with a thesaurus for object and shape description. In [Mirmehdi and Periasamy (2001)], human visual and perceptual systems are mimicked. Perceptual color features and color texture features are extracted to describe the characteristics of perceptually derived regions in the image. Wavelet-based image indexing and searching WBIIS [Wang *et al.* (1997)] is an image indexing and retrieval algorithm with partial sketch image searching capability for large image databases that are based on wavelets. The algorithm characterizes the color variations over the spatial extent of the image in a manner that provides semantically meaningful image comparisons.

2.3.1 *Semantic gap and metadata*

2.3.1.1 *Semantic gap*

The majority of the CBIR systems suffer from the "semantic gap" problem. Semantic gap is the lack of coincidence between the information that can be extracted from an image and the interpretation of that image [Dunckley (2003)]. The semantic gap exists because an image is usually described by the image signature, which is composed of features such as the color distribution, texture or shape without any additional semantical information. The semantic gap can be overcome by

- image understanding systems,
- manual annotation of the image (metadata).

2.3.1.2 *Image understanding*

A solution to the semantic gap problem is the construction of image understanding systems, which identifies objects using computer vision techniques [Winston (1992); Russell and Norvig (2003)]. This approach, which was developed in the field of AI, only functions in a narrow domain and is computationally expensive. The automatic derivation of a description from an image for CBIR is extremely difficult. Known examples of CBIR systems, which identify and annotate objects, are [Blei and Jordan (2003); Chen and Wang (2004); Li and Wang (2003b); Wang *et al.* (2001)]. Jean et al. proposed [Jeon *et al.* (2003)] an automatic approach to the annotation and retrieval of images based on a training set of images. The approach assumes that regions in an image can be described using a small vocabulary of blobs. Blobs are generated from image features using clustering. In [Li and Wang (2003a)], categorized images are employed to train a dictionary of hundreds of statistical models, in which each model represents a concept. Images of any given concept are regarded as instances of a stochastic process that characterizes the concept. To measure the extent of the association between an image and the textual description of a concept, the likelihood of the occurrence of an image based on the characterization of stochastic process is computed.

2.3.1.3 *Metadata*

The semantic gap can also be overcome by metadata. Metadata can be defined as "data about data". Metadata addresses the content structure and similarities of data. It can be represented as text using keywords to ensure that traditional text-based search engines can be utilized. The metadata and the original data need to be maintained and we need to know how to store and update the data, which is specified by multimedia standards.

2.3.1.4 *Multimedia standards*

Multimedia standards were developed to ensure interoperability and scalability. Popular examples are as follows:

- ID3 is a metadata container that is predominantly used in conjunction with the MP3 audio file format. It enables information such as the title, artist, album, track number, or other information about the file to be stored in the file[1].
- EXIF is a specification for metadata that employs an image file format that is used by digital cameras[2]. When taking a picture, the digital equipment can automatically embed information such as the date and time or GPS and other camera parameters. Typically, this metadata is directly embedded in the file. Both JPEG and TIFF file formats foresee the possibility of embedding extra information.
- A general example is the Dublin core, which provides substantial flexibility, is easy to learn and ensures interoperability with other schemes [Dunckley (2003)]. The Dublin core metadata can be used to describe the resources of an information system[3]. They can be located in an external document or loaded into a database, which enables the data to be indexed. The Dublin core metadata can also be included in the web pages within META tags, which are placed within the HEAD elements of an HTML document.
- MPEG-7 is a universal multimedia description standard. It supports abstraction levels for metadata from low-level signal characteristics to high-level semantic information. It creates a standardized multimedia description framework and enables content-

---

[1]http://*id3.org*
[2]http://*www.cipa.jp/index_e.html*
[3]http://*dublincore.org*

based access based on the descriptions of multimedia content and structure using the metadata. MPEG-7 and MPEG-21 are description standards for audio, image and video data [Manjunath *et al.* (2002)], [Kim *et al.* (2005)]; however, they do not make any assumptions about the internal storage format in a database. The MPEG-21 standard is an extension of the MPEG-7 standard by managing restrictions for digital content usage.

Note that neither MPEG-7, MPEG-21 nor any other metadata standard offers solutions to the problems of feature extraction and indexing [Dunckley (2003)]. Manuel textual annotation cannot replace automatic feature extraction because it is difficult and time-consuming. Because images do not attempt to explain their meaning, text description can be highly subjective. An image can represent different things to different people and can mean different things to the same person at different times. A person's keywords do not have to agree with the keywords of the indexer.

Chapter 3

Transform Functions

Transform functions can be used for lossy and lossless compression; they are the basis of feature extraction and of high dimensional indexing techniques.

3.1 Fourier Transform

It is always possible to translate periodic waveforms into a set of sinusoidal waveforms. Adding together a number of sinusoidal waveforms can approximate any periodic waveform. Fourier analysis tells us what particular sets of sinusoids compose a particular complex waveform by mapping the signal from the time domain to the frequency domain.

3.1.1 *Continuous Fourier transform*

The frequency is the number of occurrences of a repeating event per unit time[1]. The period is the duration of one cycle of an event and is the reciprocal of the frequency f. For example, if we count 40 events in two seconds, the frequency is

$$\frac{40}{2\ s} = \frac{20}{1\ s} = 20\ \frac{1}{s} = 20\ hertz$$

then the period is

$$T = p = \frac{1}{20}s.$$

A repeated event can be a rotation, oscillation, or a periodic wave. For periodic waves, one period corresponds to the time in which a full cycle of

---

[1]Section 3.1.1 is similar, with some slight changes, to section 9.1, section 3.1.2 is similar to section 9.2 and section 3.1.3 is similar to section 9.4 of the book Principles of Quantum Artificial Intelligence by the same author

a wave passes. A cycle is represented by the wavelength. The velocity v of the wave is represented by the wavelength λ divided by the period p. Because the frequency f is the inverse of the period, we can represent the velocity as

$$v = \frac{\lambda}{p} = \lambda \cdot f \tag{3.1}$$

and the frequency as

$$f = \frac{1}{T} = \frac{1}{p} = \frac{v}{\lambda}. \tag{3.2}$$

If something changes rapidly, then we say that it has a high frequency. If it does not change rapidly, i.e., it changes smoothly, we say that it has a low frequency. The Fourier transform changes a signal from the time domain $x(t) \in \mathbf{C}$ to the frequency domain $X(f) \in \mathbf{C}$. The representation of the signal $x(t)$ in the frequency domain $X(f)$ is the frequency spectrum. This representation has the amplitude or phase plotted versus the frequency. In a wave, the amplitude describes the magnitude of change and the phase describes the fraction of the wave cycle that has elapsed relative to the origin.

The frequency spectrum of a real valued signal is always symmetric; because the symmetric part is exactly a mirror image of the first part, the second part is usually not shown.

The complex number $X(f)$ conveys both the amplitude and phase of the frequency f. The absolute value $|X(f)|$ represents the amplitude of the frequency f. The phase is represented by the argument of $X(f)$, $arg(X(f))$. For a complex number

$$z = x + i \cdot y = |z| \cdot e^{i \cdot \theta} \tag{3.3}$$

θ is the phase

$$\theta = arg(z) = tan^{-1}\left(\frac{y}{x}\right) \tag{3.4}$$

and

$$|z| = \sqrt{x^2 + y^2} \tag{3.5}$$

the phase is an angle (radians), and a negative phase corresponds to a positive time delay of the wave. For example, if we shift the cosine function by the angle θ

$$\cos(x) \rightarrow \cos(x - \theta)$$

the phase of the cosines wave is shifted. It follows as well that

$$\sin(x) = \cos(x - \pi/2). \tag{3.6}$$

The Fourier transform of $x(t)$ is

$$X(f) = \int_{-\infty}^{\infty} x(t) \cdot e^{-2 \cdot \pi \cdot i \cdot t \cdot f} dt \tag{3.7}$$

t stands for time and f for frequency. The signal $x(t)$ is multiplied with an exponential term at some certain frequency f, and then integrated over all times. The inverse Fourier transform of $X(f)$ is

$$x(t) = \int_{-\infty}^{\infty} X(f) \cdot e^{2 \cdot \pi \cdot i \cdot t \cdot f} df. \tag{3.8}$$

3.1.2 Discrete Fourier transform

The discrete Fourier transform converts discrete time-based or space-based data into the frequency domain. Given a sequence α

$$\alpha_t : [1, 2, \cdots, n] \to C. \tag{3.9}$$

The discrete Fourier transform produces a sequence ω:

$$\omega_f : [1, 2, \cdots, n] \to C. \tag{3.10}$$

The discrete Fourier transform of $\alpha(t)$ is

$$\omega_f = \frac{1}{\sqrt{n}} \cdot \sum_{t=1}^{n} \alpha_t \cdot e^{-2 \cdot \pi \cdot i \cdot (t-1) \cdot \frac{(f-1)}{n}} \tag{3.11}$$

its wave frequency is $\frac{(f-1)}{n}$ events per sample. The inverse discrete Fourier transform of ω_f is

$$\alpha_t = \frac{1}{\sqrt{n}} \cdot \sum_{f=1}^{n} \omega_f \cdot e^{2 \cdot \pi \cdot i \cdot (t-1) \cdot \frac{(f-1)}{n}}. \tag{3.12}$$

Discrete Fourier transform (DFT) can be seen as a linear transform F talking the column vector α to a column vector ω

$$\omega = F \cdot \alpha \tag{3.13}$$

$$\begin{pmatrix} \omega_1 \\ \omega_2 \\ \vdots \\ \omega_n \end{pmatrix} = F \cdot \alpha =$$

$$= \frac{1}{\sqrt{n}} \cdot \begin{pmatrix} e^{-2\cdot\pi\cdot i\cdot(0)\cdot\frac{(0)}{n}} & e^{-2\cdot\pi\cdot i\cdot(0)\cdot\frac{(1)}{n}} & \cdots & e^{-2\cdot\pi\cdot i\cdot(0)\cdot\frac{(n-1)}{n}} \\ e^{-2\cdot\pi\cdot i\cdot(1)\cdot\frac{(0)}{n}} & e^{-2\cdot\pi\cdot i\cdot(1)\cdot\frac{(1)}{n}} & \cdots & e^{-2\cdot\pi\cdot i\cdot(1)\cdot\frac{(n-1)}{n}} \\ \vdots & \vdots & \ddots & \vdots \\ e^{-2\cdot\pi\cdot i\cdot(n-1)\cdot\frac{(0)}{n}} & e^{-2\cdot\pi\cdot i\cdot(n-1)\cdot\frac{(1)}{n}} & \cdots & e^{-2\cdot\pi\cdot i\cdot(n)\cdot\frac{(n-1)}{n}} \end{pmatrix} \cdot \begin{pmatrix} \alpha_1 \\ \alpha_2 \\ \vdots \\ \alpha_n \end{pmatrix}$$

(3.14)

and the inverse discrete Fourier transform (IDFT) can be seen as a linear transform IF talking the column vector ω to a column vector α

$$\alpha = IF \cdot \omega \tag{3.15}$$

$$\begin{pmatrix} \alpha_1 \\ \alpha_2 \\ \vdots \\ \alpha_n \end{pmatrix} = \frac{1}{\sqrt{n}} \cdot \begin{pmatrix} e^{2\cdot\pi\cdot i\cdot(0)\cdot\frac{(0)}{n}} & e^{2\cdot\pi\cdot i\cdot(0)\cdot\frac{(1)}{n}} & \cdots & e^{2\cdot\pi\cdot i\cdot(0)\cdot\frac{(n-1)}{n}} \\ e^{2\cdot\pi\cdot i\cdot(1)\cdot\frac{(0)}{n}} & e^{2\cdot\pi\cdot i\cdot(1)\cdot\frac{(1)}{n}} & \cdots & e^{2\cdot\pi\cdot i\cdot(1)\cdot\frac{(n-1)}{n}} \\ \vdots & \vdots & \ddots & \vdots \\ e^{2\cdot\pi\cdot i\cdot(n-1)\cdot\frac{(0)}{n}} & e^{2\cdot\pi\cdot i\cdot(n-1)\cdot\frac{(1)}{n}} & \cdots & e^{2\cdot\pi\cdot i\cdot(n)\cdot\frac{(n-1)}{n}} \end{pmatrix} \cdot \begin{pmatrix} \omega_1 \\ \omega_2 \\ \vdots \\ \omega_n \end{pmatrix}.$$

(3.16)

For $n = 8$

$$F = \frac{1}{\sqrt{8}} \cdot \begin{pmatrix} 1 & 1 & 1 & 1 & 1 & 1 & 1 & 1 \\ 1 & e^{-\pi\cdot i\cdot\frac{1}{4}} & -i & e^{-\pi\cdot i\cdot\frac{3}{4}} & -1 & e^{\pi\cdot i\cdot\frac{3}{4}} & i & e^{\pi\cdot i\cdot\frac{1}{4}} \\ 1 & -i & -1 & i & 1 & -i & -1 & i \\ 1 & e^{-\pi\cdot i\cdot\frac{3}{4}} & i & e^{-\pi\cdot i\cdot\frac{1}{4}} & -1 & e^{\pi\cdot i\cdot\frac{1}{4}} & i & e^{\pi\cdot i\cdot\frac{3}{4}} \\ 1 & -1 & 1 & -1 & 1 & -1 & 1 & -1 \\ 1 & e^{\pi\cdot i\cdot\frac{3}{4}} & -i & e^{\pi\cdot i\cdot\frac{1}{4}} & -1 & e^{-\pi\cdot i\cdot\frac{1}{4}} & i & e^{-\pi\cdot i\cdot\frac{3}{4}} \\ 1 & i & -1 & -i & 1 & i & -1 & -i \\ 1 & e^{\pi\cdot i\cdot\frac{1}{4}} & i & e^{\pi\cdot i\cdot\frac{3}{4}} & -1 & e^{-\pi\cdot i\cdot\frac{3}{4}} & -i & e^{-\pi\cdot i\cdot\frac{1}{4}} \end{pmatrix}.$$

(3.17)

The first row of F is the DC average of the amplitude of the input state when measured, the following rows represent the AC (difference) of the input state amplitudes. F can be simplified with

$$e^{-\pi\cdot i\cdot\frac{1}{4}} = \frac{1-i}{\sqrt{2}}$$

into

$$F = \frac{1}{\sqrt{8}} \cdot \begin{pmatrix} 1 & 1 & 1 & 1 & 1 & 1 & 1 & 1 \\ 1 & \frac{1-i}{\sqrt{2}} & -i & \frac{-1-i}{\sqrt{2}} & -1 & \frac{-1+i}{\sqrt{2}} & i & \frac{1+i}{\sqrt{2}} \\ 1 & -i & -1 & i & 1 & -i & -1 & i \\ 1 & \frac{-1-i}{\sqrt{2}} & -i & \frac{1-i}{\sqrt{2}} & -1 & \frac{1+i}{\sqrt{2}} & i & \frac{-1+i}{\sqrt{2}} \\ 1 & -1 & 1 & -1 & 1 & -1 & 1 & -1 \\ 1 & \frac{-1+i}{\sqrt{2}} & -i & \frac{1+i}{\sqrt{2}} & -1 & \frac{1-i}{\sqrt{2}} & i & \frac{-1-i}{\sqrt{2}} \\ 1 & i & -1 & -i & 1 & i & -1 & -i \\ 1 & \frac{1+i}{\sqrt{2}} & -i & \frac{-1+i}{\sqrt{2}} & -1 & \frac{-1-i}{\sqrt{2}} & i & \frac{1-i}{\sqrt{2}} \end{pmatrix}$$

(3.18)

and represented as a sum of a real and imaginary matrix

$$F = \frac{1}{\sqrt{8}} \cdot \begin{pmatrix} 1 & 1 & 1 & 1 & 1 & 1 & 1 & 1 \\ 1 & \frac{1}{\sqrt{2}} & 0 & \frac{-1}{\sqrt{2}} & -1 & \frac{-1}{\sqrt{2}} & 0 & \frac{1}{\sqrt{2}} \\ 1 & 0 & -1 & 0 & 1 & 0 & -1 & 0 \\ 1 & \frac{-1}{\sqrt{2}} & 0 & \frac{1}{\sqrt{2}} & -1 & \frac{1}{\sqrt{2}} & 0 & \frac{-1}{\sqrt{2}} \\ 1 & -1 & 1 & -1 & 1 & -1 & 1 & -1 \\ 1 & \frac{-1}{\sqrt{2}} & 0 & \frac{1}{\sqrt{2}} & -1 & \frac{1}{\sqrt{2}} & 0 & \frac{-1}{\sqrt{2}} \\ 1 & 0 & -1 & 0 & 1 & 0 & -1 & 0 \\ 1 & \frac{1}{\sqrt{2}} & 0 & \frac{-1}{\sqrt{2}} & -1 & \frac{-1}{\sqrt{2}} & 0 & \frac{1}{\sqrt{2}} \end{pmatrix} + \tag{3.19}$$

$$+ \frac{1}{\sqrt{8}} \cdot \begin{pmatrix} 0 & 0 & 0 & 0 & 0 & 0 & 0 & 0 \\ 0 & \frac{-i}{\sqrt{2}} & -i & \frac{-i}{\sqrt{2}} & 0 & \frac{i}{\sqrt{2}} & i & \frac{i}{\sqrt{2}} \\ 0 & -i & 0 & i & 0 & -i & 0 & i \\ 0 & \frac{-i}{\sqrt{2}} & -i & \frac{-i}{\sqrt{2}} & 0 & \frac{i}{\sqrt{2}} & i & \frac{-i}{\sqrt{2}} \\ 0 & 0 & 0 & 0 & 0 & 0 & 0 & 0 \\ 0 & \frac{i}{\sqrt{2}} & -i & \frac{i}{\sqrt{2}} & 0 & \frac{-i}{\sqrt{2}} & i & \frac{-i}{\sqrt{2}} \\ 0 & i & 0 & -i & 0 & i & 0 & -i \\ 0 & \frac{i}{\sqrt{2}} & -i & \frac{i}{\sqrt{2}} & 0 & \frac{-i}{\sqrt{2}} & i & \frac{-i}{\sqrt{2}} \end{pmatrix}. \tag{3.20}$$

The first row measures the DC, the second row the fractional frequency of the amplitude of the input state of $1/8$, the third that of $1/4 = 2/8$, the fourth that of $3/8$, the fifth that of $1/2 = 4/8$, the sixth that of $5/8$, the seventh that of $3/4 = 6/8$ and the eighth that of $7/8$ or, equivalently, the fractional frequency of $-1/8$. The resulting frequency of the amplitude vector ω for a real valued amplitude vector α is symmetric; $\omega_2 = \omega_6$, $\omega_3 = \omega_7$ and $\omega_4 = \omega_8$.

3.1.2.1 *Example*

We generate a list with $256 = 2^8$ elements containing a periodic signal α_t

$$\alpha_t = cos\left(\frac{50 \cdot t \cdot 2 \cdot \cdot \pi}{256}\right),$$

see Figure 3.1 (a). The discrete Fourier transform ω_f of the real valued signal α_t is symmetric. It shows a strong peak at $50 + 1$ and a symmetric peak at $256 - 50 + 1$ representing the frequency component of the signal α_t (see Figure 3.1 (b)). We add to the periodic signal α_t Gaussian random noise from the interval $[-0.5, 0.5]$.

$$\alpha_t^* = cos\left(\frac{50 \cdot t \cdot 2 \cdot \cdot \pi}{256}\right) + noise.$$

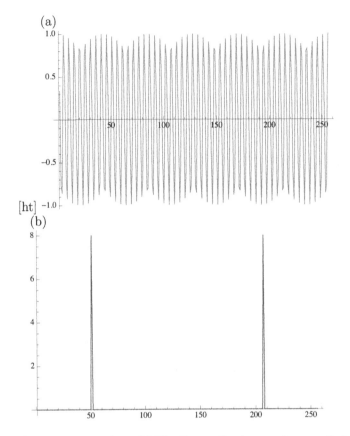

Fig. 3.1   (a) A periodic signal α_t. (b) The discrete Fourier transform ω_f. It shows two peaks at $50 + 1$ and a symmetric peak at $256 - 50 + 1$.

The represented data looks random, see Figure 3.2 (a). The frequency component of the signal α_t^* are shown in Figure 3.2 (b). A filter that reduces Gaussian noise based on DFT removes frequencies with low amplitude of ω_f (see Figure 3.3) and performs the inverse discrete Fourier transform. For dimension reduction of the signal, only a fraction of frequencies with high amplitude are represented.

3.1.3   *Fast Fourier transform*

An efficient decomposition is represented by the fast Fourier transform (FFT). Carl Friedrich Gauss invented the FFT algorithm in approximately

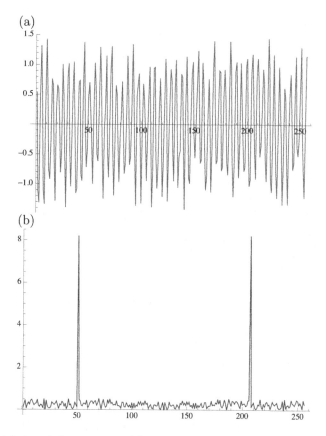

Fig. 3.2 (a) A periodic signal α_t^*. (b) The discrete Fourier transform ω_f^*. It shows a strong peak at $50 + 1$ and a symmetric peak at $256 - 50 + 1$ representing the frequency component of the signal α_t^*. The zero frequency term represents the DC average and appears at position 1 instead of at position 0.

1805. However, because the corresponding article was written in Latin, it did not gain any popularity. The FFT was several times rediscovered, and it was made popular by J. W. Cooley and J. W. Tukey in 1965 [Cooley and Tukey (1965)], [Cormen *et al.* (2001b)]. The original algorithm is limited to the DFT matrix of the size $2^m \times 2^m$, with a power of two. Variants of the algorithm for the case in which the size of the matrix is not a power of two exist. The original algorithm decomposes F_m recursively.

$$F_{m+1} = \frac{1}{\sqrt{2}} \cdot \begin{pmatrix} I_m & D_m \\ I_m & -D_m \end{pmatrix} \cdot \begin{pmatrix} F_m & 0 \\ 0 & F_m \end{pmatrix} \cdot R_{m+1} \qquad (3.21)$$

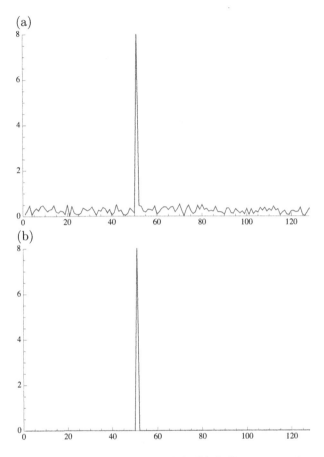

Fig. 3.3   (a) The discrete Fourier transform ω_f^*. (b) A filter removes frequencies with low amplitude, resulting in ω_f.

with the permutation matrix R_m given that $n = 2^m$

$$R_m = \begin{pmatrix} r_{11} & \cdots & r_{1n} \\ \vdots & \ddots & \vdots \\ r_{n1} & \cdots & r_{nn} \end{pmatrix} \tag{3.22}$$

with

$$r_{ab} = \begin{cases} 1 & if \quad 2 \cdot a - 1 = b \\ 1 & if \quad 2 \cdot a - n = b \\ 0 & else \end{cases} \tag{3.23}$$

and the diagonal matrix with $n \cdot 2 = 2^{m+1}$

$$D_m = \begin{pmatrix} \zeta_{n\cdot2}^0 & 0 & \cdots & 0 \\ 0 & \zeta_{n\cdot2}^1 & \cdots & 0 \\ \vdots & \vdots & \ddots & \vdots \\ 0 & 0 & \cdots & \zeta_{n\cdot2}^{n-1} \end{pmatrix}. \tag{3.24}$$

For example F_2 is decomposed with

$$D_1, \zeta_4 = e^{-2\cdot\pi\cdot i\cdot\frac{1}{4}} \rightarrow D_1 = \begin{pmatrix} e^{-\cdot\pi\cdot i\cdot\frac{0}{2}} & 0 \\ 0 & e^{-\cdot\pi\cdot i\cdot\frac{1}{2}} \end{pmatrix} = \begin{pmatrix} 1 & 0 \\ 0 & -i \end{pmatrix} \tag{3.25}$$

and

$$R_2 = \begin{pmatrix} 1 & 0 & 0 & 0 \\ 0 & 0 & 1 & 0 \\ 0 & 1 & 0 & 0 \\ 0 & 0 & 0 & 1 \end{pmatrix} \tag{3.26}$$

it follows

$$F_2 = \frac{1}{\sqrt{2}} \cdot \begin{pmatrix} 1 & 0 & 1 & 0 \\ 0 & 1 & 0 & -i \\ 1 & 0 & -1 & 0 \\ 0 & 1 & 0 & i \end{pmatrix} \cdot \frac{1}{\sqrt{2}} \cdot \begin{pmatrix} 1 & 1 & 0 & 0 \\ 1 & -1 & 0 & 0 \\ 0 & 0 & 1 & 1 \\ 0 & 0 & 1 & -1 \end{pmatrix} \cdot \begin{pmatrix} 1 & 0 & 0 & 0 \\ 0 & 0 & 1 & 0 \\ 0 & 1 & 0 & 0 \\ 0 & 0 & 0 & 1 \end{pmatrix} \tag{3.27}$$

$$F_2 = \frac{1}{2} \cdot \begin{pmatrix} 1 & 1 & 1 & 1 \\ 1 & -i & -1 & i \\ 1 & -1 & 1 & -1 \\ 1 & i & -1 & -i \end{pmatrix}. \tag{3.28}$$

The complexity of the FFT algorithm that decomposes F_m recursively is $O(n \cdot m)$.

3.1.4 *Discrete cosine transform*

The discrete Fourier transform of $\alpha(t)$ is

$$\omega_f = \frac{1}{\sqrt{n}} \cdot \sum_{t=1}^{n} \alpha_t \cdot e^{-2\cdot\pi\cdot i\cdot(t-1)\cdot\frac{(f-1)}{n}}. \tag{3.29}$$

Using the Eluer's formula

$$e^{i\cdot x} = \cos x + i \cdot \sin x \tag{3.30}$$

it can be represented as

$$\omega_f = \frac{1}{\sqrt{n}} \cdot \sum_{t=1}^{n} \alpha_t \cdot (\cos\left(-2 \cdot \pi \cdot (t-1) \cdot \frac{(f-1)}{n}\right) +$$

$$i \cdot \sin\left(-2 \cdot \pi \cdot (t-1) \cdot \frac{(f-1)}{n}\right)) \tag{3.31}$$

and

$$\omega_f = \frac{1}{\sqrt{n}} \cdot \sum_{t=1}^{n} \alpha_t \cdot (\cos\left(2 \cdot \pi \cdot (t-1) \cdot \frac{(f-1)}{n}\right) -$$

$$i \cdot \sin\left(2 \cdot \pi \cdot (t-1) \cdot \frac{(f-1)}{n}\right)). \tag{3.32}$$

For a real valued signal, the spectrum is symmetric, so half of the spectrum is redundant. However, for the reconstruction of the signal through the inverse Fourier transform, the real part and the imaginary part are both required. DCT is a Fourier-related transform similar to the discrete Fourier transform (DFT), but it only uses real numbers.

$$\gamma'_f = \frac{1}{\sqrt{n}} \cdot \sum_{t=1}^{n} \alpha_t \cdot \cos\left(2 \cdot \pi \cdot (t-1) \cdot \frac{(f-1)}{n}\right) \tag{3.33}$$

Due to normalization it is usually defined as

$$\gamma_f = w(t) \cdot \sum_{t=0}^{n-1} \alpha_t \cdot \cos\left(\pi \cdot \frac{f \cdot (2 \cdot t + 1)}{2 \cdot n}\right). \tag{3.34}$$

with

$$w(t) = \begin{cases} \frac{1}{\sqrt{n}} & for\ t = 0 \\ \sqrt{\frac{2}{n}} & else \end{cases}$$

The resulting spectrum is represented by the absolute value of real numbers and is not redundant. Due to normalization, the spectrum is defined over the entire frequency space.

3.1.4.1　*Example*

We generate a list with $n = 256 = 2^8$ elements containing a periodic signal α_t,

$$\alpha_t = sin\left(\frac{60 \cdot t \cdot 2 \cdot \pi}{256}\right).$$

The discrete Fourier transform ω_f. It shows two peaks at $60 + 1$ and a symmetric peak at $256 - 60 + 1$, however the discrete cosine not symmetric. It shows several peaks around the main peak at $2 \cdot 60 + 1$ (see Figure 3.4).

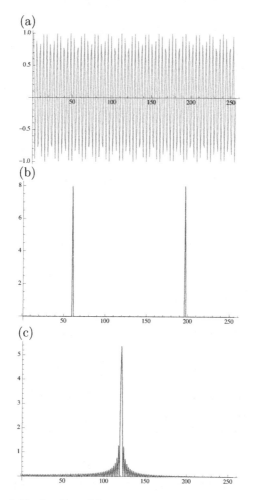

Fig. 3.4 (a) A periodic signal α_t. (b) The discrete Fourier transform ω_f. It shows two peaks at $60 + 1$ and a symmetric peak at $256 - 60 + 1$. (c) The discrete cosine transform shows several peaks around the main peak at $120 + 1$.

3.1.5 *Two dimensional transform*

The discrete Fourier transform and the discrete cosine transform can be extended to two dimensions, $\alpha_{x,y}$, with

$$\omega_{fx,fy} = \frac{1}{\sqrt{n} \cdot \sqrt{m}} \cdot \sum_{x=1}^{n} \sum_{y=1}^{m} \alpha_{x,y} \cdot e^{-2 \cdot \pi \cdot i \cdot (x-1) \cdot \frac{(f_x - 1)}{n}} \cdot e^{-2 \cdot \pi \cdot i \cdot (y-1) \cdot \frac{(f_y - 1)}{m}},$$

$$(3.35)$$

and

$$\gamma_{fx,fy} = w(x) \cdot v(y) \sum_{x=0}^{n-1} \sum_{y=0}^{m-1} \alpha_{x,y} \cdot \cos\left(\frac{\pi \cdot (2 \cdot x + 1) \cdot f_x}{2 \cdot n}\right)$$

$$\cdot \cos\left(\frac{\pi \cdot (2 \cdot y + 1) \cdot f_y}{2 \cdot m}\right) \qquad (3.36)$$

with

$$w(x) = \begin{cases} \frac{1}{\sqrt{n}} & for\ x = 0 \\ \sqrt{\frac{2}{n}} & else \end{cases}$$

and

$$v(y) = \begin{cases} \frac{1}{\sqrt{m}} & for\ y = 0 \\ \sqrt{\frac{2}{m}} & else \end{cases}.$$

3.1.5.1 *Examples*

We generate a two dimensional list with $n = 32 = 2^5$ and $m = 32$ elements containing a periodic signal $\alpha_{x,y}$,

$$\alpha_{x,y} = sin\left(\frac{15 \cdot \pi \cdot (x + y)}{32}\right).$$

The spectrum of the discrete Fourier transform $\omega_{fx,fy}$ shows two peaks, and the discrete cosine transform $\gamma_{fx,fy}$ shows only one peak (see Figure 3.5). A black and white picture of size 100×100 pixels with 256 different gray values is represented in Figure 3.6. Each pixel is represented by 8 bits; the values between 0 and 255 are normalized to lie between 0 and 1 and represent the two dimensional values $\alpha_{x,y}$. The corresponding spectrum of the discrete Fourier transform $\omega_{fx,fy}$ of the picture is shown in Figure 3.7 (a). To visualize the high range of the values of the spectrum, the logarithm of the spectrum

$$\log(|\omega_{fx,fy}|)$$

is used as shown in Figure 3.7 (b). The highest values correspond to the low frequencies represented at the four edges.

The spectrum is symmetric around the origin with

$$|\omega_{fx,fy}| = |\omega_{-fx,-fy}|.$$

Thus, it is common to indicate the origin as representing the low frequencies in the center of the spectrum (see Figure 3.8). The centered spectrum simplifies the visualization because the highest absolute values of the discrete Fourier transform $\omega_{fx,fy}$ usually correspond to low frequencies (see Figure 3.9), which are represented at the center of the spectrum. The discrete cosine transform $\gamma_{fx,fy}$ is not symmetric (see Figure 3.10) and does not need to be centred.

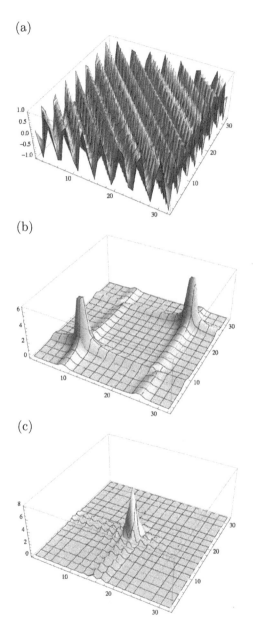

Fig. 3.5   (a) A periodic signal $\alpha_{x,y}$. (b) The spectrum of the discrete Fourier transform $\omega_{fx,fy}$. (c) The spectrum of the discrete cosine transform $\gamma_{fx,fy}$.

Fig. 3.6   A black and white picture of the size 100×100 pixels with 256 different grey values representing a painting with two girls.

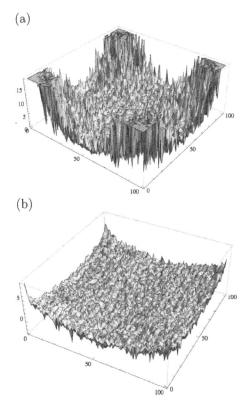

Fig. 3.7   (a) The spectrum of the discrete Fourier transform $\omega_{fx,fy}$ of Figure 3.6. (b) The logarithm of the spectrum.

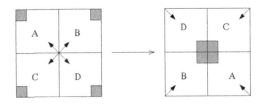

Fig. 3.8   The highest absolute values of the discrete Fourier transform $\omega_{fx,fy}$ correspond to low frequencies at the four edges. Because the spectrum is symmetric around the origin, it is common to indicate the origin as representing the low frequencies in the center of the spectrum.

(a)

(b)

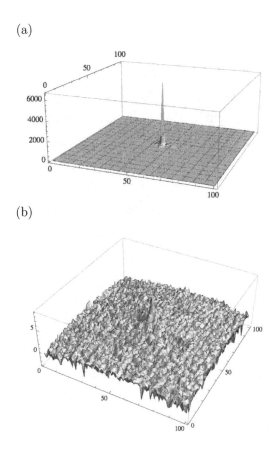

Fig. 3.9   (a) The centered spectrum of the picture of Figure 3.6. (b) The logarithm of the centered spectrum of the picture.

(a)

(b)

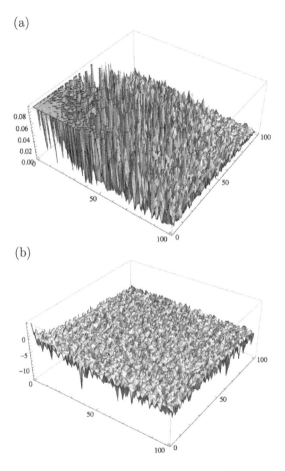

Fig. 3.10 a) The discrete cosine transform of the picture of Figure 3.6. (b) The logarithm of the discrete cosine transform the picture.

3.2 Wavelet Transform

3.2.1 *Short-term Fourier transform*

Signals whose frequency content does not change in time are called stationary signals. For non-stationary signals, frequency content does change over time (see Figure 3.11). The Fourier transform gives the spectral content of

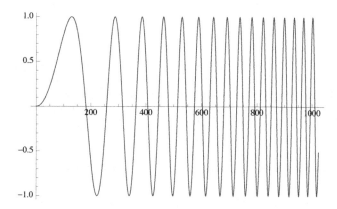

Fig. 3.11 Non stationary signal $f(t) = \sin(100 \cdot t^2)$.

a signal, but it gives no information regarding where in time those spectral components appear. The Fourier transform of $x(t)$ is

$$X(f) = \int_{-\infty}^{\infty} x(t) \cdot e^{-2 \cdot \pi \cdot i \cdot t \cdot f} dt \qquad (3.37)$$

t stands for time and f for frequency. The signal $x(t)$, is multiplied with an exponential term, at some certain frequency f and then integrated over all times. The information provided by the integral, corresponds to all time instances. No matter where in time the component with frequency f appears, it will affect the result of the integration equally as well. Whether the frequency component f appears at time t_1 or t_2, it will have the same effect on the integration (see Figure 3.12). A signal can be analyzed through narrow windows, assuming that it is stationary in those areas. The width of the windows should be equal to the segment of the signal where it is stationary. The signal is divided into small enough segments, where these segments of the signal are assumed to be stationary. This approach is called

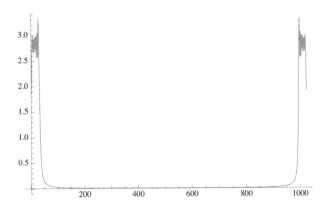

Fig. 3.12   Fourier transform of $f(t) = \sin(100 \cdot t^2)$, it gives the spectral content of the signal, but it gives no information regarding where in time those spectral components appear. (The frequency spectrum of a real valued signal is always symmetric).

the short-term Fourier transform (STFT) or short-time Fourier transform.

$$STFT_X(t', f) = \int_{-\infty}^{\infty} x(t) \cdot w(t - t') \cdot e^{-2 \cdot \pi \cdot i \cdot t \cdot f} dt \qquad (3.38)$$

$x(t)$ is the signal, $w(t)$ is the window function, and, for every t' and f, a new STFT coefficient is computed. The STFT of the signal is the Fourier transform of the signal multiplied by a window function, which is nonzero for only a short period of time. Usually, the Gaussian window function $w(t)$ is used with

$$w(t) = e^{-s \cdot t^2 / 2} \qquad (3.39)$$

where s determines the length of the window. The function represents a centered bell. In the discrete time case for a sequence α

$$\alpha_t : [1, 2, \cdots, n] \to C. \qquad (3.40)$$

the discrete Short Time Fourier transform of $\alpha(t)$ is

$$STFT_\omega(t', f) = \frac{1}{\sqrt{n}} \cdot \sum_{t=1}^{n} \alpha_t \cdot w(t - t') \cdot e^{-2 \cdot \pi \cdot i \cdot (t-1) \cdot \frac{(f-1)}{n}}, \qquad (3.41)$$

it produces a sequence $\omega(t', f)$. A spectrogram is a visual representation of the spectrum of frequencies in a signal as they vary with time, with

$$spectrogram_\omega(t', f) = |STFT_\omega(t', f)|^2, \qquad (3.42)$$

it is represented as a graph with two dimensions; the x-axis represents time, and the y-axis represents frequency [Deller *et al.* (1993)]. The absolute values of the amplitude of a particular frequency correspond to the intensity of each point in the image. Large absolute values are shown darker. Using the STFT, the time intervals in which certain bands of frequencies exist can be known. However, the exact time-frequency representation of a signal cannot be known. The problem with the STFT is that it has a fixed resolution, defined by the window function. The width of the window function w determines how the signal is represented. With a wide window, a good frequency resolution is present, but the time resolution is poor. In contrast, with a narrow window, a good time resolution is present, but the frequency resolution is poor (see Figure 3.13). High temporal resolution and frequency resolution cannot be achieved at the same time; this uncertainty principle is called the Gabor limit or Heisenberg-Gabor limit [Gabor (1946)]. If a window has a fixed size, for example 64, it covers the points 1

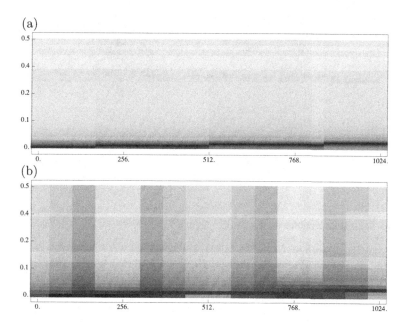

Fig. 3.13 With a wide window, a good frequency resolution is present, but the time resolution is poor. In contrast, with a narrow window, a good time resolution is present, but the frequency resolution is poor. The short term Fourier transform of $f(t) = \sin(100 \cdot t^2)$. (a) The spectrogram with a non-overlapping Gaussian window of size 256. (b) The spectrogram with a non-overlapping Gaussian window of size 64.

to 64 and then the points 65 to 128. An event that is represented between the points 60 and 123 is not covered by the window. Overlapping windows solve this problem; the overlap is indicated by the offset. The offset determines the shift of the window; the bigger the offset, the less overlap is present. A heuristic[2] that determines the window size ws and the offset of a signal of length T is given by

$$ws = 2^{\lfloor \log_2(\sqrt{T})+0.5 \rfloor +1} \tag{3.43}$$

and the offset is

$$\left\lfloor \frac{ws}{3} + 0.5 \right\rfloor. \tag{3.44}$$

According to the equation for a signal length of $T = 1024$, the size of the window is $ws = 64$ and the offset is 21 (see Figure 3.14). The sound

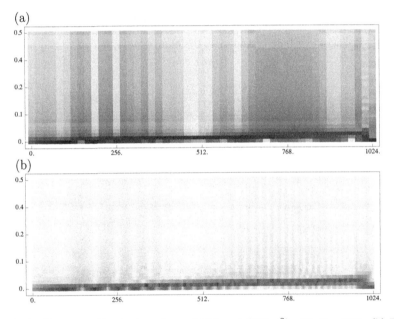

Fig. 3.14   Short term Fourier transform of $f(t) = \sin(100 \cdot t^2)$ with $T = 1024$. (b) The spectrogram with an overlapping Gaussian window of size 64 with offset 21. (b) With a smaller offset, more details are shown. The spectrogram with an overlapping Gaussian window of size 64 with offset 4.

signal "Houston, we have a problem", spoken during the Apollo 13 mission, and the corresponding spectral representation using the equation that determines the window size and the offset are shown in the Figure 3.15.

[2]http://reference.wolfram.com/mathematica/ref/Spectrogram.html

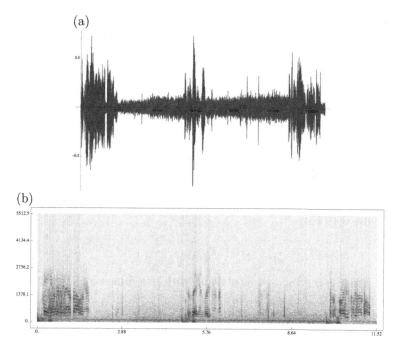

Fig. 3.15   (a) The sound signal "Houston, we have a problem", spoken during the Apollo 13 mission. (b) Corresponding spectral representation.

3.2.2   *Continuous wavelet transform*

The uncertainty principle can be overcome by analyzing the signal at different frequencies with different resolutions. This approach is called the multi-resolution analysis (MRA) [Gonzales and Woods (2001)]. An example of the multi-resolution analysis is the continuous wavelet transform given by the continuous walvelet transform (CWT),

$$CWT(s, \tau) = \frac{1}{\sqrt{|s|}} \int_{-\infty}^{\infty} x(t) \cdot \psi^* \left(\frac{t - \tau}{s} \right) dt \qquad (3.45)$$

the transformed signal is a function of two variables, τ translation and s scale. Translation τ corresponds to time information in the transform domain. It is used as t' in the STFT, which that represents the location of the window function $w(t)$. Translation τ represents the location of the transforming function $\psi(t)$. The scale parameter s is defined as

$$s = \frac{1}{f}. \qquad (3.46)$$

The transforming function $\psi(t)$ is called the mother wavelet. The term wavelet means a small wave, in reference to the transforming function being oscillatory and of finite length [Hubbard (1998)]. The term mother implies that the transforming function is a prototype for generating other transformation functions with different regions of width. Known examples of wavelets that are used in the continuous wavelet transform are the Mexican hat wavelet and the Morlet wavelet. The Mexican hat wavelet is defined as (see Figure 3.16 (a))

$$\psi(t) = \frac{-2}{\pi^{1/4} \cdot \sqrt{3 \cdot \sigma}} \cdot \left(\frac{t^2}{\sigma^2} - 1 \right) \cdot e^{-\left(\frac{t^2}{2 \cdot \sigma^2} \right)} \tag{3.47}$$

with width σ; in our examples, $\sigma = 1$. The Morlet wavelet is defined as (see Figure 3.16 (b))

$$\psi(t) = \frac{1}{\pi^{1/4}} \cdot \cos \left(t \cdot \pi \cdot \sqrt{\frac{2}{\log 2}} \right) \cdot e^{-\left(\frac{t^2}{2} \right)}. \tag{3.48}$$

A scalogram is represented as a graph with two dimensions, where the x-

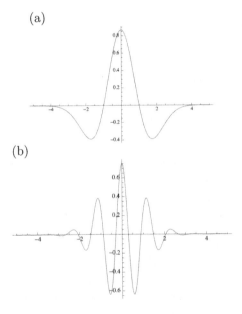

Fig. 3.16 (a) The Mexican hat wavelet with $\sigma = 1$. (b) The Morlet wavelet.

axis represents translation and the y-axis represents the scale. The absolute values of the amplitude of a particular scale (inverse frequency) correspond to the intensity of each point in the image. Large absolute values are shown darker. In Figure 3.17, we indicate the continuous wavelet transform of $f(t) = \sin(100 \cdot t^2)$ with the Mexican hat wavelet and Morlet wavelet.

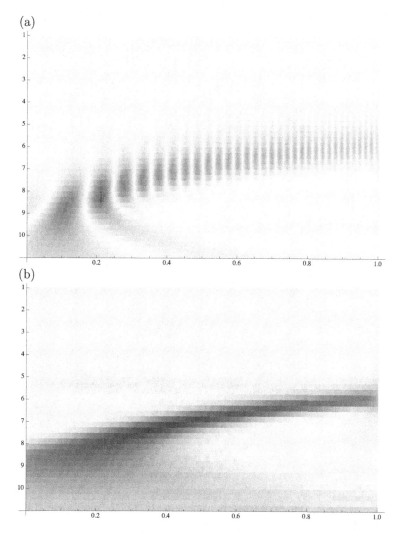

Fig. 3.17 (a) Continuous wavelet transform of $f(t) = \sin(100 \cdot t^2)$ with the Mexican hat wavelet with $\sigma = 1$. (b) Continuous wavelet transform of $f(t) = \sin(100 \cdot t^2)$ with the Morlet wavelet.

In Figure 3.18, we indicate the continuous wavelet transform of a stationary signal $f(t) = \sin(100 \cdot t)$ with the Morlet wavelet. In Figure 3.19, we

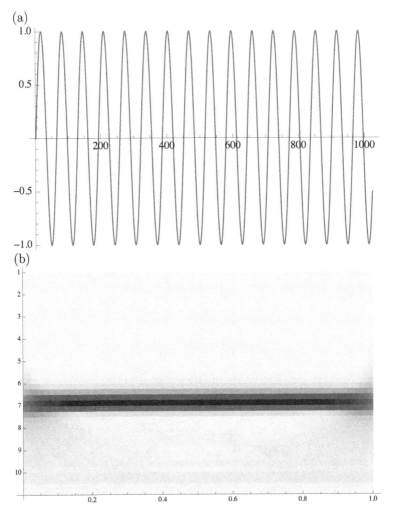

Fig. 3.18 (a) The stationary signal $f(t) = \sin(100 \cdot t)$. (b) Continuous wavelet transform of the stationary signal with Morlet wavelet.

show the scalogram representing the continuous wavelet transform of the sound signal "Houston, we have a problem", spoken during the Apollo 13 mission, with the Mexican hat wavelet with $\sigma = 1$ and the Morlet wavelet.

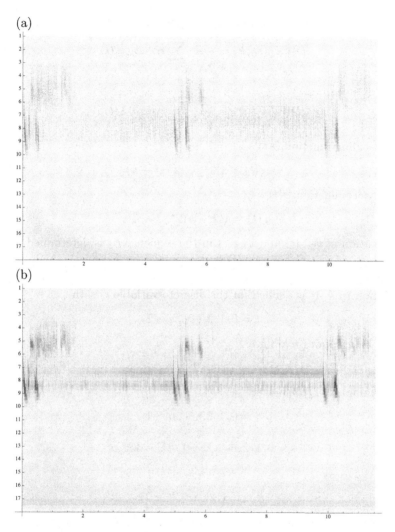

Fig. 3.19 Continuous wavelet transform of the sound signal "Houston, we have a problem", spoken during the Apollo 13 mission. (a) With the Mexican hat wavelet with $\sigma = 1$. (b) With the Morlet wavelet.

3.2.3 Discrete wavelet transform

We can discretize the continuous wavelet transformation by discretizing τ, translation, and s, scale. For a sequence α

$$\alpha_t : [0, 2, \cdots, n-1] \to C \tag{3.49}$$

the discrete wavelet transformation is defined as a DWT pair

$$DWT_\phi(s_0, k) = \frac{1}{\sqrt{n}} \cdot \sum_t \alpha_t \cdot \phi_{s_0,k}(t) \qquad (3.50)$$

and

$$DWT_\psi(s, k) = \frac{1}{\sqrt{n}} \cdot \sum_t \alpha_t \cdot \psi_{s,k}(t) \qquad (3.51)$$

with a scaling function $\phi(t)$

$$\phi_{s,k}(t) = \sqrt{2^s} \cdot \phi\left(2^s \cdot t - k\right) \qquad (3.52)$$

and wavelet function $\psi(t)$

$$\psi_{s,k}(t) = \sqrt{2^s} \cdot \psi\left(2^s \cdot t - k\right). \qquad (3.53)$$

The location of $\phi_{s,k}(t)$ and $\psi_{s,k}(t)$ in the sequence α_t is determined by k. The width of $\phi_{s,k}(t)$ and $\psi_{s,k}(t)$ is determined by s, and the high of the amplitude is represented by 2^s. The shape of $\phi_{s,k}(t)$ and $\psi_{s,k}(t)$ changes in relation to s. It is defined for the discrete variable t, with

$$t = 0, 1, 2, \cdots, n - 1$$

with n being power two for a Σ

$$n = 2^\Sigma.$$

The summation is done over

$$t = 0, 1, 2, \cdots, n - 1$$

$$s = 0, 1, 2, \cdots, \Sigma - 1, \quad \Sigma = \log_2 n$$

and

$$k = 0, 1, 2, \cdots, 2^s - 1,$$

the discrete wavelet transform coefficients are defined on a dyadic grid. The Haar's mother wavelet ψ and the Haar's unit-width scale function ϕ are defined as (see a well Figure 3.20)

$$\psi(t) = \begin{cases} -1 \text{ if } \frac{1}{2} \leq t < 1 \\ 1 \ \text{ if } 0 \leq t < \frac{1}{2} \end{cases} \qquad (3.54)$$

and

$$\phi(t) = \begin{cases} 1 \text{ if } 0 \leq t < 1 \\ 0 \quad \text{else} \end{cases} \qquad (3.55)$$

The Haar scale function is one in the interval

(a)

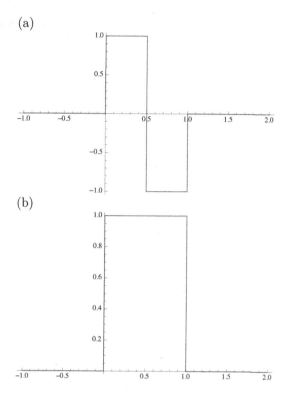

(b)

Fig. 3.20 (a) The the Haar's mother wavelet (b) The Haar's unit-width scale function.

$$[0, 1)$$

and zero outside. The interval $[0, 1)$ is the width of the function; the support of the function is 1 inside the interval and 0 outside. For the example

$$\alpha_0 = 2, \alpha_1 = 4, \alpha_2 = 8, \alpha_3 = 0$$

with $n = 4$ are distributed over the support of the basis scale function, either by $\phi_{0,0}\left(\frac{t}{n}\right) = \phi\left(\frac{t}{4}\right)$ or the Haar's basis scale function width is not one but four. With $n = 4$ and $\Sigma = \log_2 4 = 2$, with $s_0 = 0$ with summation over $t = 0, 1, 2, 3$ and for $s = 0$

$$for \quad s = 0, \quad k = 0$$

and

$$for \quad s = 1, \quad k = 0, k = 1$$

The four samples of with the Haar's wavelet and the Haar's scale function with

$$\phi_{s_0,k}(t) = \phi_{0,0}(t) = \sqrt{2^s} \cdot \phi\left(2^s \cdot t - k\right) = \phi(t)$$

$$DWT_\phi(0,0) = \frac{1}{\sqrt{4}} \cdot \sum_{t=0}^{3} \alpha_t \cdot \phi_{s_0,k}\left(\frac{t}{n}\right) = \frac{1}{2} \cdot \sum_{t=0}^{3} \alpha_t \cdot \phi_{0,0}\left(\frac{t}{4}\right)$$

$$= \frac{1}{2} \cdot (2 \cdot 1 + 4 \cdot 1 + 8 \cdot 1 + 0 \cdot 1) = 7 \qquad (3.56)$$

and for the Haar's wavelet,

$$\psi_{s,k}(t) = \psi_{0,0}(t) = \sqrt{2^0} \cdot \psi\left(2^0 \cdot t - 0\right) = \psi(t)$$

$$DWT_\psi(0,0) = \frac{1}{2} \cdot \sum_t \alpha_t \cdot \psi_{0,0}\left(\frac{t}{4}\right) \qquad (3.57)$$

$$\frac{1}{2} \cdot (2 \cdot 1 + 4 \cdot 1 + 8 \cdot (-1) + 0 \cdot (-1)) = -1$$

and

$$\psi_{1,0}(t) = \sqrt{2} \cdot \psi\left(2 \cdot t\right)$$

$$DWT_\psi(1,0) = \frac{1}{2} \cdot \sum_t \alpha_t \cdot \psi_{1,0}\left(\frac{t}{4}\right) \qquad (3.58)$$

$$\frac{1}{2} \cdot \left(2 \cdot \sqrt{2} + 4 \cdot \left(-\sqrt{2}\right) + 8 \cdot 0 + 0 \cdot 0\right) = -\cdot \sqrt{2} = -1.4142$$

$$\psi_{1,1}(t) = \sqrt{2} \cdot \psi\left(2 \cdot t - 1\right)$$

$$DWT_\psi(1,1) = \frac{1}{2} \cdot \sum_t \alpha_t \cdot \psi_{1,1}\left(\frac{t}{4}\right) \qquad (3.59)$$

$$\frac{1}{2} \cdot \left(2 \cdot 0 + 4 \cdot 0 + 8 \cdot \sqrt{2} + 0 \cdot \left(-\sqrt{2}\right)\right) = 4 \cdot \sqrt{2} = 5.6459$$

The discrete wavelet transform of the example is represented by the transform coefficients

$$7, -1, -1.4142, 5.6459.$$

The coefficients of the example can be as well represented by a scalogram (see Figure 3.21), the x-axis represents translation (location) and the y-axis the scale (width). The original function can be reconstructed from the

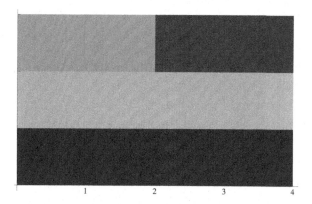

Fig. 3.21 The coefficients $7, -1, -1.4142, 5.6459$ of the Haar wavelet and scaling function, the x-axis represents translation (location) and the y-axis the scale (width). Large absolute values are shown darker.

coefficients for $s \geq s_0$ by

$$\alpha_t = \frac{1}{\sqrt{n}} \cdot \sum_k DWT_\phi(s_0, k) \cdot \phi_{s_0,k}(t) + \frac{1}{\sqrt{n}} \cdot \sum_{s=s_0}^{\infty} \sum_k DWT_\psi(s, k) \cdot \psi_{s,k}(t)$$

$$(3.60)$$

for our example

$$\alpha_t = \frac{1}{\sqrt{4}} \cdot \left(DWT_\phi(0,0) \cdot \phi_{0,0}\left(\frac{t}{4}\right) + DWT_\psi(0,0) \cdot \psi_{0,0}\left(\frac{t}{4}\right) + \right.$$

$$\left. DWT_\psi(q,0) \cdot \psi_{1,0}\left(\frac{t}{4}\right) + DWT_\psi(1,1) \cdot \psi_{1,1}\left(\frac{t}{4}\right) \right)$$

$$(3.61)$$

for $t = 2$

$$\alpha_2 = \frac{1}{\sqrt{4}} \cdot (7 \cdot 1 - 1 \cdot (-1) - \sqrt{2} \cdot 0 + 4 \cdot \sqrt{2} \cdot \sqrt{2} = 8)$$

We can represent the discrete wavelet transformation of Haar's wavelet and the Haar's scale function by the Haar transformation matrix, for $n = 4$

$$H_4 = \frac{1}{\sqrt{4}} \cdot \begin{pmatrix} 1 & 1 & 1 & 1 \\ 1 & 1 & -1 & -1 \\ \sqrt{2} & -\sqrt{2} & 0 & 0 \\ 0 & 0 & \sqrt{2} & -\sqrt{2} \end{pmatrix}.$$

$$(3.62)$$

The discrete wavelet transformation of Haar's wavelet and Haar's scale function can be seen as a linear transform H taking the column vector α to a column vector ω, in our example

$$\omega = H_4 \cdot \alpha$$

$$(3.63)$$

$$\begin{pmatrix} \omega_0 \\ \omega_1 \\ \omega_2 \\ \omega_3 \end{pmatrix} = \frac{1}{\sqrt{4}} \cdot \begin{pmatrix} 1 & 1 & 1 & 1 \\ 1 & 1 & -1 & -1 \\ \sqrt{2} & -\sqrt{2} & 0 & 0 \\ 0 & 0 & \sqrt{2} & -\sqrt{2} \end{pmatrix} \cdot \begin{pmatrix} \alpha_0 \\ \alpha_1 \\ \alpha_2 \\ \alpha_3 \end{pmatrix}$$

$$\begin{pmatrix} 7 \\ -1 \\ -1.4142 \\ 5.6459 \end{pmatrix} = \frac{1}{\sqrt{4}} \cdot \begin{pmatrix} 1 & 1 & 1 & 1 \\ 1 & 1 & -1 & -1 \\ \sqrt{2} & -\sqrt{2} & 0 & 0 \\ 0 & 0 & \sqrt{2} & -\sqrt{2} \end{pmatrix} \cdot \begin{pmatrix} 2 \\ 4 \\ 8 \\ 0 \end{pmatrix}.$$

The Haar transform matrix contains the Haar basis function $h_k(t)$ with

$$t \in [0,1], \quad n = 2^\Sigma$$

and

$$k = 2^p + q - 1, \quad 0 \le p \le \Sigma - 1$$

with

$$q = 0 \vee q = 1 \ \text{if } p = 0$$

$$1 \le q = \le 2^p \ \text{if } p \ne 0$$

and is defined as

$$h_0(t) = h_{00}(t) = \frac{1}{\sqrt{n}} \tag{3.64}$$

and

$$h_k(t) = h_{pq}(t) = \frac{1}{\sqrt{n}} \cdot \begin{cases} 2^{p/2} & \text{if } \frac{q-1}{2^p} \le t < \frac{q-1/2}{2^p} \\ -2^{p/2} & \text{if } \frac{q-1/2}{2^p} \le t < \frac{q}{2^p} \\ 0 & \text{otherwise} \end{cases} \tag{3.65}$$

with

$$t = 0/n, 1/n, 2/n, \cdots, (n-1)/n.$$

For $n = 2$,

$$k = 0 = 2^0 + 0 - 1, \quad p = 0, q = 0$$

$$k = 1 = 2\ 0 + 0 - 1, \quad p = 0, q = 1$$

with

$$t = 0/2, t = 1/2$$

Table 3.1   The values for p and q in relation to k.

k	0	1	2	3	4	5	6	7
p	0	0	1	1	2	2	2	2
q	0	1	1	2	1	2	3	4

and the Haar transform matrix is given by

$$H_2 = \frac{1}{\sqrt{2}} \cdot \begin{pmatrix} 1 & 1 \\ 1 & -1 \end{pmatrix}. \tag{3.66}$$

The Haar transform matrix is real and orthogonal with

$$H \cdot H^T = H \cdot H^{-1} = I. \tag{3.67}$$

For a linear transform H

$$\omega = H \cdot \alpha \tag{3.68}$$

and H^{-1}

$$\alpha = H^{-1} \cdot \omega \tag{3.69}$$

For $n = 8$ the corresponding values for p and q are shown in the Table 3.1 and with t,

$$t = 0/8, 1/8, 2/8, 3/8, 4/8, 5/8, 6/8, 7/8$$

the Haar transform matrix H_8 is

$$H_8 = \begin{pmatrix} \frac{1}{2\sqrt{2}} & \frac{1}{2\sqrt{2}} & \frac{1}{2\sqrt{2}} & \frac{1}{2\sqrt{2}} & \frac{1}{2\sqrt{2}} & \frac{1}{2\sqrt{2}} & \frac{1}{2\sqrt{2}} & \frac{1}{2\sqrt{2}} \\ \frac{1}{2\sqrt{2}} & \frac{1}{2\sqrt{2}} & \frac{1}{2\sqrt{2}} & \frac{1}{2\sqrt{2}} & -\frac{1}{2\sqrt{2}} & -\frac{1}{2\sqrt{2}} & -\frac{1}{2\sqrt{2}} & -\frac{1}{2\sqrt{2}} \\ \frac{1}{2} & \frac{1}{2} & -\frac{1}{2} & -\frac{1}{2} & 0 & 0 & 0 & 0 \\ 0 & 0 & 0 & 0 & \frac{1}{2} & \frac{1}{2} & -\frac{1}{2} & -\frac{1}{2} \\ \frac{1}{\sqrt{2}} & -\frac{1}{\sqrt{2}} & 0 & 0 & 0 & 0 & 0 & 0 \\ 0 & 0 & \frac{1}{\sqrt{2}} & -\frac{1}{\sqrt{2}} & 0 & 0 & 0 & 0 \\ 0 & 0 & 0 & 0 & \frac{1}{\sqrt{2}} & -\frac{1}{\sqrt{2}} & 0 & 0 \\ 0 & 0 & 0 & 0 & 0 & 0 & \frac{1}{\sqrt{2}} & -\frac{1}{\sqrt{2}} \end{pmatrix} \tag{3.70}$$

and $H_8^{-1} = H_8^T$ is

$$H_8^T = \begin{pmatrix} \frac{1}{2\sqrt{2}} & \frac{1}{2\sqrt{2}} & \frac{1}{2} & 0 & \frac{1}{\sqrt{2}} & 0 & 0 & 0 \\ \frac{1}{2\sqrt{2}} & \frac{1}{2\sqrt{2}} & \frac{1}{2} & 0 & -\frac{1}{\sqrt{2}} & 0 & 0 & 0 \\ \frac{1}{2\sqrt{2}} & \frac{1}{2\sqrt{2}} & -\frac{1}{2} & 0 & 0 & \frac{1}{\sqrt{2}} & 0 & 0 \\ \frac{1}{2\sqrt{2}} & \frac{1}{2\sqrt{2}} & -\frac{1}{2} & 0 & 0 & -\frac{1}{\sqrt{2}} & 0 & 0 \\ \frac{1}{2\sqrt{2}} & -\frac{1}{2\sqrt{2}} & 0 & \frac{1}{2} & 0 & 0 & \frac{1}{\sqrt{2}} & 0 \\ \frac{1}{2\sqrt{2}} & -\frac{1}{2\sqrt{2}} & 0 & \frac{1}{2} & 0 & 0 & -\frac{1}{\sqrt{2}} & 0 \\ \frac{1}{2\sqrt{2}} & -\frac{1}{2\sqrt{2}} & 0 & -\frac{1}{2} & 0 & 0 & 0 & \frac{1}{\sqrt{2}} \\ \frac{1}{2\sqrt{2}} & -\frac{1}{2\sqrt{2}} & 0 & -\frac{1}{2} & 0 & 0 & 0 & -\frac{1}{\sqrt{2}} \end{pmatrix}. \tag{3.71}$$

The first row of the H_8 matrix measures the average value of the input vector multiplied by $\sqrt{2}$. The second row measures a low frequency component. The next two rows are sensitive to the first and second half of the input vector, respectively, which correspond to moderate frequency components. The remaining four rows are sensitive to the four sections of the input vector that correspond to high frequency components. A known example of a wavelet for the discrete wavelet transform, besides the Haar wavelet, is the Daubechies wavelet and its corresponding scale function (see Figure 3.22). It is not possible to write down the Daubechies wavelet and the scale function in closed form. The graphs in Figure 3.22 were generated using an iterative algorithm [Daubechies (1992)].

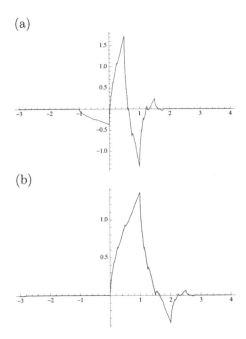

Fig. 3.22　(a) The Daubechies mother wavelet (b) The corresponding scale Daubechies function.

In Figure 3.23, we indicate the scalogram of the discrete wavelet transform of $f(t) = \sin(100 \cdot t^2)$ with the Haar wavelet and Daubechies wavelet. The discrete wavelet transform coefficients are defined on a dyadic grid; the windows do not overlap. Events that are represented between the windows are not covered. A scalogram is represented as a graph with two dimensions, where the x-axis represents translation and the y-axis represents the scale. The absolute values of the amplitude of a particular scale (inverse frequency) correspond to the intensity of each point in the image. Large absolute values are shown darker.

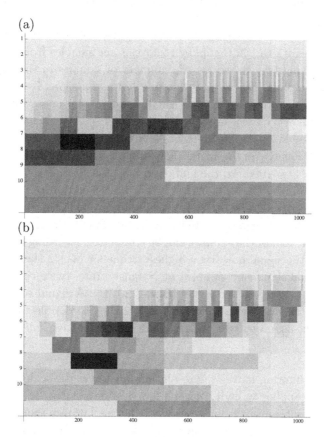

Fig. 3.23 (a) Discrete wavelet transform of $f(t) = \sin(100 \cdot t^2)$ with the Haar wavelet and scale function. The scaling function corresponding to the averaging function multiplied by $\sqrt{2}$, represented in row 12 of the scalogram. (b) Discrete wavelet transform of $f(t) = \sin(100 \cdot t^2)$ with the Daubechies wavelet and scale function. There are three scaling functions in row 12.

3.2.4   *Fast wavelet transform*

In the fast wavelet transform, the signal is passed through a series of high pass filters to analyze the high frequencies, and it is passed through a series of low pass filters to analyze the low frequencies. The filtering operations change the resolution of the signal. The scale is changed by down sampling and up sampling. The resolution of the signal, which is a measure of the amount of detail and information in the signal, is changed by the filtering operations. The scale is changed by up sampling and down sampling (subsampling) operations. Subsampling removes some samples from the signal, and subsampling by two reduces the number of samples in the signal two times. Up sampling increases the sampling rate of a signal by adding new samples, and up sampling by two usually adds a zero or an interpolated value between every two samples of the signal.

A half band low pass filter removes all frequencies that are above half of the highest frequency in the signal. For example, if a signal has a maximum component of $\omega = 2000$ Hz, the half band low pass filtering removes all the frequencies above $\omega/2 = 1000$ Hz. Thus, the resolution of the signal is changed; it is halved. The high frequency information is removed; however, the scale itself is unchanged. After passing the signal through a half band low pass filter, half of the samples can be eliminated according to Nyquist's rule because the signal now has a highest frequency of $\omega/2$ Hz instead of ω Hz. The signal should be sampled at Nyquist's rate, twice the maximum frequency that exists in the signal [Black (2013)]. A signal sampled at ω Hz contains the maximum frequency of $\omega/2$ Hz. To double the scale, we subsample the signal by two; the resulting signal will have half the number of points.

- The filtering halves the resolution but leaves the scale unchanged. This applies to high pass and low pass filters.
- The subsampling does not affect the resolution because removing half of the spectral components from the signal makes half the number of samples redundant according to Nyquist's rule.

This sub band coding can be repeated for further decomposition[3] [Polikar (1996)]. At every level, the filtering and subsampling will result in half the number of samples. Suppose that the original signal has $N = 512$ sample points, spanning a frequency band of zero to ω Hz.

---

[3]http://engineering.rowan.edu/ polikar/WAVELETS/WTtutorial.html

- The signal is passed through the low pass and high pass filters followed by subsampling by 2. The output of the high pass filter has 512 points with frequencies $\omega/2$ Hz to ω Hz; after subsampling by 2, it has 256 points.
- These 256 samples of the high pass filter constitute the first level of DWT coefficients. They represent the high frequency components and 256 translation steps.
- The output of the low pass filter has 512 points with frequencies 0 Hz. to $\omega/2$ Hz; after subsampling by 2, it has 256 points.
- This signal is passed through the low pass and high pass filters followed by subsampling by 2.
- The output of the high pass filter has 256 points with frequencies $\omega/4$ Hz to $\omega/2$ Hz; after subsampling by 2, it has 128 points. These 128 samples of the high pass filter constitute the second level of DWT coefficients. They represent the high frequency components and 128 translation steps.
- The output of the low pass filter has 128 points with frequencies 0 Hz. to $\omega/4$ Hz; after subsampling by 2, it has 128 points.
- This process is repeated until the number of points after subsampling by 2 is 1. The 1 sample of the high pass filter and the 1 sample of the low pass filter constitute the ninth and tenth levels of DWT coefficients.

When this process is repeated, it forms a sequence of ten points

$$256, 128, 64, 32, 16, 8, 4, 2, 1, 1$$

with frequencies $\omega/2$ Hz to ω Hz, $\omega/4$ Hz to $\omega/2$ Hz, $\cdots$, $\omega/512$ Hz to $\omega/256$ and, finally, 0 to $\omega/512$ Hz. This decomposition can be represented by a tree known as a filter bank of depth $\log_2 n$; in our case, the depth is 9. More samples are used at high frequencies so that the time resolution increases and the frequency resolution decreases. Fewer samples are used at lower frequencies so that the time resolution decreases but the frequency resolution increases.

Filtering a signal corresponds to the mathematical operation of convolution. The convolution of the discrete signal α_t with the impulse response of the filter $h(t)$ is defined as

$$\alpha_t * h(t) = \sum_{i=0}^{n-1} \alpha_i \cdot h(t - i). \tag{3.72}$$

For the example with $n = 4$ and

$$\alpha_0 = 2, \alpha_1 = 4, \alpha_2 = 8, \alpha_3 = 0$$

and with two filters $h_\phi(t)$ and $h_\psi(t)$ corresponding to the Haar scaling and wavelet vectors

$$h_\phi(t) = \begin{cases} \frac{1}{\sqrt{2}} & \text{if} \quad t = 0 \\ \frac{1}{\sqrt{2}} & \text{if} \quad t = 1 \\ 0 & \text{otherwise} \end{cases} \tag{3.73}$$

and

$$h_\psi(t) = \begin{cases} \frac{1}{\sqrt{2}} & \text{if} \quad t = 0 \\ -\frac{1}{\sqrt{2}} & \text{if} \quad t = 1 \\ 0 & \text{otherwise} \end{cases} \tag{3.74}$$

the convolution for the filter $h_\phi(t)$ is represented as

$$(\alpha * h_\phi)(0) = \alpha_0 \cdot h_\phi(0) + \alpha_1 \cdot h_\phi(-1) + \alpha_2 \cdot h_\phi(-2) + \alpha_3 \cdot h_\phi(-3) =$$

$$(\alpha * h_\phi)(0) = 2 \cdot \frac{1}{\sqrt{2}} + 4 \cdot 0 + 8 \cdot 0 + 0 \cdot 0 = \sqrt{2}$$

$$(\alpha * h_\phi)(1) = \alpha_0 \cdot h_\phi(1) + \alpha_1 \cdot h_\phi(0) + \alpha_2 \cdot h_\phi(-1) + \alpha_3 \cdot h_\phi(-2) = 3 \cdot \sqrt{2}$$

$$(\alpha * h_\phi)(2) = \alpha_0 \cdot h_\phi(2) + \alpha_1 \cdot h_\phi(1) + \alpha_2 \cdot h_\phi(0) + \alpha_3 \cdot h_\phi(-1) = 6 \cdot \sqrt{2}$$

$$(\alpha * h_\phi)(3) = \alpha_0 \cdot h_\phi(3) + \alpha_1 \cdot h_\phi(2) + \alpha_2 \cdot h_\phi(1) + \alpha_3 \cdot h_\phi(0) = 4 \cdot \sqrt{2}$$

$$(\alpha * h_\phi)(4) = \alpha_0 \cdot h_\phi(4) + \alpha_1 \cdot h_\phi(3) + \alpha_2 \cdot h_\phi(2) + \alpha_3 \cdot h_\phi(1) = 0,$$

the convolution for the filter $h_\psi(t)$ is computed in the same manner. The convolution operation can be represented by a matrix multiplication

$$\begin{pmatrix} (\alpha * h_\phi)(0) \\ (\alpha * h_\phi)(1) \\ (\alpha * h_\phi)(2) \\ (\alpha * h_\phi)(3) \\ (\alpha * h_\phi)(4) \end{pmatrix} = \begin{pmatrix} \frac{1}{\sqrt{2}} & 0 & 0 & 0 \\ \frac{1}{\sqrt{2}} & \frac{1}{\sqrt{2}} & 0 & 0 \\ 0 & \frac{1}{\sqrt{2}} & \frac{1}{\sqrt{2}} & 0 \\ 0 & 0 & \frac{1}{\sqrt{2}} & \frac{1}{\sqrt{2}} \\ 0 & 0 & 0 & \frac{1}{\sqrt{2}} \end{pmatrix} \cdot \begin{pmatrix} \alpha_0 \\ \alpha_1 \\ \alpha_2 \\ \alpha_3 \end{pmatrix} \tag{3.75}$$

and

$$\begin{pmatrix} (\alpha * h_\psi)(0) \\ (\alpha * h_\psi)(1) \\ (\alpha * h_\psi)(2) \\ (\alpha * h_\psi)(3) \\ (\alpha * h_\psi)(4) \end{pmatrix} = \begin{pmatrix} -\frac{1}{\sqrt{2}} & 0 & 0 & 0 \\ \frac{1}{\sqrt{2}} & -\frac{1}{\sqrt{2}} & 0 & 0 \\ 0 & \frac{1}{\sqrt{2}} & -\frac{1}{\sqrt{2}} & 0 \\ 0 & 0 & \frac{1}{\sqrt{2}} & -\frac{1}{\sqrt{2}} \\ 0 & 0 & 0 & \frac{1}{\sqrt{2}} \end{pmatrix} \cdot \begin{pmatrix} \alpha_0 \\ \alpha_1 \\ \alpha_2 \\ \alpha_3 \end{pmatrix} \tag{3.76}$$

The high pass filters are represented by wavelet functions, and the low pass filter is represented by the scale function. For the example

$$\alpha_0 = 2, \alpha_1 = 4, \alpha_2 = 8, \alpha_3 = 0$$

we will compute the Fast Wavelet Transform (FWT) using two stage filter banks represented by the Haar scaling and wavelet vectors

- The signal is passed through the low pass and high pass filters followed by subsampling by 2.
- The output of the high pass filter $h_\psi(t)$ is

$$-\sqrt{2}, -\sqrt{2}, -2 \cdot \sqrt{2}, 4 \cdot \sqrt{2}, 0$$

after subsampling by 2 it is

$$-\sqrt{2}, 4 \cdot \sqrt{2}$$

These 2 samples of the high pass filter constitute the first level of DWT coefficients. They represent the high frequency components and 2 translation steps.

- The output of the low pass filter $h_\phi(t)$ is

$$\sqrt{2}, 3 \cdot \sqrt{2}, 6 \cdot \sqrt{2}, 4 \cdot \sqrt{2}, 0$$

after subsampling by 2 it is

$$3 \cdot \sqrt{2}, 4 \cdot \sqrt{2}$$

and after subsampling by 2.The values correspond to the average value of the input vector multiplied by $\sqrt{2}$

$$\frac{2+4}{2} \cdot \sqrt{2}, \frac{8+0}{2} \cdot \sqrt{2}$$

This signal is passed in the next step through the low pass and high pass filters followed by subsampling by 2.

- The output of the high pass filter $h_\psi(t)$ is

$$-3, -1, -4$$

after subsampling by 2 it is

$$-1$$

- The output of the low pass filter $h_\phi(t)$ is

$$3, 7, 4$$

after subsampling by 2 it is

$$7$$

The 1 sample of the high pass filter and the 1 sample of the low pass filter constitute the ninth and tenth level of DWT coefficients.

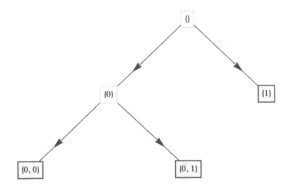

Fig. 3.24   The filter bank decomposition is represented by a tree of depth 2. The left branch represents the low pass filter, represented by the Haar scale function $\phi(x)$. The right branch represents the high pass filter, represented by the Haar wavelet $\psi(x)$.

This decomposition can be represented by a tree (filter bank) of depth $\log_2 4 = 2$, as shown in Figure 3.24, where the left branch represents the low filter and the right branch represents the high filter. The components of the tree are

$$\{0\} \implies \{4.24264, 5.65685\},$$

$$\{1\} \implies \{-1.41421, 5.65685\},$$

$$\{0, 0\} \implies \{7\},$$

$$\{0, 1\} \implies \{-1\}.$$

Mathematically, the fast wavelet transform (FWT) exploits the relationship between the coefficients of DWT and scales. $\phi(t)$ can be expressed as a refinement equation

$$\phi(t) = \sum_{\nu} h_\phi(\nu) \cdot \sqrt{2} \cdot \phi \left(2 \cdot t - \nu \right) \tag{3.77}$$

with scaling function coefficients $h_\phi(\nu)$. The expansion function of any subspace can be composed from double resolution copies of themselves. With the Haar scaling function

$$h_\phi(t) = \begin{cases} \frac{1}{\sqrt{2}} & \text{if} \quad t = 0 \\ \frac{1}{\sqrt{2}} & \text{if} \quad t = 1 \\ 0 & \text{otherwise} \end{cases}$$

we get

$$\phi(t) = \frac{1}{\sqrt{2}} \cdot \sqrt{2} \cdot \phi(2 \cdot t) + \frac{1}{\sqrt{2}} \cdot \sqrt{2} \cdot \phi(2 \cdot t - 1)$$

$$\phi(t) = \phi(2 \cdot t) + \phi(2 \cdot t - 1). \tag{3.78}$$

With translation k and scaling values 2^s for t and $\mu = 2 \cdot k + \nu$

$$\phi(2^s \cdot t - k) = \sum_{\nu} h_\phi(\nu) \cdot \sqrt{2} \cdot \phi(2 \cdot (2^s \cdot t - k) - \nu) \tag{3.79}$$

$$\phi(2^s \cdot t - k) = \sum_{\mu} h_\phi(\mu - 2 \cdot k) \cdot \sqrt{2} \cdot \phi(2^{s+1} \cdot t - \mu). \tag{3.80}$$

By similar operations we get

$$\psi(2^s \cdot t - k) = \sum_{\mu} h_\psi(\mu - 2 \cdot k) \cdot \sqrt{2} \cdot \phi(2^{s+1} \cdot t - \mu). \tag{3.81}$$

With

$$DWT_\psi(s, k) = \frac{1}{\sqrt{n}} \cdot \sum_{t} \alpha_t \cdot \psi_{s,k}(t)$$

and with translation k and scaling values 2^s for t and $\mu = 2 \cdot k + \nu$

$$DWT_\psi(s, k) = \frac{1}{\sqrt{n}} \cdot \sum_{t} \alpha_t \cdot 2^{s/2} \cdot \psi(2^s \cdot t - k). \tag{3.82}$$

By replacing $\psi(2^s \cdot t - k)$ with Equation 3.81

$$DWT_\psi(s, k) = \frac{1}{\sqrt{n}} \cdot \sum_{t} \alpha_t \cdot 2^{s/2} \cdot \left(\sum_{\mu} h_\psi(\mu - 2 \cdot k) \cdot \sqrt{2} \cdot \phi(2^{s+1} \cdot \cdot t - \mu) \right). \tag{3.83}$$

By rearranging the terms we get

$$DWT_\psi(s, k) = \sum_{\mu} h_\psi(\mu - 2 \cdot k) \cdot \left(\frac{1}{\sqrt{n}} \cdot \sum_{t} \alpha_t \cdot 2^{(s+1)/2} \cdot \phi(2^{s+1} \cdot t - \mu) \right) \tag{3.84}$$

and we can simplify into

$$DWT_\psi(s, k) = \sum_{\mu} h_\psi(\mu - 2 \cdot k) \cdot DWT_\phi(s + 1, \mu) \tag{3.85}$$

the coefficients of DWT at scale s are represented by DWT coefficients at scale $k + 1$. In similar way

$$DWT_\phi(s, k) = \sum_{\mu} h_\phi(\mu - 2 \cdot k) \cdot DWT_\phi(s + 1, \mu). \tag{3.86}$$

The complexity of FWT is

$$O(n + \frac{n}{2} + \frac{n}{3} + \cdots + \frac{n}{n - 1} + 1 = O(n).$$

3.2.5 *Discrete wavelet transform and images*

In two dimensions, the two-dimensional scaling function and wavelet functions are represented by a product of one dimensional scaling and wavelet functions. There are four possible combinations, the scaling function

$$\phi(x,y) = \phi(x) \cdot \phi(y) \qquad (3.87)$$

and three direction sensitive wavelets, the horizontal sensitive wavelet

$$\psi^H(x,y) = \psi(x) \cdot \phi(y) \qquad (3.88)$$

the vertical sensitive wavelet

$$\psi^V(x,y) = \phi(x) \cdot \psi(y) \qquad (3.89)$$

and the diagonal sensitive wavelet

$$\psi^D(x,y) = \psi(x) \cdot \psi(y) \qquad (3.90)$$

measure the variations among different directions. We can discretise the continuous wavelet transformation by discretising τ translation and s scale. The discrete Fourier transform and the discrete cosine transform can be extended to two dimensions of $\alpha_{x,y}$ with

$$DWT_\phi(s_0, k, l,) = \frac{1}{\sqrt{n} \cdot \sqrt{m}} \cdot \sum_x \sum_y \alpha_{x,y} \cdot \phi_{s_0, k, l}(x, y) \qquad (3.91)$$

and

$$DWT_\psi^H(s, k, l) = \frac{1}{\sqrt{n} \cdot \sqrt{m}} \cdot \sum_x \sum_y \alpha_{x,y} \cdot \psi_{s,k,l}^H(x, y), \qquad (3.92)$$

$$DWT_\psi^V(s, k, l) = \frac{1}{\sqrt{n} \cdot \sqrt{m}} \cdot \sum_x \sum_y \alpha_{x,y} \cdot \psi_{s,k,l}^V(x, y), \qquad (3.93)$$

$$DWT_\psi^D(s, k, l) = \frac{1}{\sqrt{n} \cdot \sqrt{m}} \cdot \sum_x \sum_y \alpha_{x,y} \cdot \psi_{s,k,l}^D(x, y) \qquad (3.94)$$

with a scaling function $\phi(x, y)$

$$\phi_{s,k,l}(x, y) = \sqrt{2^s} \cdot \phi\left(2^s \cdot x - k, 2^s \cdot x - l\right) \qquad (3.95)$$

and wavelet function $\psi(x, y)$

$$\psi_{s,k}^H(x, y) = \sqrt{2^s} \cdot \psi^H\left(2^s \cdot x - k, 2^s \cdot x - l\right), \qquad (3.96)$$

$$\psi_{s,k}^V(x, y) = \sqrt{2^s} \cdot \psi^V\left(2^s \cdot x - k, 2^s \cdot x - l\right), \qquad (3.97)$$

$$\psi^D_{s,k}(x,y) = \sqrt{2^s} \cdot \psi^D \left(2^s \cdot x - k, 2^s \cdot x - l\right). \tag{3.98}$$

The original function can be reconstructed from the coefficients for $s \geq s_0$ by

$$\alpha_{x,y} = \frac{1}{\sqrt{n} \cdot \sqrt{m}} \cdot \sum_k \sum_l DWT_\phi(s_0, k, l) \cdot \phi_{s_0,k,l}(x,z) +$$

$$\frac{1}{\sqrt{n} \cdot \sqrt{m}} \cdot \sum_{s=s_0}^{\infty} \sum_k \sum_l DWT_\psi^H(s, k, l) \cdot \psi^H_{s,k,l}(x,z) +$$

$$\frac{1}{\sqrt{n} \cdot \sqrt{m}} \cdot \sum_{s=s_0}^{\infty} \sum_k \sum_l DWT_\psi^V(s, k, l) \cdot \psi^V_{s,k,l}(x,z) +$$

$$\frac{1}{\sqrt{n} \cdot \sqrt{m}} \cdot \sum_{s=s_0}^{\infty} \sum_k \sum_l DWT_\psi^D(s, k, l) \cdot \psi^D_{s,k,l}(x,z). \tag{3.99}$$

The two dimensional Haar's mother wavelet ψ and the Haar's unit-width scale function ϕ are shown is Figure 3.25. A black and white picture of the

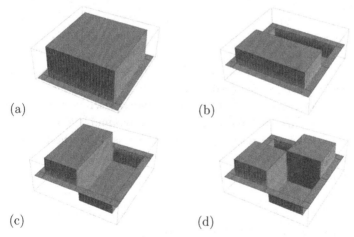

(a)   (b)

(c)   (d)

Fig. 3.25   (a) (a) The Haar scaling function $\phi(x,y)$. (b) The horizontal sensitive wavelet $\psi^H(x,y)$. (c) The vertical sensitive wavelet $\psi^V(x,y)$. (d) The diagonal sensitive wavelet $\psi^D(x,y)$.

size 100×100 with 256 different grey values is represented in Figure 3.26. A convolution of four filters and subsampling by 2 is done (see Figure 3.27). The filters are defined by the Haar scaling function $\phi(x,y)$ (low pass filter),

Fig. 3.26   A black and white picture of the size 100×100 with 256 different grey values.

the horizontal sensitive wavelet $\psi^H(x, y)$ (high pass filter), the vertical sensitive wavelet $\psi^V(x, y)$ and the diagonal sensitive wavelet $\psi^D(x, y)$. The FWT of an image can be represented by a tree (filter bank). In Figure 3.28, a tree of depth 2 is shown, where the left branch represents the low pass filter and the right branch represents the high filters. The components of the tree of Figure 3.28 are represented as image lot wavelet image coefficients in a grid layout in Figure 3.29. The 2 dimensional discrete wavelet transform image coefficients are usually arranged in a pyramid layout (see Figure 3.30). For compression of an image only a FWT is done, the frequencies with low amplitude are discarded. The image can be then reconstructed from the coefficients.

3.3   The Karhunen-Loève Transform

The Karhunen-Loève transform is a linear transform that maps possibly correlated variables into a set of values of linearly uncorrelated variables. This transformation is defined in such a way that the first principal component has the largest possible variance. In contrast to a Fourier transform that is based on sinusoidal functions, the Karhunen-Loève transform is based on orthogonal basis functions determined by the covariance matrix.

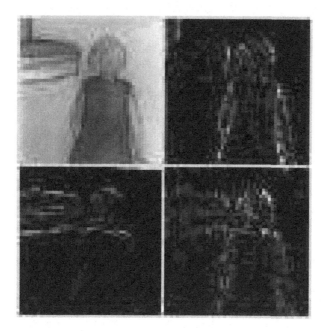

Fig. 3.27 Convolution of four filters and subsampling by 2. The filters are defined by he Haar scaling function $\phi(x, y)$ (low pass filter), the horizontal sensitive wavelet $\psi^H(x, y)$ (high pass filter), the vertical sensitive wavelet $\psi^V(x, y)$ and the diagonal sensitive wavelet $\psi^D(x, y)$.

3.3.1 *The covariance matrix*

The sample size denoted by n, is the number of data items in a sample of a population. The goal is to make inferences about a population from a sample. Sample covariance indicates the relationship between two variables of a sample.

$$cov(X, Y) = \frac{\sum_{k=1}^n (x_k - \overline{x}) \cdot (y_k - \overline{y})}{n - 1} \tag{3.100}$$

with $\overline{x}$ and $\overline{y}$ being the arithmetic mean of the two variables of the sample. The arithmetic mean is the average value; the sum of all values in the sample divided by the number of values. For the whole population, the covariance is

$$cov(X, Y) = \frac{\sum_{k=1}^n (x_k - \overline{x}) \cdot (y_k - \overline{y})}{n}. \tag{3.101}$$

The sample covariance has $n - 1$ in the denominator rather than n due to Bessel's correction. The sample covariance relies on the difference between each observation and the sample mean. The sample mean is slightly

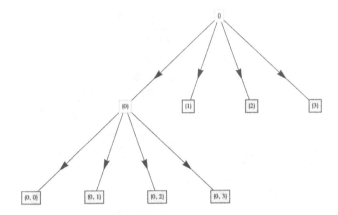

Fig. 3.28 The filter bank decomposition is represented by a tree of depth w. The left branch represents the low pass filter, represented by the Haar scale function $\phi(x, y)$. The right branches represent the high pass filters, represented by the Haar wavelet $\psi^H(x, y)$, $\psi^V(x, y)$, $\psi^D(x, y)$.

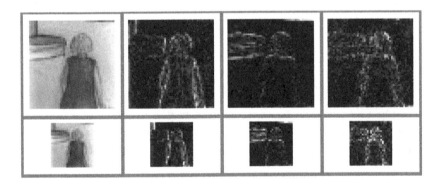

Fig. 3.29 The components of the tree are $\{0\}, \{1\}, \{2\}, \{3\}$ in the first row, and $\{0, 0\}, \{0, 1\}, \{0, 2\}, \{0, 3\}$ in the second row.

correlated with each observation because it is defined in terms of all observations. The sample mean is always smaller or equal to the population mean. In computer science, the sample covariance is usually used and is therefore also used in this paper without further indication; for example, when we introduce the covariance matrix, we will not distinguish between the sample covariance matrix and the population covariance matrix. Co-

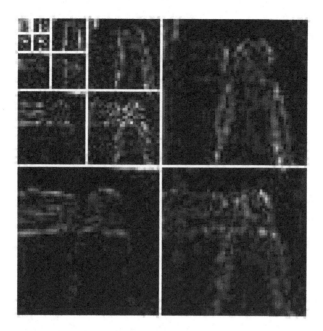

Fig. 3.30   The 2 dimensional discrete wavelet transform image coefficients arranged in a pyramid layout of depth four (see Figure 3.26).

variance is a measure of how much two random variables change together. In a linear relationship, either the high values of one variable are paired with the high values of another variable or the high values of one variable are paired with the low values of another variable. For example, for a list of two variables, (X, Y),

$$\Sigma = \{(2.1, 2), (2.3, 2), (2.9, 3), (4.1, 4), (5, 4.8), (2, 2.5), (2.2, 1.5),$$

$$(4, 5), (4, 2), (2.8, 4), (3, 3.4), (3.5, 3.8), (4.5, 4.7), (3.5, 3)\}$$

represents the data set Σ. The sample covariance of the data set is 0.82456. Ordering the list by X, we notice that the ascending X values are matched by ascending Y values (see Figure 3.31). The covariance matrix measures the tendency of two features, x_i and x_j, to vary in the same direction. The covariance between features x_i and x_j is estimated for n vectors as

$$c_{ij} = \frac{\sum_{k=1}^{n} (x_{k,i} - \overline{x_i}) \cdot (y_{k,j} - \overline{y_j})}{n - 1} \tag{3.102}$$

with $\overline{x_i}$ and $\overline{y_j}$ being the arithmetic mean of the two variables of the sample. Covariances are symmetric; $c_{ij} = c_{ji}$. The resulting covariance matrix C is

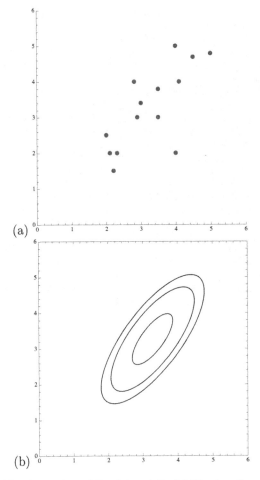

Fig. 3.31   (a) The data points of the data set Σ. (b) The two dimensional distribution Σ can be described by three ellipse that divide the data points in four equal groups.

symmetric and positive-definite,

$$C = \begin{pmatrix} c_{11} & c_{12} & \cdots & c_{1m} \\ c_{21} & c_{22} & \cdots & c_{2m} \\ \vdots & \vdots & \ddots & \vdots \\ c_{m1} & c_{m2} & \cdots & c_{mm} \end{pmatrix}. \tag{3.103}$$

The covariance matrix of the data set Σ is given by

$$C = \begin{pmatrix} 0.912582 & 0.82456 \\ 0.82456 & 1.34247 \end{pmatrix}. \tag{3.104}$$

3.3.2 *The Karhunen-Loève transform*

A real matrix M is positive definite if $\mathbf{z}^\top \cdot M \cdot \mathbf{z}$ is positive for any non-zero column vector $\mathbf{z}$ of real numbers. A symmetric and positive-definite matrix can be diagonalized. It follows that

$$U^{-1} \cdot C \cdot U = \Lambda = diag(\lambda_1, \lambda_2, \cdots .\lambda_m) \qquad (3.105)$$

U is an orthonormal matrix of the dimension $m \times m$,

$$U^\top \cdot U = I \qquad (3.106)$$

$$U^\top \cdot C \cdot U = \Lambda = diag(\lambda_1, \lambda_2, \cdots .\lambda_m) \qquad (3.107)$$

and

$$U \cdot \Lambda = C \cdot U. \qquad (3.108)$$

There are m eigenvalues and eigenvectors with

$$(\lambda_i \cdot I - C) \cdot \mathbf{u}_i = 0 \qquad (3.109)$$

and

$$C \cdot \mathbf{u}_i = \lambda_i \cdot \mathbf{u}_i \qquad (3.110)$$

An eigenvector can have two directions, it is either $\mathbf{u}_i$ or $-\mathbf{u}_i$.

$$C \cdot (-\mathbf{u}_i) = \lambda_i \cdot (-\mathbf{u}_i) \qquad (3.111)$$

The eigenvectors are always orthogonal, and their length is arbitrary. The normalized eigenvectors define the orthonormal matrix U of dimension $m \times m$. Each normalized eigenvector is a column of U with

$$U^\top \cdot U = I.$$

The matrix U defines the Karhunen-Loève transform. The Karhunen-Loève transform rotates the coordinate system in such a way that the new covariance matrix will be diagonal

$$\mathbf{y} = U^\top \cdot \mathbf{x} \qquad (3.112)$$

The squares of the eigenvalues represent the variances along the eigenvectors. The eigenvalues corresponding to the covariance matrix of the data set Σ are

$$\lambda_1 = 1.97964, \quad \lambda_2 = 0.275412$$

and the corresponding normalized eigenvectors are

$$\mathbf{u}_1 = \begin{pmatrix} 0.611454 \\ 0.79128 \end{pmatrix}, \quad \mathbf{u}_2 = \begin{pmatrix} -0.79128 \\ 0.611454 \end{pmatrix}.$$

The define the matrix U with

$$U = \begin{pmatrix} 0.611454 & -0.79128 \\ 0.79128 & 0.611454 \end{pmatrix}. \qquad (3.113)$$

The Karhunen-Loève transform for the data set Σ is given by

$$\mathbf{y} = U^\top \cdot \mathbf{x} = \begin{pmatrix} 0.611454 & 0.79128 \\ -0.79128 & 0.611454 \end{pmatrix} \cdot \mathbf{x}, \qquad (3.114)$$

it rotates the coordinate system in such a way that the new covariance matrix will be diagonal (see Figure 3.32).

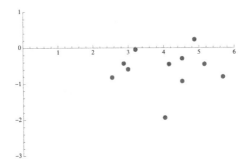

Fig. 3.32   The Karhunen-Loève transform for the the data set Σ. It rotates the coordinate system (the points) in such a way rhat the new covariance matrix will be diagonal.

3.3.3   *Principal component analysis*

Principal component analysis (PCA) is a technique that is useful for the compression of data. The purpose is to reduce the dimensionality of a data set by finding a new set of variables, smaller than the original set of variables, that nonetheless retains most of the sample's information. The first principal component corresponds to the normalized eigenvector with the highest variance. Uncorrelated features with higher variance, represented by λ_i, contain more information. In principal component analysis (PCA), the significant eigenvectors define the principal components. Accordingly to the Kaiser criterion, the eigenvectors whose eigenvalues are below 1 are discarded [de Sá (2001)]. Each of the s non-discarded eigenvectors is a column of the matrix W of dimension $s \times m$ with the linear mapping from $\mathbf{R}^m \to \mathbf{R}^s$,

$$\mathbf{z} = W^\top \cdot \mathbf{x} \tag{3.115}$$

with $dim(s) \leq dim(m)$. The resulting principal components are linear transformation of the original features. The Principal component analysis for the data set Σ is given by

$$\mathbf{z} = W^\top \cdot \mathbf{x} = \left(0.611454\, 0.79128 \right) \cdot \mathbf{x} \tag{3.116}$$

(see Figure 3.33). For a dimension reduction, it desirable that $dim(s) \ll dim(m)$. It is difficult to attach any semantic meaning to the principal components. For new data that is added to the dataset, the PCA has to be recomputed.

Fig. 3.33   The data set Σ is projected onto one dimension.

3.3.3.1   *Examples*

Suppose we have a covariance matrix:

$$C = \begin{pmatrix} 3 & 1 \\ 1 & 21 \end{pmatrix} \qquad (3.117)$$

What is the corresponding matrix of the K-L transformation? First, we have to compute the eigenvalues. The system has to become linear depend-able (singular). The determinant has to become zero.

$$|\lambda \cdot I - C| = 0. \qquad (3.118)$$

Solving the Equation

$$\lambda^2 - 24 \cdot \lambda + 62 = 0 \qquad (3.119)$$

we get the two eigenvalues

$$\lambda_1 = 2.94461, \quad \lambda_2 = 21.05538.$$

To compute the eigenvectors we have to solve two singular, dependent systems

$$|\lambda_1 \cdot I - C| = 0$$

and

$$|\lambda_2 \cdot I - C| = 0.$$

For $\lambda_1 = 2.94461$ we get

$$\left(\begin{pmatrix} 2.94461 & 0 \\ 0 & 2.94461 \end{pmatrix} - \begin{pmatrix} 3 & 1 \\ 1 & 21 \end{pmatrix} \right) \cdot \begin{pmatrix} u_1 \\ u_2 \end{pmatrix} = 0 \qquad (3.120)$$

and we have to find a nontrivial solution for

$$\begin{pmatrix} -0.05538 & -1 \\ -1 & -18.055 \end{pmatrix} \cdot \begin{pmatrix} u_1 \\ u_2 \end{pmatrix} = 0 \qquad (3.121)$$

Because the system is linear dependable, the left column is a multiple value of the right column, and there are infinitely many solution. We only have to determine the direction of the eigenvectors; if we simply suppose that $u_1 = 1$,

$$\begin{pmatrix} -0.05538 & -1 \\ -1 & -18.055 \end{pmatrix} \cdot \begin{pmatrix} 1 \\ u_2 \end{pmatrix} = 0$$

and

$$\begin{pmatrix} -0.05538 \\ -1 \end{pmatrix} = \begin{pmatrix} 1 \\ 18.055 \end{pmatrix} \cdot u_2$$

with

$$\mathbf{u}_1 = \begin{pmatrix} u_1 \\ u_2 \end{pmatrix} = \begin{pmatrix} 1 \\ -0.05539 \end{pmatrix}.$$

For $\lambda_2 = 21.05538$ we get

$$\begin{pmatrix} 18.055 & -1 \\ -1 & 0.05538 \end{pmatrix} \cdot \begin{pmatrix} u_1 \\ u_2 \end{pmatrix} = 0 \tag{3.122}$$

with

$$\mathbf{u}_2 = \begin{pmatrix} u_1 \\ u_2 \end{pmatrix} = \begin{pmatrix} 1 \\ 18.055 \end{pmatrix}.$$

The two normalized vectors $\mathbf{u}_1$, $\mathbf{u}_2$ define the columns of the matrix U

$$U = \begin{pmatrix} 0.998469 & 0.0553016 \\ -0.0553052 & 0.99847 \end{pmatrix}.$$

Because $\lambda_1 = 2.94461 < \lambda_2 = 21.05538$ the second eigenvector is more significant, however we can not apply the Kaiser criterion.

For the data set (see Figure 3.34)

$$\Psi = \{(1,1), (2,2), (3,3), (4,4), (5,5), (6,6)\}$$

the covariance matrix is

$$C = \begin{pmatrix} 3.5 & 3.5 \\ 3.5 & 3.5 \end{pmatrix}. \tag{3.123}$$

The two two eignvalues are

$$\lambda_1 = 7, \quad \lambda_2 = 0$$

and the two normalized eigenvectors are

$$\mathbf{u}_1 = \begin{pmatrix} \frac{1}{\sqrt{2}} \\ \frac{1}{\sqrt{2}} \end{pmatrix}, \quad \mathbf{u}_2 = \begin{pmatrix} -\frac{1}{\sqrt{2}} \\ \frac{1}{\sqrt{2}} \end{pmatrix}.$$

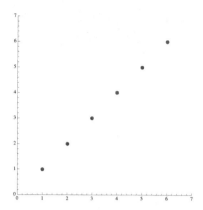

Fig. 3.34 The data points of the data set Ψ.

The matrix that describes the K-L transformation is given by

$$U = \begin{pmatrix} \frac{1}{\sqrt{2}} & \frac{1}{\sqrt{2}} \\ \frac{1}{\sqrt{2}} & -\frac{1}{\sqrt{2}} \end{pmatrix} = \frac{1}{\sqrt{2}} \cdot \begin{pmatrix} 1 & 1 \\ 1 & -1 \end{pmatrix} = \sqrt{2} \cdot \begin{pmatrix} \frac{1}{2} & \frac{1}{2} \\ \frac{1}{2} & -\frac{1}{2} \end{pmatrix}. \qquad (3.124)$$

The K-L transformation maps the two dimensional data set Ψ in one dimension because λ_2 is zero (see Figure 3.35). For example, the data point $(1,1)$ is mapped on the $x - axis$

$$\begin{pmatrix} \sqrt{2} \\ 0 \end{pmatrix} = \begin{pmatrix} \sqrt{2} \cdot \frac{1+1}{2} \\ \sqrt{2} \cdot \frac{1-1}{2} \end{pmatrix} = \sqrt{2} \cdot \begin{pmatrix} \frac{1}{2} & \frac{1}{2} \\ \frac{1}{2} & -\frac{1}{2} \end{pmatrix} \cdot \begin{pmatrix} 1 \\ 1 \end{pmatrix} \qquad (3.125)$$

with the value $\sqrt{2} \approx 1.4142$ corresponding to the length of the vector $(1,1)$.

Fig. 3.35 The data set Ψ projected onto one dimension.

3.4 Clustering

Clustering is a useful tool for data compression. Instead of reducing the dimensionality of a data set, clustering reduces the number of data points. It groups the data points into clusters according to a distance function. The points are similar to one another within the same cluster and dissimilar to the objects in other clusters. The cluster centers (also called centroids) represent the compressed data set. Usually, the number of clusters k is much smaller than the number of data points.

3.4.1 _k-means_

The most popular clustering method is k-means clustering. We map n data points, represented by vectors of dimension m, into k centroids with

$$k \ll n$$

of dimension m. The Euclidean norm induced by the inner product

$$\|\mathbf{x}\| = \sqrt{\langle \mathbf{x} | \mathbf{x} \rangle}. \tag{3.126}$$

and Euclidean distance function

$$d_2(\mathbf{x}, \mathbf{z}) = \|x - z\| = \sqrt{\sum_{i=1}^{m} (x_i - z_i)^2}. \tag{3.127}$$

In k-means clustering with k centroids

$$\mathbf{c}_1, \mathbf{c}_2 \cdots, \mathbf{c}_k$$

and k clusters

$$C_1, C_2 \cdots, C_k.$$

each cluster is defined as the set of points with

$$C_j = \{\mathbf{x} | d_2(\mathbf{x}, \mathbf{c}_j) = \min_t d_2(\mathbf{x}, \mathbf{c}_t)\}. \tag{3.128}$$

Each cluster C_j contains the points that are closest to the centroid $\mathbf{c}_j$. The centroid $\mathbf{c}_j$ is represented by the mean value of all the points of C_j

$$\mathbf{c}_j = \frac{1}{|C_j|} \cdot \sum_{x \in C_j} \mathbf{x}. \tag{3.129}$$

The error or cost function

$$E = \sum_{j=1}^{k} \sum_{x \in C_j} d_2(\mathbf{x}, \mathbf{z}) \tag{3.130}$$

for the partial derivative of E is

$$\frac{\partial E}{\partial \mathbf{c}_j} = -\sum_{x \in C_j} (\mathbf{x} - \mathbf{c}_j) \tag{3.131}$$

with the solution for the local minima

$$0 = \frac{\partial E}{\partial \mathbf{c}_j}, \quad \mathbf{c}_j = \frac{1}{|C_j|} \cdot \sum_{x \in C_j} \mathbf{x}. \tag{3.132}$$

Determination of the $\mathbf{c}_j$ vectors is computationally difficult. However, an efficient iterative algorithm exists that minimizes the error function E. The algorithm is called the standard algorithm or Lloyd's algorithm [Lloyd (1982)]. The algorithm starts with a random initialization of centroids $\mathbf{c}_j$ and moves them iteratively in the direction of the center of the clusters. An unknown value is the number of clusters k that has to be defined by the user. The algorithm is given by

Standard k-measn

random initialisation of k centroids;
do
    {
        assign to each $\mathbf{x}_i$ in the dataset the nearest centroid $\mathbf{c}_j$ according to d_2;
        compute all new centroids $\mathbf{c}_j = \frac{1}{|C_j|} \cdot \sum_{x \in C_j} \mathbf{x}$;
    }
until ($|E_{new} - E_{old}| < \epsilon$ or number of iterations *max* iterations).

To choose the value k, we have to know our data. Repeated runs of k-means clustering on the same data can lead to quite different partition results due to the random initialization. There are many alternative ways to determine the value of k or to initialize the centroids $\mathbf{c}_j$. One simple way is to choose a maximum radius r within every data point that should have a cluster seed after completion of the initialization phase. In a single sweep, one goes through the data and assigns the cluster seeds according to the chosen radius r. A data point becomes a new cluster seed if it is not covered by the spheres with the chosen radius of the other already assigned seeds [Sommer and Wichert (2002)]. k represents an unsupervised learning; it is an unsupervised classification because no predefined classes are present. For large data sets, the adaptive k-means learning algorithm according to Equation 3.131 is given by

k-means for large data sets

random initialisation of k centroids;
do

{
    chose $\mathbf{x}_i$ from the dataset;
    determine the nearest centroid $\mathbf{c}_j^*$ according to d_2;
    compute the new centroid $\mathbf{c}_j^{*new} = \mathbf{c}_j^{*old} + \frac{1}{|C_{*j}^{old}|+1} \cdot (\mathbf{x}_i - \mathbf{c}_j^{*old})$;
}
until ($|E_{new} - E_{old}| < \epsilon$ or number of iterations *max* iterations).

3.4.1.1 *Color reduction*

k-means can be used for color reduction for RGB images. k would indicate the number of the reduced colors, and the dimension would be there for R, G, B. $x_i = R_i, G_i, B_i$ would correspond to the pixel at position i in a one dimensional array. Color segmentation represents a weak segmentation, in which the segmented parts (the same color) do not correspond necessarily to objects.

Chapter 4

Compression

Multimedia objects are represented by digital information (numbers, vectors). The size of a multimedia object may be large; a high-quality colored image requires 6 MB and five minutes of a high-quality video clip with 30 FPS would require 54 GB. Compression is a clever method for encoding information using fewer bits than required by the original representation. Two categories of compression exist: lossless compression and lossy compression. Both types of compression can reduce the amount of the source information. Although no information is lost in lossless compression, this is not the case with lossy compression. When the compressed information is decompressed in lossy compression, a minor loss of information and quality occurs from the identification of unnecessary or unimportant information, which can be removed.

4.1 Lossless Compression

Lossless compressions are independent of the type of information that is compressed. It either transforms the representation or identifies redundancy by statistical encoding.

4.1.1 *Transform encoding*

Transform encoding transforms the information from one representation into another representation without loss of information that is associated with the transformation. Transformations can be applied to signals to obtain additional information about the signal that is not readily available in the raw signal. In many cases, the most distinguished information is hidden in the frequency content of the signal. One type of transformation is the Fourier transform. For example, if we consider the Fourier transform of the electric current that we use in our houses, we will observe a spike at 50 Hz in European houses and a spike at 60 Hz in American houses. The signal only has a 50 Hz or 60 Hz frequency component. Other popular and simple transform encodings include the run-length encoding for binary strings and differential encoding.

Run-length encoding Run-length encoding of a binary string can be employed when the ones and zeros appear grouped [Halsall (2001)]. Run-length encoding (RLE) is a very simple form of data compression for binary strings, in which the same value occurs in many consecutive positions. A single value and count are stored. For a binary string,

$$00000001111111110000011$$

the value and counts are represented by

$$(0,7)(1,10)(0,5)(1,2).$$

For a representation of 0 and 1, we can simplify the representation to

$$7, 10, 5, 2.$$

Pointer coding If a small number of 1s is equally distributed over the coordinates of the vectors, a sparse code is given. For a binary string with more zeros then ones, pointer coding can be utilized. In pointer coding, only the positions of the vector components that are unequal to zero are represented.

$$01000110000$$

The pointer representation of ones is given by

$$2, 6, 7.$$

Inverted index The pointer representation is related to the inverted index or inverted file for non binary strings. In an inverted index, the position of some content in a string is represented. For binary strings, the inverted index corresponds to the pointer coding.

Differential encoding The amplitude of a value of a signal encompasses a large range. The difference in amplitude between successive values is relatively small. Instead of representing amplitude by large code words, a set of smaller code words can be employed, in which each code word indicates the difference in amplitude between current values. For example, we need 12 bits to represent a signal but the maximum difference in amplitude between successive samples can be represented by 3 bits.

Table 4.1

M	S
A	00
B	01
C	10
D	11

4.1.2 *Lempel-Ziv*

The Lempel-Ziv (LZ) compressing algorithm employs entire strings as the basis of the coding operation [Halsall (2001)]. For the compression of a text, a table that contains all possible words that occur in the text is stored by the encoder and the decoder. Because each word occurs in the text, the word is represented by a unique code that is shorter than the word. Each code corresponds to a word in the dictionary. Most word-processing packages contain a dictionary for spell checking and LZ compression. In the Lempel-Ziv-Welsh (LZW) coding algorithm, the contents of the dictionary are dynamically extended. Initially, the dictionary contains only the character code; the remaining entries in the dictionary are subsequently and dynamically constructed.

4.1.3 *Statistical encoding*

The transmitted messages are usually not included in the alphabet of the original message M. For example, in Morse code, spaced short and long electrical pulses or light flashes are used as a signal alphabet S to transmit the message's alphabet M. Using an example, we explain how to efficiently convert messages into a signal alphabet. The message alphabet is named M and consists of the four characters A, B, C, and D. The signal alphabet is named S and consists of the characters 0 and 1. We assume that the signal channel can transmit 100 characters from S each second. This rate is referred to as the channel capacity. Subject to these constraints, the goal is to maximize the transmission rate of characters from M. Using the conversion from M to S in Table 4.1, the message ABC would be transmitted using the sequence 000110. Each character from M is represented by two characters from S. Because the channel capacity is 100 characters from S each second, this communication scheme can transmit 50 characters from M each second. We disregard the fact that characters are employed with varying frequencies in most alphabets. For example, in typical English text, the letter e occurs approximately 200 times as frequently as the

Table 4.2

M	S
A	0
B	10
C	110
D	111

letter z. Thus, one method for improving the efficiency of a signal transmission is to use shorter codes for the more frequent characters, as occurs in Morse code. We assume that generally one-half of the characters in the messages that we wish to send comprise the letter A, one-quarter of the characters comprise the letter B, one-eighth of the characters consist of the letter C, and one-eighth of the characters comprise the letter D. Using the conversion in Table 4.2, the message ABC would be transmitted using the sequence 010110, which also contains six characters. To demonstrate that this second encoding is better on *average* than the first encoding requires a longer message. For a message of 120 characters, we would use a sequence of 240 signal characters in the first coding and 210 in the second. We can determine for each message m_i the probability of its presence $p(m_i)$ if we assume that this probability remains fixed. From any finite sample, we can estimate the true fraction and calculate the accuracy of our estimation [Topsoe (1974); Wichert (2013a)]. This approach is referred to as the frequentist approach. The large is the probability that we receive a message, the lower is the degree that we are surprised. Surprise of a message m_i is defined as the inverse probability

$$s_i = \frac{1}{p(m_i)}. \tag{4.1}$$

Information is defined as

$$I_i = log_2(s_i) = -log_2(p(m_i)) \tag{4.2}$$

Probabilities are multiplied and information is summed. The theoretical minimum average number of bits that are required to transmit (represent) information is known as the Shannon's entropy. With n as the number of different messages m_i and $p(m_i)$ as the probability of occurrence of the symbol, the theoretical minimum average number of bits is computed using Shannon's formula of entropy

$$H = -\sum_{i}^{n} p(m_i) \cdot \log_2 p(m_i). \tag{4.3}$$

Table 4.3

M	S
A	10
B	11
C	000
D	001
E	010
F	011

The relationship between $\log_2$ and any other base b involves multiplication by a constant,

$$\log_2 x = \frac{log_b x}{log_b 2} = \frac{log_{10} x}{log_{10} 2}.$$ (4.4)

If we measure Shannon's entropy in decimal numbers with the base $b = 10$, it differs by a constant $1/log_{10}2 = 3.3219\cdots$ from the entropy measured in bits with $b = 2$ with

$$H = -\frac{1}{log_{10} 2} \cdot \sum_i^n p(m_i) \cdot \log_{10} p(m_i). = -\sum_i^n p(m_i) \cdot \log_2 p(m_i).$$ (4.5)

The efficiency of a particular encoding scheme is frequently computed as a ratio of the entropy of the source to the average number of bits per codeword required for the scheme

$$\sum_i^n N_i \cdot p(m_i).$$ (4.6)

where N_i is the number of bits to message m_i. For example, for six letters (messages) A, B, C, D, E and F with $p(A) = p(B) = 0.25$ and $p(C) = p(D) = p(E) = p(F) = 0.125$, using the conversion of Table 4.3 the average number of bits per codeword is

$$\sum_i^6 N_i \cdot p(m_i) =$$ (4.7)

$$2 \cdot 0.25 + 2 \cdot 0.25 + 4 \cdot 0.125 + 4 \cdot 0.125 + 4 \cdot 0.125 + 4 \cdot 0.125 = 2.5$$

and the entropy of the source is

$$H = -\sum_i^6 p(m_i) \cdot \log_2 p(m_i) =$$ (4.8)

$$-2 \cdot (0.25 \cdot log_2(0.25)) - 4 \cdot (0.125 \cdot log_2(0.125)) = 2.5 \; bits.$$

The ratio of the entropy of the source to the average number of bits per codeword in our example is one.

For the decoding operation to properly function, a shorter codeword in the set S does not form the beginning of a longer code word. This property is referred to as the *prefix property*. A greedy algorithm constructs an optimal code with the prefix property. The resulting code is the Huffman code [Cormen *et al.* (2001b)]. A string composed of the message alphabet to be compressed is analyzed. The relative frequencies of the messages are determined and a Huffman code tree is constructed. The first two less-frequent messages are assigned to the 1 and 0 branches. The two leaf nodes are subsequently replaced by a branch node; the weight of the branch node is the sum of the weights of the two leaf nodes. This procedure is repeated until two nodes remain. The resulting Huffman code tree is a binary tree with branches with values 0 and 1. The base of the tree is the root node, and the point at which a branch divides is the branch node. The termination point of a branch is the leaf node with the message m_i. Each branch divides a binary value 0 or 1 is assigned to the new branch. The binary code words of S are determined by tracing the path from the root node to each leaf m_i. The resulting code has a prefix property; for each leaf, only one unique path from the root exists. In Figure 4.1, we indicate the steps for Huffman's algorithm for given frequencies.

4.2 Lossy Compression

Most lossy compression algorithms are base on human perceptual features.

4.2.1 *Digital images*

Image compression may be characterized as lossy or lossless compression. Lossless compression can be based on run-length encoding and entropy coding. Lossy compression can reduce the color space and can be based on transform coding, which is based on the limitations of the human eye. The Joint Photographic Experts Group (JPEG) is a common lossy compression for digital images. The JPEG defines a range of different compression methods [Halsall (2001)]. We describe the lossy sequential mode, which is also known as the baseline method. Several principles of lossless and lossy compression are integrated into the baseline method, namely,

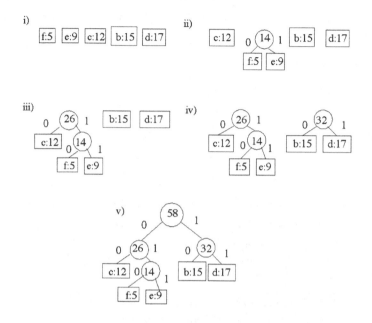

Fig. 4.1 The frequencies are given in i). The words of S are sorted by the order of increasing frequency. Each word corresponds to a tree or a leaf: i) represents the initial set, in which each word is a tree. ii) to iv) are internal stages. In each step, two trees with the lowest frequency are merged. A left edge connection is denoted as 0 and a right connection is denoted as 1. v) is the final tree, which represents the coding $f = 010$, $e = 011$, $c := 00$, $b = 10$ and $d = 11$.

- transform coding and the sensitivity of the human eye,
- run-length coding,
- Huffman coding,
- differential encoding.

In the first step, the two-dimensional matrix of pixel values is transformed into an equivalent matrix of spatial frequency components. Because it would be too time-consuming to compute the transformed values of each position of the total matrix that represents the image, the matrix that represents the image is divided into smaller 8×8 submatrices. Each submatrix consists of a block of 64 values.

The discrete cosine transform for two dimensions of $\alpha_{x,y}$ for 8×8 is

$$\gamma_{fx,fy} = w(x) \cdot v(y) \sum_{x=0}^{7} \sum_{y=0}^{7} \alpha_{x,y} \cdot \cos\left(\frac{\pi \cdot (2 \cdot x + 1) \cdot f_x}{16}\right)$$

$$\cdot \cos\left(\frac{\pi \cdot (2 \cdot y + 1) \cdot f_y}{16}\right) \tag{4.9}$$

with

$$w(x) = \begin{cases} \frac{1}{\sqrt{8}} & for\ x = 0 \\ \sqrt{\frac{2}{8}} & else \end{cases}$$

and

$$v(y) = \begin{cases} \frac{1}{\sqrt{8}} & for\ y = 0 \\ \sqrt{\frac{2}{8}} & else \end{cases}.$$

For $f_x = 0$ and $f_y = 0$, the two cosine terms are both 0. Because $\cos(0) = 1$, the value in $\gamma_{0,0}$ of the transformed matrix is simply a summation of all values in the input matrix, which is known as the DC coefficient. Because the values in all other locations of the transformed matrix have a frequency coefficient, they are known as AC coefficients.

- For $f_y = 0$ only horizontal frequency coefficients
- For $f_x = 0$ only vertical frequency coefficients.

If the magnitude of a higher frequency coefficient is below a certain threshold, the human eye will not detect it. Spatial coefficients below a threshold are set to zero, which results in lossy compression. The sensitivity of the eye is related to the spatial frequency. The amplitude threshold below which the eye will detect a particular spatial frequency varies. For each of the 8×8 DCT coefficients, a threshold value exists that is represented by a quantization table with 8×8 entries. The resulting 8×8 integer matrix is mapped into a vector because the run-length encoding algorithm operates on a vector. By scanning the matrix line by line, the resulting vector contains a combination of nonzero and zero values. A zig-zag scan creates a vector with long strings of zeros. The first component of the 64 dimensional vector is the DC coefficient; the remaining 63 components are the AC coefficients. The 63 AC coefficients are run-length encoded. For the vector represented as a row

$$(12, 0, 0, 0, 0, 0, 0, 0, 0, 0, 13, 0, 0, 0, 0, 0, 0, 0, 11, \cdots)$$

12 is the DC component and the remaining 63 AC integer coefficients of a block are run-length encoded as

$$(0, 9), (13, 1), (0, 7), (11, 1), \cdots$$

For each run-length encoded AC coefficient in the block, the bits are encoded using the Huffman code. The DC coefficients for all blocks of the image are differentially encoded; for example,

$$12, 13, 11, 11, 10, \cdots$$

are represented as

$$12, 1, -2, 0, -1, \cdots$$

The frame builder encapsulates all information.

4.2.2 Digital audio signal

Perceptual encoders use a psychoacoustic model that exploits a number of limitations of the human ear. Only the features that are perceptible by the ear are represented.

4.2.2.1 Adaptive differential

An additive technique known as sub-band coding breaks a signal into a number of different frequency bands and independently encodes each band [Halsall (2001)]. For example the audio input signal is passed through two filters that divide them into two separate signals of equal bandwidth:

- lower sub-band signal (50 Hz- 3.5 kHz),
- upper sub-band signal (3.5 kHz - 7 kHz).

Each signal is independently sampled and encoded. The sampling frequency should be more than twice the maximum frequency component of the signal. Otherwise, the original signal's information may not be completely recoverable from the sampled signal. A lower sub-band is a signal sampled at 8 kHz, whereas an upper sub-band signal is sampled at 16 kHz. The use of two sub-bands has the advantage that different bit rates can be employed for each sub-band. Because the frequency components that are present in the lower sub-band signal, have a higher perceptual importance for humans compared with the frequency components in the higher sub-band, they are represented by a larger number of bits. Lossy compression occurs because the upper sub-band signal is represented by a lower number of bits. The two bit streams are then multiplexed (merged) in such a manner that the decoder is capable of dividing them. The decomposition into different frequency bands is the basis of the perceptual encoders for digital audio encoding, such as an MPEG-1 Audio Layer 3 (MP3). An MP3 is an audio coding format for digital audio, which employs a form of lossy data compression.

4.2.2.2   *Perceptual encoders*

Perceptual encoders have been designed for the compression of general audio [Halsall (2001)]. They use a psychoacoustic model to exploit a number of the limitations of the human ear; only features that are perceptible to the ear are transmitted. A signal is usually quantized, and the sampling rate and the number of bits per sample are determined by the specific application. The bandwidth that is available is divided into a number of frequency sub-bands using a bank of analysis filters. The processing associated with both frequency and temporal masking is performed by the psychoacoustic model that is currently performed with the filtering operations based on

- sensitivity of the ear,
- frequency masking,
- temporal masking.

Sensitivity of the ear   The human ear is sensitive to signals in the range 15 Hz through 20 kHz. The maximal minimal amplitude of the signal is measured in decibels (dB). It is the dynamic range of the sound that an ear can hear from the loudest sound to the quietest sound. The region of sensitivity is approximately 96 dB; however, the sensitivity of the ear varies with the frequency of the signal and is nonlinear (refer to Figure 4.2).

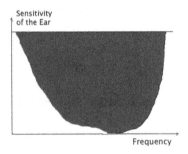

Fig. 4.2   The region of sensitivity of the ear varies with the frequency of the signal and is nonlinear (dark area).

Frequency masking When an audio sound consists of multiple frequency signals, the sensitivity of the ear changes and varies with the relative amplitude of the signals. The sensitivity of the ear changes in the vicinity of a loud signal. When a sufficiently loud signal is present at one frequency, the ear will not hear the weaker signals at nearby frequencies. If signal a is larger in amplitude than signal b, the sensitivity curve of the ear is distorted in the region of the signal a so prevent the signal b from being heard (refer to Figure 4.3). The frequency masking varies with the frequency, and the width of each curve is known as the critical band.

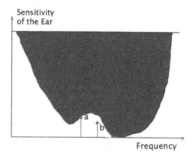

Fig. 4.3   If the amplitude of signal a is larger than the amplitude of signal b, the sensitivity curve of the ear is distorted in the region of the signal a to prevent signal b from being heard.

Temporal masking The cochlea, or the inner ear, is a fluid-filled spiral-shaped structure that contains auditory receptors (hair cells). The sound waves are channeled into the ear canal and strike the tympanic membrane, which causes it to vibrate and convert the sound waves to mechanical energy. The middle ear components mechanically amplify sound, and the stapes moves in and out of the oval window of the cochlea creating a fluid motion. The fluid movement is recognized by the hair cells. A specific amount of time is required for a hair cell to rise. If an ear hears a loud sound, a short period of time passes before it can hear a quieter sound (refer to Figure 4.4).

4.2.3   *Digital video*

Video is also referred to as moving pictures or frames. When we apply a JPEG to each frame (picture) of the video, the format is known as a

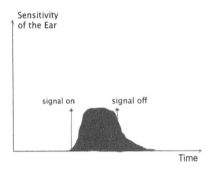

Fig. 4.4   A specific amount of time is required for a hair cell to rise. If an ear hears a loud sound, a short period of time passes before it can hear a quieter sound (dark area represents the inaudible signal amplitude).

moving JPEG or a MJPG. In addition to the spatial redundancy in each frame in practice, considerable redundancy frequently exists between a set of pictures [Halsall (2001)]. A typical scene in a movie consists of approximately 3 seconds, a frame refreshing rate of 60 frames per second, and a scan of 180 frames. Considerable redundancy frequently exists between a set of frames because only small portion of each frame changes. By only representing information related to these changes, considerable compression can be achieved. Instead of representing the video as a set of compressed frames, only a selection is represented in this form and only the difference between the actually frame contents and the predicted contents is represented. The accuracy of the prediction is determined by how well any movement between successive frames is estimated. Two basic types of frames exist:

- I-frames are represented as separate images; they are encoded without any reference to any other frame,
- P-frames are represented relative to the contents of either a preceding I-frame or a preceding P-frame. P-frames estimate the movement between successive frames.

The number of frames between a P-frame and the immediately preceding I- or P-frame is referred to as a group of pictures (GOP). Because the error of the first P-frame will propagate to the next P-frame, the GOP should not exceed 12. A typical GOP value ranges from 3 to 12.

4.2.3.1 *Motion estimation for P-frame*

Target frames are compared on a pixel-by-pixel basis with the contents of the corresponding macro block in the preceding I- or P-frame (reference frame). The reference frame and the target frame are divided into macro blocks with a size of 16×16 pixels. A macro block of the reference frame is compared with the macro blocks of the target frame pixel by pixel. If a close match is found, only the position of the macro block is encoded; otherwise, the search is extended to cover an area around the macro blocks of the target frame. Because the YCbCr color space is used, only the Y part of the image that corresponds to the greyscale is employed for the matching operation. A match is found if the distance between the macro block target frame is less than a given threshold. For a match, two parameters are encoded, which is known as the motion vector. The first parameter is the position and the second parameter is the prediction error. It contains different values between the target macro blocks and the set of pixels in the search area that produce the close match. The motion vectors are encoded using differential encoding; the resulting codewords are subsequently Huffman encoded. A segment can move outside of the search region. To facilitate this movement, B-frames that perform bidirectional prediction are employed in addition to P-frames. The H.261 video compression standard uses only I and P frames, whereas theH.263 video compression standard also uses B frames [Halsall (2001)].

4.2.3.2 *Video Compression Standard*

A Motion Picture Expert Group (MPEG) was formed to formulate a set of standards relating to a range of multimedia applications. It has standardized the following compression formats [Halsall (2001)]:

- MPEG-1: Initial video and audio compression standard that uses I, P, and B frames. It includes the popular Layer 3 (MP3) audio compression format. Three levels of processing, which are known as layers 1, 2, 3, exist. For example, layer 1 does not include temporal masking but is present in layers 2 and 3.
- MPEG-2: Transport, video and audio standards for broadcast-quality television. Used for over-the-air digital television and for

DVDs (with slight modifications)

- MPEG-3: Originally designed for HDTV but abandoned when MPEG-2 became sufficient for HDTV.
- MPEG-4: Expands MPEG-1 and MPEG-2, support objects, 3D content, low bit rate encoding and digital rights management.
- MPEG-7: A formal system for describing multimedia content.
- MPEG-21: Expands MPEG-7 to support digital rights management.

Chapter 5

Feature Extraction

The extraction of primitive out of media data is referred to as feature extraction. The set of features represents the relevant information about the input data in a certain context. The context is dependent on the desired task that uses the reduced representation instead of the original input. The set of primitives is usually described by a feature vector. Feature extraction is related to compression algorithms and is frequently based on transform functions, as described in the previous chapter. During content-based media retrieval, the feature vectors are used to determine the similarities among the media objects. The extracted features represent the signature of the media object. Feature extraction is a crucial step in content-based media retrieval.

5.1 Basic Image Features

In traditional content-based image retrieval methods, features that describe important properties of the images, such as color, texture and shape, are employed [Flickner *et al.* (1995)], [Smeulders *et al.* (2000)], [Smeulders *et al.* (2000)], [Quack *et al.* (2004)], [Dunckley (2003)]. For example, the color distribution can be described by a color histogram and the shape can be extracted by edge detection algorithms.

5.1.1 *Color histogram*

To construct a histogram, we divide the range between the highest and lowest values in a distribution into several bins of equal size. The height of a rectangle in a frequency histogram represents the number of values in the corresponding bin. The histogram in Figure 5.1 indicates the number

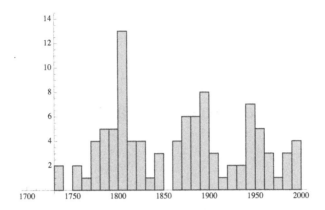

Fig. 5.1 Number of chemical elements discovered each decade from 1700 to 2000.

of chemical elements that were discovered each decade from 1700 to 2000. A histogram of a digital image with gray levels in the range $[1, L]$ is a discrete function $h(g_k)$. A black and white digital image with 256 different grey values requires 8 bits per pixel with gray levels in the range of $[1, 256]$. For example, for a pixel, the g_k indicates its gray level, with k as the kth gray level from the interval $[1, L]$. The number of pixels with gray level g_k is indicated by the number n_k. A common practice involves normalizing a histogram by dividing its value by the total number of pixels as denoted by n with

$$p(g_k) = \frac{n_k}{n}, \tag{5.1}$$

$p(g_k)$ estimates the probability of occurrence of the gray level g_k. The histogram $h(g_k)$ represents an L dimensional vector, which represents the gray level distribution of the digital image. If the background and the observed object have considerably different gray levels, then both regions can be separated by looking at relative frequencies in the histogram [Paulus and Hornegger (2003)]. Color images in the red, green, and blue (RGB) color space consist of colored pixels defined by three numbers: one for red, one for green and one for blue. A RGB image can be approximately transformed into a gray image by computing the mean value of the three numbers of each pixel, which represents the colors red, green and blue (refer to 5.2). The range of different colors, which can be produced is dependent on the pixel depth. For a 24 bit pixel depth, 8 bits per primary color yields

$$2^8 \cdot 2^8 \cdot 2^8 = 16777216$$

Fig. 5.2 Example of an RGB image, represented as a gray image. The transformation was performed by computing the mean value of the three numbers of each pixel, which represent the colors red, green and blue.

16 million colors. For a color histogram for each color channel, which includes red, green and blue, a histogram is computed (refer to Figure 5.3). The three histograms for each RGB channel are concatenated

$$2^8 + 2^8 + 2^8 = 768.$$

A histogram of a digital RGB image with RGB levels in the range $[1, L]$ is a discrete function $h(R_k) + h(G_k) + h(B_k)$. The pixel R_k, G_k, B_k indicates its RGB level. The histogram $h(R_k, G_k, B_k)$ represents a $3 \cdot L$ dimensional vector, which represents the RGB level distribution of the digital color RGB image (refer to Figure 5.3). An image can be divided into k subimages and a k color histogram of the sub images can be determined. We obtain

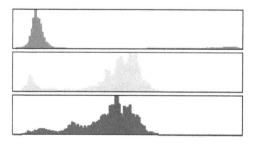

Fig. 5.3 Three histograms that represent the RGB level distribution of the digital color RGB image represented in Figure 5.2.

additional information about the color distribution of an image. For an image of size $z = n \times m$ as k approaches z, more spatial information about the color distribution is presented.

5.1.1.1 Scaled RGB images

An extreme case is $k = z$, which is the entire image. Scaled RGB images represent an extreme example of naïve features. All images have to be mapped into a three-band RGB (red, green, blue) representation in which each color is represented by 8 bits and scaled to a fixed size by a bilinear method [Gonzales and Woods (2001)].

5.1.2 Texture

No accurate definition for the texture of a digital image is available [Gonzales and Woods (2001)]. We refer to the texture as images or patterns with some type of structure. According to Linda G. Shapiro and George C. Stockman [Shapiro and Stockman (2001)], "Image texture provides information about the spatial arrangement of color or the intensity of an image or selected region of an image." We can define texture as

- repetition,
- stochastic,
- stochastic repetition,
- fractal.

We can classify images by regions with certain textures. Texture-based segmentation divides an image into regions with uniform texture. The basic elements that form the texture are sometimes referred to as "texels"; however, these primitives do not always exist and are not always. Some textures may exhibit structures in several resolutions, whereas fractals exhibit a similar structure in each resolution. Textures may be recognized by a Fourier transform in small windows of the image or by a wavelet transform. By analyzing their spectrum, the periodicity and directionality can be determined. The variance σ^2 of a sample window can be used to measure the relative smoothness s with

$$s = 1 - \frac{1}{1 + \sigma^2} \tag{5.2}$$

For constant intensity $s, \approx 0$ and s approaches one for rough texture with varying levels.

5.1.3 *Edge detection*

An image may be converted into a set of curves or edges. The basic idea behind edge detection is to localize the discontinuities of the intensity function in the image. Many approaches to edge detection are based on the rapid changes and discontinuities in the gray level. If we represent the gray levels as two-dimensional functions, the discontinuities can be detected using maxima in the first derivative or zero-crossing in the second derivative. In one dimension, the largest change corresponds to the derivative that has the maximum magnitude (second derivative is zero). In two dimensions, the derivative is represented by the gradient [Paulus and Hornegger (2003)]. The gradient of a continuous function $f(x, y)$ that represents an image is given by

$$\bigtriangledown f(x, y) = \left(\frac{\partial f}{\partial x}, \frac{\partial f}{\partial y} \right). \tag{5.3}$$

It points in the direction of the most rapid change in intensity. The magnitude of the gradient defines the edge direction and the edge strength. The edge direction is usually defined to be orthogonal to the gradient. The gradient direction is given by

$$\bigtriangledown f(x, y) = \left(\frac{\partial f}{\partial x}, \frac{\partial f}{\partial y} \right). \tag{5.4}$$

and edge strength is given by the gradient magnitude

$$\| \bigtriangledown f(x, y) \| = \sqrt{\left(\frac{\partial f}{\partial x} \right)^2 + \left(\frac{\partial f}{\partial y} \right)^2}. \tag{5.5}$$

A digital image can be differentiate either by reconstruct a continuous image $f(x, y)$ and then computing the gradient or by discrete derivative, computing a finite difference

$$\frac{\partial f}{\partial x}(x, y) \approx f(x + 1, y) - f(x, y) \tag{5.6}$$

and

$$\frac{\partial f}{\partial y}(x, y) \approx f(x, y + 1) - f(x, y). \tag{5.7}$$

The equations can be interpreted as a symmetric masks h_x, h_y

$$h_x = \begin{pmatrix} -1 & 0 & 1 \end{pmatrix} \tag{5.8}$$

and

$$h_y = \begin{pmatrix} -1 \\ 0 \\ -1 \end{pmatrix} \tag{5.9}$$

or as functions

$$h_x(x,y) = \begin{cases} -1 & \text{if} & x = 0 \\ 0 & \text{if} & x = 1 \\ 1 & \text{if} & x = 2 \\ 0 & \text{if } (x < 0) \vee (x > 2) \end{cases} \tag{5.10}$$

and

$$h_y(x,y) = \begin{cases} -1 & \text{if} & y = 0 \\ 0 & \text{if} & y = 1 \\ 1 & \text{if} & y = 2 \\ 0 & \text{if } (y < 0) \vee (y > 2) \end{cases} \tag{5.11}$$

For image f of the size $n \times m$ and the masks h_x and h_y the derivative is simply computed by convolution

$$\frac{\partial f}{\partial x}(x,y) \approx f * h_x = \sum_{i=0}^{n-1} f(i,y) \cdot h_x(x - i, y) \tag{5.12}$$

and

$$\frac{\partial f}{\partial y}(x,y) \approx f * h_y \sum_{j=0}^{m-1} f(x,j) \cdot h_x(x, y - j). \tag{5.13}$$

Since the distance from the central point where the derivative is estimated is one pixel to the right, the computation yields only half of the derivative. Better approximations of the derivatives are represented by the Sobel operators (masks)

$$s_x = \begin{pmatrix} -1 & 0 & 1 \\ -2 & 0 & 2 \\ -1 & 0 & 1 \end{pmatrix} \tag{5.14}$$

and

$$s_y = \begin{pmatrix} 1 & 2 & 1 \\ 0 & 0 & 0 \\ -1 & -2 & -1 \end{pmatrix} = s_x^T \tag{5.15}$$

with

$$\frac{\partial f}{\partial x}(x,y) \approx f * \left(\frac{1}{8} \cdot s_x \right) \tag{5.16}$$

and

$$\frac{\partial f}{\partial y}(x,y) \approx f * \left(\frac{1}{8} \cdot s_y \right). \tag{5.17}$$

we multiplay the Sobel operator with the term $1/8$ to approximate the right gradient value. For edge detection this normalisation factor is not required (see Figure 5.4).

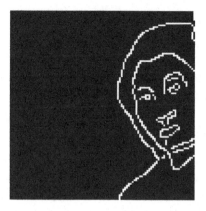

Fig. 5.4   Gradient image computed with the Sobel operator on the image represented in the Figure 5.2.

5.1.4   *Measurement of angle*

In a circle a measurement is represented by an angle α and a more exact one by the angle β with $\alpha > \beta$ (see Figure 5.5). The information gain is

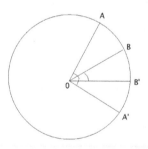

Fig. 5.5   In a circle a measurement is represented by two angles.

$$I\left(\frac{\alpha}{\beta}\right) = \log_2\left(\frac{\alpha}{\beta}\right) \tag{5.18}$$

bits. The angle measure of a direction must lie between 0 and $2 \cdot \pi$. With a priori knowledge $\alpha = 2 \cdot \pi$ only one measurement β is required [Resnikoff (1989)]

$$I\left(\frac{2 \cdot \pi}{\beta}\right) = \log_2\left(\frac{2 \cdot \pi}{\beta}\right). \tag{5.19}$$

For a straight line $\beta = \pi$ and the information content is

$$I(\pi) = \log_2 \left(\frac{2 \cdot \pi}{\pi} \right) = 1 \; bit. \tag{5.20}$$

The observed direction lies in one half-of the planes. Smaller angles correspond to greater information, $I(\pi/2) = 2 \; bits, \quad I(\pi/4) = 3 \; bits$.

5.1.5   *Information and contour*

By edge detection or weak colour segmentation we can extract some shape information that can define contours. To measure the information of a contour we divide it into short segments of equal length. Each segmenting point can be thought as the vertex of an angle formed with two neighboring points [Resnikoff (1989)]. Associated with that angle is its measure of information gain. In a simple example there are three points P, Q, R (see Figure 5.6). We move on a line from P to Q. The corresponding information is 1 bit. The information gain passing from one straight line to the next is

$$I\left(\frac{\pi}{\pi} \right) = 0 \; bits$$

since the angle remains unchanged. When the right angle at vertex Q is reached, there is a positive gain of information

$$I\left(\frac{\pi}{\pi/2} \right) = 1 \; bits.$$

At the next step, passing from right angle to the straight angle there is an information loss

$$I\left(\frac{\pi/2}{\pi} \right) = -1 \; bits.$$

In the example the right angle is where the contour changes its direction. Corners yield the greatest information, more strongly curved points yield more information.

5.1.5.1   *Histogram of corners*

An image can be described by a histogram of corners. A histogram of a digital image with corner information (represented in bits) in the range $[0, B]$ is a discrete function $h(\theta_b)$. For example a corner θ_b indicate a corner with b bits of information. The number of corners with information b bits is indicated by the number n_b.

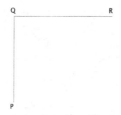

Fig. 5.6 There are three points P, Q, R.

5.2 Image Pyramid

The representation of images at several resolutions corresponds to a structure that is named the "image pyramid" in digital image processing [Burt and Adelson (1983)], [Gonzales and Woods (2001)]. The base of the pyramid contains an image with a high resolution; its apex is a low-resolution approximation of the image. For an image of size $n \times n$ (n a power of two.) with a base level $J = \log_2 n$ there exist $J + 1$ levels with

$$0 \geq j \geq J$$

with apex of one pixel of the size 1×1. The total number of pixels is given by

$$n^2 \cdot \left(1 + \frac{1}{4^1} + \frac{1}{4^2} + \cdots + \frac{1}{4^J}\right) = n^2 \cdot \left(\sum_{j=0}^{J} \frac{1}{4^j}\right) = n^2 \cdot \frac{1 - \left(\frac{1}{4}\right)^{J+1}}{1 - \frac{1}{4}} \leq n^2 \cdot \frac{4}{3}$$

$$(5.21)$$

The reduced representation is achieved by filtering the input image and by downsampling. Different filter operations can be employed, including wavelet scale functions, neighborhood averaging, which corresponds to the Haar's scale function and results in the mean pyramid (refer to Figure 5.7).

The series of reduced images that form the Gaussian image pyramid begins with the original image. This image is blurred by a Gaussian filter (Gaussian blur) and is subsequently sampled to form the image at a lower spatial resolution and size. The Gaussian filter $G(x, y)$ is defined as

$$G(x, y) = \frac{1}{2 \cdot \pi \cdot \sigma^2} \cdot e^{-\frac{x^2 + y^2}{2 \cdot \sigma^2}} \tag{5.22}$$

with σ being the standard deviation of the Gaussian distribution. In Figure 5.8 see the Gaussian filter $G(x, y)$ with $\sigma = 2$. Although Gaussian

Fig. 5.7   Mean image pyramid.

filters have infinite support, they decay at a rapid rate. As a result, a simple rectangular window function that performs the truncation is employed. Figure 5.9 shows the Gaussian filter $G(x, y)$ with $\sigma = 2$ and the rectangular window function of size 5×5. The corresponding Gaussian filter can be represented by a matrix G of size 5×5 (mask)

$$G = \begin{pmatrix} 0.0917044 & -0.0611669 & -0.23164 & -0.0611669 & 0.0917044 \\ -0.0611669 & 0.0220649 & 0.11488 & 0.0220649 & -0.0611669 \\ -0.23164 & 0.11488 & 0.501297 & 0.11488 & -0.23164 \\ -0.0611669 & 0.0220649 & 0.11488 & 0.0220649 & -0.0611669 \\ 0.0917044 & -0.0611669 & -0.23164 & -0.0611669 & 0.0917044 \end{pmatrix}$$

$$(5.23)$$

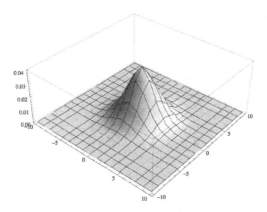

Fig. 5.8   Gaussian filter $G(x, y)$ with $\sigma = 2$.

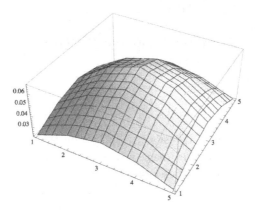

Fig. 5.9   Gaussian filter $G(x, y)$ with $\sigma = 2$ and the rectangular window function of size 5×5.

where $\sigma = 2$. The convolution of an image $I(x, y)$ and the Gaussian mask G is defined as

$$I(x, y) * G. \qquad (5.24)$$

After the convolution, the image is downsampled by a factor of 2 and the process is repeated. An image pyramid is related to a discrete wavelet transform of images. In each resolution, different operations such as a color histogram texture or edge determination can be applied.

5.2.1 *Scale space*

An image pyramid is related to the scale space. In an image pyramid, the scale is sampled in both space and scale, whereas in scale space, the subsampling stage is coupled with the multi-scale representation [Burger and Burge (2011)]. An image can be represented at any scale. The Gaussian scale space is defined by the Gaussian kernel $G(x, y, s)$ on the scale s

$$G(x, y, s) = \frac{1}{2 \cdot \pi \cdot s} \cdot e^{-\frac{x^2 + y^2}{2 \cdot s}} \tag{5.25}$$

The convolution of an image $I(x, y)$ and the Gaussian kernel at the scale s is defined as

$$L(x, y, s) = G(x, y, s) * I(x, y). \tag{5.26}$$

The Gaussian kernel $G(x, y, s)$ is related to the Gaussian filter $G(x, y)$ with $s = \sigma^2$, since the standard deviation is $\sigma = \sqrt{s}$. In Figure 5.10 we indicate the Gaussian scale representation of the image of Figure 5.2. With the growing scale parameter, the details from the image are removed and the size of the image remains unchanged.

5.3 SIFT

A scale-invariant feature transform (SIFT) generates local features of an image that are invariant to image scaling and rotation and illumination [Lowe (2004)]. An image is described by several vectors of fixed dimension 128. Each vector represents an invariant key feature descriptor of the image.

In the first step of the SIFT algorithm, keypoints are detected. Keypoints are locations that are invariant to scale change [Lowe (2004)]. They correspond to stable features across different scales s of the scale space. The difference of two scales $s \cdot k_i$ and $s \cdot k_j$ is given by

$$D(x, y, s) = (G(x, y, s \cdot k_i) - G(x, y, s \cdot k_j)) * I(x, y) \tag{5.27}$$

with

$$L(x, y, s \cdot k_i) = G(x, y, s \cdot k_i) * I(x, y) \tag{5.28}$$

it can be computed by a simple subtraction between the smoothed images $L(x, y, s \cdot k_i)$ and $L(x, y, s \cdot k_j)$

$$D(x, y, s) = L(x, y, s \cdot k_i) - L(x, y, s \cdot k_j). \tag{5.29}$$

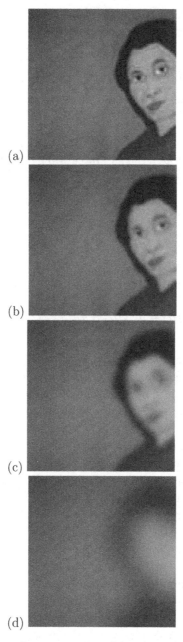

(a)

(b)

(c)

(d)

Fig. 5.10   Gaussian scale representation of the image of Figure 5.2. (a) With $s = 1$, (b) $s = 2$, (c) $s = 4$ and (d) $s = 16$.

The difference of two scales $D(x, y, s)$ is called Difference-of-Gaussian (DoG). It is an approximation to the scale-normalized Laplacian of Gaussian

$$D(x, y, s) \approx ((k - 1) \cdot s \cdot \nabla^2 G) * I(x, y). \tag{5.30}$$

with $k = \frac{k_i}{k_j}$. It follows from the relationship of the heat diffusion equation in which $\sigma = \sqrt{s}$

$$\sigma \cdot \nabla^2 G = \frac{\partial G}{\partial \sigma} \approx \frac{G(x, y, \sigma \cdot k) - G(x, y, \sigma)}{(\sigma \cdot k - \sigma)}. \tag{5.31}$$

The Laplace operator is a second-order differential operator that is given by the sum of the second partial derivatives of the function with respect to each independent variable.

$$\nabla^2 L = L_{xx} + L_{yy} = \nabla \left(\frac{\partial L}{\partial x}, \frac{\partial L}{\partial y} \right) = \nabla \left(\frac{\partial L}{\partial x_1}, \frac{\partial L}{\partial x_2} \right) = \sum_{i=1}^{2} \frac{\partial L}{\partial x_i} \tag{5.32}$$

and

$$\nabla^2_{norm} L(x, y; \sigma) = \sigma \cdot (L_{xx} + L_{yy}) \approx D(x, y, \sigma). \tag{5.33}$$

The scale-normalized Laplacian of Gaussian is useful for detecting edges that appear at various image scales, as shown in Figure 5.11. In the next step, the local maxima and minima of $D(x, y, \sigma)$ are determined by the SIFT algorithm ($\sigma = \sqrt{s}$). They correspond to the local extrema with respect to both space and scale. However, some of the determined keypoint candidates are not accurate extrema due to the manner in which the SIFT algorithm actually determines the extrema.

Each image is convolved with Gaussian blurs at different scales, the range of the scales corresponds to the doubling of the value of $\sigma = \sqrt{s}$, which is achieved by selecting the value k_i and k_j. The group of the corresponding images is referred to as an octave. In the group of the images, an octave is subsampled by two images. This process is repeated and produces an octave pyramid; for each octave, there is a fixed number of convolved images. For each image represented in an octave, the Difference-of-Gaussian computed by subtracting the Gaussian blurred image that produces a Difference-of-Gaussian pyramid. In extrema selection, each point of an image is compared with eight neighbors in the image, with nine neighbors in the scale below and with nine neighbors in the scale above. A point is selected as an extrema if it is larger or smaller than all 26 neighbors. The cost of the SIFT algorithm is minimal. By selecting k_i

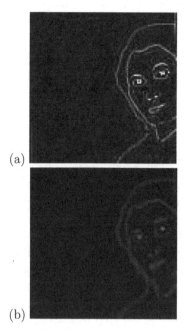

(a)

(b)

Fig. 5.11 Scale-normalized Laplacian of Gaussian of the image of Figure 5.2. (a) With $s = 1$, (b) $s = 2$.

and k_j, the reduction of a continuous function $D(x, y, \sigma)$ to a discrete function is achieved. The determined extrema are the extrema of the discrete function. To verify whether the error of the determined extrema is not to large in relation to the true extrema of the continuous function $D(x, y, \sigma)$, a detailed fit to the nearby data for a location is performed using the Taylor expansion of $D(x, y, \sigma)$ to the quadratic terms. The Taylor expansion is a representation of the function $f(x)$ as a sum of the terms that are calculated from the values of the function's derivatives at a single point a. A function is frequently approximated by a finite number of terms of its Taylor series, such as

$$f(x) \approx f(a) + \frac{f'(x)}{1!} \cdot (x - a)^1 + \frac{f''(x)}{2!} \cdot (x - a)^2 + \frac{f'''(x)}{3!} \cdot (x - a)^3. \quad (5.34)$$

The Taylor expansion of $D(x, y, \sigma)$ up to the quadratic terms with origin being the sample point is given as

$$D(\mathbf{x}) = D + \frac{\partial D^T}{\partial \mathbf{x}} \cdot \mathbf{x} + \frac{1}{2} \cdot \mathbf{x}^T \cdot \frac{\partial^2 D}{\partial \mathbf{x}^2} \cdot \mathbf{x} \quad (5.35)$$

with derivatives at the sample point and

$$\mathbf{x}^T = (x, y, \sigma)$$

is the offset of the sample point. The accurate extrema is given by the zero derivative of the Taylor expansion

$$\frac{\partial D}{\partial \mathbf{x}} + \frac{\partial^2 D}{\partial \mathbf{x}^2} \cdot \mathbf{x} = 0 \qquad (5.36)$$

with the solution

$$\mathbf{x'} = \frac{\partial D}{\partial \mathbf{x}} \cdot \frac{\partial^2 D}{\partial \mathbf{x}^2} \qquad (5.37)$$

If an offset of $\mathbf{x'}$ from the sampling point (the determined extrema) is too large (larger than 0.5), then the keypoint should be a different sampling point. As a consequence, the determined extrema corresponds to an inaccurate keypoint and is sorted out.

In the next step, two filters are used to discard the low contrast keypoints and poorly located edge responses. Low contrast is sensitive to noise. The corresponding keypoints are eliminated if the value of the determined extremum $D(\mathbf{x'})$ is below a threshold that is empirically determined. For normalized pixel values in the range $[0, 1]$, the estimated threshold is 0.03, which is approximately one-third of the maximal value. The keypoint is discarded if

$$|D(\mathbf{x'})| < 0.03. \qquad (5.38)$$

Keypoints that correspond to edges are poorly determined and unstable in the presence of small amounts of noise. These keypoints exhibit a large principal curvature that can be computed from a 2×2 Hessian matrix. A Hessian matrix is a square matrix of second-order partial derivatives of a function

$$\mathbf{H} = \begin{pmatrix} D_{xx} & D_{xy} \\ D_{xy} & D_{yy} \end{pmatrix}. \qquad (5.39)$$

We can compute the sum of the two eigenvalues λ_1 and λ_2 from the trace of H and their product from the determinant

$$Tr(\mathbf{H}) = D_{xx} + D_{yy} = \lambda_1 + \lambda_2 \qquad (5.40)$$

and

$$Det(\mathbf{H}) = D_{xx} \cdot D_{yy} - D_{xy} \cdot D_{yy} = \lambda_1 \cdot \lambda_2 \qquad (5.41)$$

if the determinant is negative then the key point is discarded. We define the ratio between the larger eigenvalue and the smaller one as

$$\lambda_1 = r \cdot \lambda_2. \qquad (5.42)$$

With

$$\frac{T(\mathbf{H})^2}{Det(\mathbf{H})} = \frac{(\lambda_1 + \lambda_2)^2}{\lambda_1 \cdot \lambda_2} = \frac{(r \cdot \lambda_2 + \lambda_2)^2}{r \cdot \lambda_2^2} = \frac{(r+1)^2}{r} \qquad (5.43)$$

it was shown by Harris that to check if the ratio of principal curvatures is below some threshold r we need to check if

$$\frac{T(\mathbf{H})^2}{Det(\mathbf{H})} < \frac{(r+1)^2}{r}. \qquad (5.44)$$

If $r < 10$ then the ratio is too great and the key point is discarded, the value 10 was determined by empirical experiments.

In the next steps, we determine the orientation of the key points. Within a region around the keypoint, the gradient's magnitude and orientation of the sample points are computed. The scale of the keypoint σ is used to select the Gaussian smoothed image to compute the gradient magnitude of the sample points in a region around the key point using pixel differences.

$$m(x,y) = \sqrt{(L(x+1,y) - L(x-1,y))^2 + L(x,y+1) - L(x,y-1)^2} \qquad (5.45)$$

and the orientation

$$\theta(x,y) = \tan^{-1}\left(\frac{L(x,y+1) - L(x,y-1)}{L(x+1,y) - L(x-1,y)}\right). \qquad (5.46)$$

We define a histogram with each bin covering 10 degrees, which results in 36 bins. For each sample point of the region around the key point, the orientation $\theta(x,y)$ is determined, weighted and added to the histogram. The value is weighted by its gradient magnitude $m(x,y)$ and multiplied with $3/2$ of the selected scale value σ

$$weight = \frac{m(x,y) \cdot 3 \cdot \sigma}{2}$$

The peaks in this histogram correspond to dominant orientations, in which each keypoint can be assigned one or more orientations. The orientations that correspond to the highest peak and local peaks that are within 80% of the highest peaks are assigned to the keypoint. For more than one orientations, additional keypoints are created with the same location and scale as the original keypoints but with different orientations. In Figure 5.12, we indicate the determined keypoint locations at particular scales and orientations of the image in Figure 5.2. The corresponding keypoints ensure invariance to image location, scale and rotation. In the next step, a descriptor that is represented by a vector of dimension 128 is constructed for

Fig. 5.12 Keypoints of the image of Figure 5.2. They are displayed as vectors indicating scale, orientation and location.

each key point. The descriptor is highly distinctive and partially invariant to the remaining variations, such as illumination and the position of the viewpoint. The scale of the keypoint σ is employed to select the Gaussian smoothed image. The image gradients $m(x, y)$ with orientations $\theta(x, y)$ are sampled over 16×16 array of locations of the key point in scale space σ. We represent 4×4 the subregions of the 16×16 array of locations by 16 histograms. Each histogram represents 8 main orientations that cover 45 degrees. The added value is weighted by its gradient magnitude $m(x, y)$ and multiplied with 0.5 of the selected scale value σ added to the histogram

$$weight = \frac{m(x, y) \cdot \sigma}{2}.$$

As result, a key point descriptor is represented by a 128 dimensional vector

$$16 \ (histograms) \times 8 \ (bins).$$

To enhance the invariance, the 128 dimensional vector is normalized to the unit length. To minimize the effect of the nonlinear illumination, a threshold of 0.2 is applied and the vector is again normalized. Note that all values were determined by empirical experiments [Lowe (2004)].

An image or an object is described by a set of descriptor vectors (such as Bag-of-Descriptors). For object recognition in a database of images, a minimum of 3 key points of the query have to match the corresponding candidate image. The match is determined by the nearest neighbor with a Euclidean distance function.

5.4 GIST

Observers recognize a real-world scene at a single glance; the GIST is a corresponding concept of a descriptor and is not a unique algorithm. It is a low-dimensional representation of a scene that does not require any segmentation [Oliva and Torralba (2001)]. It is related to the SIFT descriptor. The scaled image of a scene is partitioned into coarse cells, and each cell is described by a common value. An image pyramid is formed with l levels. A GIST descriptor is represented by a vector of the dimension

$$grid \times grid \times l \times orientations \qquad (5.47)$$

For example, the image is scaled to the size 32×32 and segmented into a 4×4 grid. From the grid orientation, histograms are extracted on three scales, $l = 3$. We define a histogram with each bin covering 18 degrees, which results in 20 bins (orientations=20). The dimension of the vector that represents the GIST descriptor is 960. In another example, the image is scaled to the size 128×128 and segmented into a 4×4 grid. Five frequencies ($5 = l$) at six orientations are determined, which produces a vector of dimension 480. Each image is described by one GIST descriptor.

5.5 Recognition by Components

The visual input is matched against structural representations of simple 2D or 3D geometric elements, such as cylinders, bricks, wedges, cones, circles and rectangles, which correspond to the simple parts of an object. This simple 2D or 3D form is referred to as a geon [Biederman (1987)]. Geons are directly recognized from edges based on their non accidental properties (i.e., 3D features that are usually preserved by a projective imaging process), as shown in Figure 5.13.

This type of description supports generalization and is noise-sensitive. Binary vectors can represent objects. A one represents a GEON at the corresponding position of a binary vector; its absence is denoted by a zero (as a Bag-of-Descriptors). The geon set A, B, C, D, E, F, G, H, I, J, K is represented by a binary vector with dimension 11. The presence of features C and E is represented by the binary vector [0 0 1 0 1 0 0 0 0 0 0].

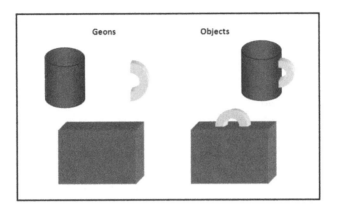

Fig. 5.13 Recognition by Components theory is an example of how objects can be broken down into geons.

5.6 Speech

The speech (sound) signal is sampled to a discrete signal and represented by the frequency spectrum. For speech recognition, the short-term Fourier transform is applied; a window (frame) is usually computed every 10 ms [Lieberman and Blumstein (1988)]. The vocal cords form quasi-periodic pulses from the relatively constant air flow of the lungs. The supralaryngeal vocal tract that consists of the airways of the mouth and the nose and pharynx forms an variable acoustic filter, as shown in Figure 5.14.

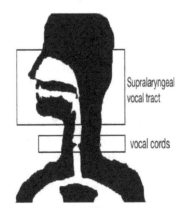

Fig. 5.14 Physiologic components of speech production.

5.6.1 *Formant frequencies*

The acoustic filter enables proportionally more acoustic energy at certain frequencies. These frequencies, which are named format frequencies, correspond to the energy maxima of the spectrum. The first three format frequencies characterize the speech represented by the spectrum. Because the format frequencies are related to the size of the supra laryngeal vocal tract, different people with different sizes of the supra laryngeal vocal tract produce different formant frequencies. Large differences among men and women and children are observed. During spoken language, the rate at which the vocal cords open and close determines the period of air and the fundamental frequency. The fundamental frequency is the lowest frequency of a periodic waveform, which is also indicated by f_0. The perception of fundamental frequency is referred to as the pitch; it is the relative highness or lowness of a tone as perceived by the ear [Lieberman and Blumstein (1988)]. The fundamental frequency can vary

- from 80 to 200 Hz for a male voice,
- from 150 to 450 Hz for a female voice,
- from 200 to 600 Hz for a child's voice.

The fundamental frequency does not remain constant during speech; it is controlled by the subglottal air pressure. There is a relationship between the fundamental frequency and the energy of spectrum of the speech. The energy only pertains to multiple values of fundamental frequency. The supra laryngeal vocal tract that forms a variable acoustic filter. It only allows multiple values of fundamental frequency to pass through it. A certain format frequency that defines a spoken signal can be undefined because its value is not a multiple value of fundamental frequency. To identify the formant frequencies of the spectrum, the maxima of the spectrum and its shape should be analyzed.

5.6.2 *Phonemes*

Most human languages consist of various different sound units, which are named the phonemes. A phoneme is the smallest unit of a language. It is characterized by a change in the meaning of words. Different languages and dialects considerably vary in the number of phonemes. English contains $34 - 45$ phonemes (generally, American English to Australian English) and German contains approximately 35 phonemes. Phonemes are divided into vowels and consonants. Vowels are classified according to the position of the tongue, whereas the consonants are classified according to air flow. Vowels can be described by the first two formant frequencies [Lieberman and Blumstein (1988)]. The formant frequencies are dependent on the size of the supra laryngeal vocal tract. For example, the listener will have difficulty distinguishing among different vowels if they are unable to estimate the size of the laryngeal vocal tract; substantial confusion arises if the listener does not know if the speaker is a man, woman or child. The estimation of the corresponding size is essential in the definition of the two-dimensional frequency parameter vowel space. In contrast with vowels, consonants cannot be described by formant frequencies because their formant frequency transitions over time are dependent on the following vowels. The formant frequency transitions of the same consonants are different for different vowels, as shown in Figure 5.15. Phonemes are dependent on human

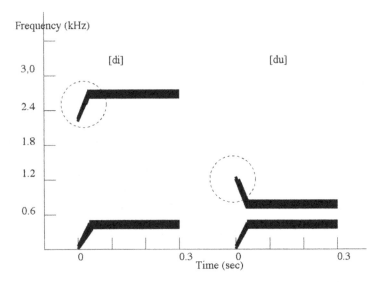

Fig. 5.15   Two formant frequencies of the consonant d, which represents the sounds [di] and [du]. The second formant frequency transition and value differ.

speech; however, the human speech cannot be segmented at the acoustic level. Their acoustic features cannot be identified in speech signals. For example, in the spoken word "bat" that is recorded on a magnetic tape, isolating a "b" or "t" is impossible. The listener will only hear an "a". The initial and final consonants comprise the modulations of formant frequencies of the vowel "a" [Lieberman and Blumstein (1988)]. The phonemes of every syllable are generated by the human mind, whereas the features are distributed over the entire signal that represents a word.

5.7 Feature Vector

Descriptors such as histograms that represent multimedia objects are frequently represented as feature vectors of a fixed dimension.

5.7.1 *Contours*

Contours (two-dimensional) can be represented by a polar coordinate system using a vector of a fixed dimension. The polar coordinates r and θ are defined in terms of two-dimensional coordinates x and y

$$r = \sqrt{x^2 + y^2} \tag{5.48}$$

and

$$\theta = \tan^{-1}\left(\frac{x}{y}\right) \tag{5.49}$$

with r being the radial distance from the origin and θ the counterclockwise angle from the x-axis (see Figure 5.16) and in therms Cartesian coordinates

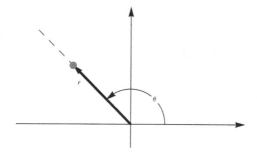

Fig. 5.16   With r being the radial distance from the origin and θ the counterclockwise angle from the x-axis.

$$x = r \cdot \cos\theta, \quad y = r \cdot \sin\theta \tag{5.50}$$

The fixed point (analogous to the origin of a Cartesian system) is called the pole. To represent a contour we determine it's centroid coordinate, it becomes the fixed point. The perimeter of the contour are sampled at a fixed rate represented by an angle γ and the values r_i are stored in a vector. The dimension m of the vector is determined by the sampling rate with

$$m = \frac{2 \cdot \pi}{\gamma}.$$

5.7.2 *Norm*

A norm is a function given a vector space V that maps a vector into a real number with

$$\|v\| \geq 0$$

and with α scalar

$$\|\alpha \cdot \mathbf{x}\| = |\alpha| \cdot \|\mathbf{x}\|$$

$$\|\mathbf{x} + \mathbf{y}\| \leq |\mathbf{x}| + |\mathbf{y}|.$$

The l_p norm is defined as the following (for $p = 2$ it is the Euclidean norm):

$$\|\mathbf{x}\|_p = (|x_1|^p + |x_2|^p + \cdots + |x_m|^p)^{\frac{1}{p}} \tag{5.51}$$

l_p norms are equivalent and the following relation holds for $0 < q < p$

$$\|\mathbf{x}\|_p \leq \|\mathbf{x}\|_q \leq m^{\frac{1}{q} - \frac{1}{p}} \cdot \|\mathbf{x}\|_p \tag{5.52}$$

and

$$m^{\frac{1}{p} - \frac{1}{q}} \cdot \|\mathbf{x}\|_q \leq \|\mathbf{x}\|_p \leq \|\mathbf{x}\|_q. \tag{5.53}$$

The maximum l_∞ norm is defined as

$$\|\mathbf{x}\|_\infty = max\left(|x_1|, |x_2|, \cdots, |x_m|\right). \tag{5.54}$$

5.7.3 *Distance function*

Metric defines a distance between two vectors with

$$d(\mathbf{x}, \mathbf{y}) \geq 0$$

symmetry

$$d(\mathbf{x}, \mathbf{y}) = d(\mathbf{y}, \mathbf{x})$$

and the triangle inequality

$$d(\mathbf{x}, \mathbf{y}) \leq d(\mathbf{x}, \mathbf{z}) + d(\mathbf{z}, \mathbf{y}).$$

The l_p norm induces the distance between two points (metric)

$$d_p(\mathbf{x}, \mathbf{y}) = \|\mathbf{x} - \mathbf{y}\|_p = (|x_1 - y_1|^p + |x_2 - y_2|^p + \cdots + |x_m - y_m^p)^{\frac{1}{p}} \quad (5.55)$$

The most popular metrics are the Taxicab or Manhattan metric d_1 with

$$d_1(\mathbf{x}, \mathbf{y}) = \|\mathbf{x} - \mathbf{y}\|_1 = |x_1 - y_1| + |x_2 - y_2| + \cdots + |x_m - y_m| \quad (5.56)$$

and the Euclidean metric

$$d_2(\mathbf{x}, \mathbf{y}) = \|\mathbf{x} - \mathbf{y}\|_2 = \sqrt{|x_1 - y_1|^2 + |x_2 - y_2|^2 + \cdots + |x_m - y_m|^2}. \quad (5.57)$$

The Euclidean norm is induced by the inner product

$$\|\mathbf{x}\|_2 = \sqrt{\langle \mathbf{x}|\mathbf{x}\rangle} \quad (5.58)$$

and defines a Hilbert space, which extends the two or three dimensional Euclidean space to spaces with any finite or infinite number of dimensions. Often one writes for Euclidean distance function and norm simply

$$d(\mathbf{x}, \mathbf{y}) = \|\mathbf{x} - \mathbf{y}\| = \sqrt{|x_1 - y_1|^2 + |x_2 - y_2|^2 + \cdots + |x_m - y_m|^2}. \quad (5.59)$$

By normalising the vector to the length one the Euclidean distance function is constrained to the unit sphere

$$0 \leq d\left(\frac{\mathbf{x}}{\|\mathbf{x}\|}, \frac{\mathbf{y}}{\|\mathbf{y}\|}\right) = \left\|\frac{\mathbf{x}}{\|\mathbf{x}\|} - \frac{\mathbf{y}}{\|\mathbf{y}\|}\right\| \leq \sqrt{2} \quad (5.60)$$

and corresponds to the angle ω between the vectors

$$\cos\omega = \frac{\langle \mathbf{x}|\mathbf{y}\rangle}{\|\mathbf{x}\| \cdot \|\mathbf{y}\|} \quad (5.61)$$

with a similarity function

$$0 \leq sim(\mathbf{x}, \mathbf{y}) = \cos\omega \leq 1 \quad (5.62)$$

called the cosine similarity.

5.7.4 *Data scaling*

Let DB be a database of s multimedia objects $\mathbf{x}_k$ represented by vectors of dimension m in which the index k is an explicit key identifying each object,

$$\{\mathbf{x}_k \in DB | k \in \{1..s\}\}.$$

Such data can be pre transformed, like for example by the principal component analysis (PCA). However such a transformation induce the loss of information. A lossless transformation is the Z-score normalization, it consists of subtracting the mean of each dimension $\bar{x}_i$ and dividing by the standard deviation (of the sample) of each dimension s_i of the data base DB

$$y_{k,i} = \frac{x_{k,i} - \overline{x}_i}{s_i}. \tag{5.63}$$

In the min-max normalization the range of intervals for each dimension i is changed from the old range specified by min_i^{old} and max_i^{old} into y min_i^{new} and max_i^{new}

$$y_{k,i} = \frac{x_{k,i} - min_i^{old}}{max_i^{old} - min_i^{old}} \cdot (max_i^{new} - min_i^{new}) + min_i^{new}. \tag{5.64}$$

One has to be careful when scaling vectors, because the operation fail to preserve distances.

5.7.5 *Similarity*

Let DB be a database of s multimedia objects $\mathbf{x}_k$ represented by vectors of dimension m in which the index k is an explicit key identifying each object with

$$\mathbf{x}_1, \mathbf{x}_2, \mathbf{x}_3, \cdots, \mathbf{x}_s.$$

Two vectors $\mathbf{y}$ and $\mathbf{x}_q$ are called NN-similar with respect to a database DB if and only if

$$\forall \mathbf{x}_k \in DB : d(\mathbf{y}, \mathbf{x}_q) \leq d(\mathbf{y}, \mathbf{x}_k) \tag{5.65}$$

The ϵ-similarity is defined for a range queries. For a vector $\mathbf{y}$ *all* vectors $\mathbf{x}_j$ are ϵ-similar to $\mathbf{y}$ according to the distance function d with

$$d(\mathbf{x}_j, \mathbf{y}) < \epsilon. \tag{5.66}$$

To find ϵ-similar objects a range query is preformed. For meaningful results an appropriate ϵ value is required. If the ϵ value is to small, no ϵ-similar objects are determined. If the ϵ value is to big, the output consists in the whole data base DB. If the database DB is large, big value of s and a high value of m, it would be desirable to develop a data structure, which for given a query vector $\mathbf{y}$ finds the neared neighbour in DB according to a distance function with a logarithmic time in s. We know that for $m = 1$ this can be achieved by a search tree. Is such a structure possible for values $m \gg 1$? We will try to answer this question in the next chapters starting from the classical decision trees.

5.8 Time Series

A disadvantage of distance functions such as the Euclidean distance is that the lengths of the vectors must identical. This problem can be handled by re-interpolating the vectors to equal length, such as subsampling or up-sampling by linear interpolation of values between points. This approach is preferred. In some cases, elastic distance measures such as dynamic time warping for word recognition in speech and the longest common subsequence in computational biology (DNA sequences) yield better results.

5.8.1 *Dynamic time warping*

Dynamic time warping enables nonlinear alignment of the points of time series [Jelinek (1998)]. DTW computes the optimal match between two given sequences, as shown in Figure 5.17. DWT is not a metric because

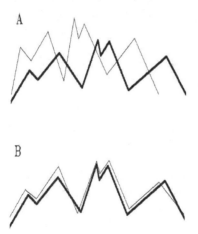

Fig. 5.17   (A) Two sequences before the aligning. (B) After the aligning by DTW.

the triangle inequality does not hold. The Euclidean distance between two sequences Q and C of the same length is given by

$$d(Q, C) = \sqrt{\sum_{i=1}^{m} |x_i - y_i|^2}. \tag{5.67}$$

The DTW is defined recessively for as

$$D(i,j) = \begin{cases} 0 & \text{if } i = j = 0 \\ \infty & \text{if } i = 0, j > 0 \text{ or } i > 0, j = 0 \\ d(q_i, c_j) + min \begin{cases} D(i-1, j-1) \\ D(i-1, j) \\ D(j, i-1) \end{cases} & \text{if } i, j > 1 \end{cases}$$

(5.68)

For example for a sequence Q of length m and sequence C of length n we call recursively $D(m, n)$ with

$$d(q_i, c_j) = |q_i - c_j|.$$

(5.69)

5.8.2　Dynamic programming

A recursive function with a memoization method is an example of dynamic programming. Memoization is the technique of saving values that have already been calculated [Cormen *et al.* (2001b)]. With $n > m$, the computing costs are quadratic with $O(n^2)$. The longest common subsequence (LCS) similarity measure is a variation of edit distance. The similarity between two time series is calculated as a function of the length of the longest matching subsequence. The edit distance with a non-negative cost satisfies the axioms of a metric.

$$L(i,j) = \begin{cases} 0 & \text{if } i = 0 \text{ or} j = 0 \\ 1 + L(i-1, j-1) & \text{if } i, j > 0 \text{ and } |q_i - c_j| \leq \epsilon \\ \max(L(i-1), j), L(i, j-1)) & \text{if } i, j > 0 \text{ and } |q_i - c_j| > \epsilon \end{cases} .$$

(5.70)

With $n > m$, the computing costs of LCS are quadratic with $O(n^2)$. Due to the heavy computational costs, re-interpolating the vectors to equal lengths should be preferred when handling large multimedia databases.

Chapter 6

Low Dimensional Indexing

For the fast access of large data, divide and conquer methods that are based on hierarchical structures are employed. For numbers, a tree can be utilized to prune branches in the processing queries. The access is fast: it is logarithmic in relation to the size of the database that represents the numbers. For low-dimensional vectors, metric index trees, such as kd-trees and R-trees can be employed. Alternatively, an index structure that is based on space-filling curves can be constructed.

6.1 Hierarchical Structures

The principles of hierarchical organization appear in nature, for example, the structure of matter itself is hierarchically organized including elementary particles, atomic nuclei, atoms, and molecules [Resnikoff (1989)]. The idea of hierarchical structures is based on the decomposition of a hierarchy into simpler parts. One of the most effective ways to structure knowledge is the taxonomic arrangement of the biological information that represents it [Resnikoff (1989)].

6.1.1 *Example of a taxonomy*

In 1887 Professor Harry Govier Seeley grouped all dinosaurs into the Saurischia and Ornithischia groups according to their hip design [Haines (1999)]. In Figure 6.1 and we 6.2 can see some examples of the two categories [Wichert (2000)].

The saurischian were divided later into two subgroups: the carnivorous, bipedal theropods and the plant-eating, mostly quadruped sauropodomorphs. The ornithischians were divided into the subgroups

Fig. 6.1 Tyranonosaurus is an example of the category coelurosaurian theropod dinosaur.

Fig. 6.2 Parasaurolophus is an example of the category ornithopod of the group of ornithischian dinosaurs.

birdlike ornithopods, armored thyreophorans, and margginoncephalia. The subgroups can be divided into suborders and then into families and finally into genus. The genus includes the species. It must be noted that in this taxonomy many relations are only guesswork, and many paleontologists have different ideas about how the taxonomy should look [Lambert (1983, 1993)] (see Figure 6.3).

6.1.2 *Origins of hierarchical structures*

We wish to create a communication system which will enable each node to communicate with every other one. There are in total s nodes, what could be a possible solution for this problem? We could connect each node with the other one resulting in

$$\frac{s \cdot (s - 1)}{2} \qquad (6.1)$$

connections. The value of the connections growths quadratic, for big s vales this could be problematic. Another solution would be to connect each node

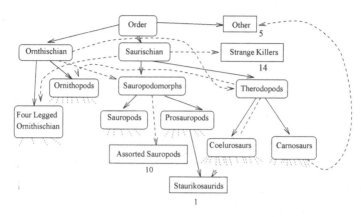

Fig. 6.3 Taxonomy of dinosauria. The number written below the rectangular boxes represents the categories which are not divided, the species. Uncertain categories are represented by dotted arrows.

to a single central node, for s nodes this would require only s connections, ee Figure 6.5 (a). The central node would determine the corresponding communication line, it would act as a kind of a telephone operator, see Figure 6.4 [Resnikoff (1989)]. We can set the central node at the top of the diagram and interpret the structure as a hierarchical arrangement with one level and two layers, layer zero and layer one, see Figure 6.5 (b). We can

Fig. 6.4 A telephone operator works a switchboard. The operator converses with the caller, who informs the operator to whom he or she would like to speak, the operator places then the front cord in the associated jack.

s=9

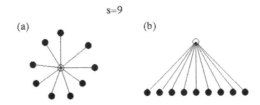

Fig. 6.5 Example with $s = 9$,(a) Each node is connected to a single central node, for 9 nodes this would require only 9 connections. (b) We can set the central node at the top of the diagram and interpret the structure as a hierarchical arrangement with one level and two layers, layer zero and layer one.

extend the hierarchy to two levels. The central node is connected to d sub nodes and each of the sub nodes is connected to s/d nodes. In this case there are $s + d$ connections, see Figure 6.6. The value of d has to be chosen

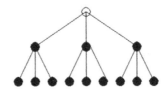

Fig. 6.6 We can extend the hierarchy to two levels. The central node is connected to d sub nodes and each of the sub nodes is connected to $9/3$ nodes. In this case there are $3 + 9$ connections.

so that

$$d \cdot d = s. \tag{6.2}$$

The solution for the value of d is

$$d = \sqrt{s}. \tag{6.3}$$

The cost of a search of the correct node would be

$$cost = 2 \cdot d = 2 \cdot \sqrt{s}. \tag{6.4}$$

A requirement for search by this kind of hierarchical organisation is that the nodes as well as the sub nodes can be ordered in such a way that a search in ascending order of the stored values can be preformed. It means that each node contains a value v and that its left neighbour (if existing) with the value v_l satisfies the relation

$$v_l \leq v.$$

From the requirement it follows that a right neighbour (if existing) with the value v_r satisfies the relation

$$v \leq v_r.$$

The values of the sub-nodes are usually represented in keys. We can extend the hierarch to several levels. Each level hierarchy corresponds to some sub nodes with their corresponding key values, see Figure 6.7. For a hierarchy

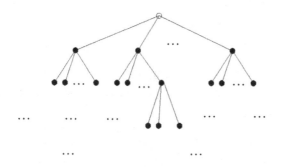

Fig. 6.7   We can extend the hierarch to several levels. Each level hierarchy corresponds to some sub nodes.

of t levels d is chosen so that

$$d = s^{\frac{1}{t}} \tag{6.5}$$

and the cost of a search of the correct node would be

$$cost = t \cdot d = t \cdot s^{\frac{1}{t}}. \tag{6.6}$$

For each level r there are

$$s(r) = d^r = s^{\frac{r}{t}} \tag{6.7}$$

nodes with $s(t) = s$. For a search of an object out of s, at each level d questions must be answered $(t \cdot d)$, with $d^t = s$ we can represent t in relation to s

$$cost = \frac{\log(s)}{\log(d)} \cdot d = t \cdot d. \tag{6.8}$$

Is there a d for which the cost becomes minimal? If we suppose that the tree is an ideal tree in which the branching factor can be an irrational number, then the solution is

$$0 = \frac{\partial cost}{\partial d} = \frac{\log(s)}{\log(d)} - \frac{\log(s)}{\log(d)^2} \qquad (6.9)$$

with

$$d = \mathbf{e} = 2.7182818...$$

which corresponds to Euler's number. The closest whole number is three, followed by two. Euler's number minimizes the cost of an idealistic search in a hierarchical structure.

6.2 Tree

A tree is represented by nodes and edges. The initial state defines the root of the tree. From each node ν, either d_ν nodes can be reached or the node is a leaf. d_ν represents the branching factor of the node v. Every node besides the root has a unique node from which it was reached, called the parent. The parent is the node above it and is connected by an edge. Each parent ν has d_ν children. The depth of a node ν is the number of edges to the root node. Nodes with the same depth r define the level r. For a tree with a constant branching factor d, each node at each level r has d children and at each level k there are $d \cdot r$ nodes [Nilsson (1982)], [Luger and Stubblefield (1993)], [Russell and Norvig (2010)]. The nodes are organized in levels, the root of the tree corresponds to the level 0, and each node at each level has d children, which means that, at each level r, there are d^r nodes. A has the highest level t, and there are $d^t = s$ leaves that correspond to the s represented objects. The leaves have the same depth, it is a perfect balanced tree[1].

6.2.1 *Search tree*

A requirement for search by a tree is that the nodes of each level can be ordered in such a way that a search in ascending order of the stored values can be preformed. A parent node can contains several keys with values.

---

[1]In a perfect balanced tree every path from root to leaf node has the same length, each leaf has the same depth. In balanced tree the depth of the left and right subtrees of every node differ by 1 or less.

For any key value v the values w_l stored in its left subtree
$$w_l \leq v,$$
and the values w_r stored in its right subtree satisfy
$$v \leq w_r.$$
Each subtree of a search tree is by itself again a search tree. For a search tree with a constant branching factor of d each node belonging to a given level has the same number of children. The cost for a search in such a tree are

$$s(0) = 1, \quad s(1) = d, \quad s(2) = d^2, \quad \cdots, \quad s(r) = d^r, \quad \cdots, \quad s = s(t) = d^t. \tag{6.10}$$

and

$$d = \frac{s(r)}{s(r-1)}, \tag{6.11}$$

$$cost = t \cdot d = \frac{s(1)}{s(0)} + \frac{s(2)}{s(1)} + \cdots + \frac{s(r)}{s(r-1)} + \cdots + \frac{s(t)}{s(t-1)} \tag{6.12}$$

with

$$t = \frac{\log(s)}{\log(d)} \tag{6.13}$$

the costs are logarithmic in s.

6.2.2 *Decoupled search tree*

Imagine the search of leaves would be wighted be some additional costs represented by $n \gg s$

$$cost = n \cdot \frac{s(1)}{s(0)} + \frac{s(2)}{s(1)} + \cdots + \frac{s(r)}{s(r-1)} + \cdots + \frac{s(t)}{s(t-1)} \tag{6.14}$$

it follows

$$cost = n \cdot d + \left(\frac{\log(s)}{\log(d)}\right) \cdot d - d \tag{6.15}$$

If n can be represented by n ordered nodes and its order is decoupled fro the s nodes, then we can reduce the costs of $n \cdot d$ by an additional search tree with a constant branching [Wichert *et al.* (2010); Wichert and Moreira (2015)]. The final costs are

$$cost = \log_d(n \cdot d) \cdot d + \log_d(s) \cdot d - d \tag{6.16}$$

simplified with

$$cost = (\log_d(n) + 1) \cdot d + (\log_d(s) - 1) \cdot d \tag{6.17}$$

and

$$cost = (\log_d(n \cdot s)) \cdot d \tag{6.18}$$

If s and n nodes are decoupled we are able to search first for the solution in the set of s nodes, then in the set of n nodes or vice versa.

6.2.3 *B-tree*

A B-tree enables the search of ordered sets in logarithmic time. It is a generalization of the binary search that halves the number of items to verify each iteration during the search. The cost of a binary search is logarithmic. In each iteration, the algorithm compares the key value of the middle element of an ordered array of key values. If the search value does not match the key value and is smaller than the key value, then the algorithm repeats its action on the sub-array to the left of the middle key. In the case in which the search value is larger than the key value, the algorithm repeats its action on the sub-array to the right of the middle key. The procedure is repeated until the search value is obtained or an empty sub-array exists. A sub-array indicates that the search value does not exist. In B-trees, the nodes store ordered ranges of numbers that represent sets of keys. B-trees [Comer (1979); Cormen *et al.* (2001a)] may have a variable number of keys and children. A key in a non leaf node has a left child pointer and a right child pointer (branch). The left pointer is the root of a subtree. It contains nodes with a lower or equal number of keys; it is the right child pointer of the proceeding key. The right pointer is the subtree that contains all keys greater than any keys in that node; it is the left child pointer of the following key (refer to Figure 6.8).

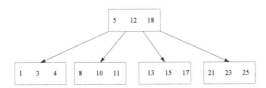

Fig. 6.8   In B-trees, the keys are ranges of numbers, they are stored in non-decreasing order in a node. The left pointer of a key is the root of a sub tree which contains nodes with keys less than or equal to it, the right pointer is the a sub tree containing all keys greater than any keys in that node.

The root node of the tree serves as an entry point for query processing. The information is stored in the leaves and the keys. The leaves are referred to as data pages and the nodes of the tree are referred to as directory pages. During the search operation to a given point, the correct child is selected by a linear search of the key values in the node. A key value greater than or equal to the desired value is searched. If it exists, the child pointer to the immediate left of this value is followed; otherwise, the rightmost child pointer is followed.

A B-tree of order w is the tree where each node may have a maximum number of w children, in which

- the number w should always be odd;
- the number of keys in each nonleaf node is one less than the number of its children;
- the keys in each nonleaf node partition the keys in the children in the manner of a search tree;
- the root is either a leaf node or contains two to w children;
- all nonleaf nodes have at least $\lceil \frac{w}{2} \rceil$ children, with the exception of the root;
- all leaves are on the same level (it is a perfectly balanced tree);
- a leaf node contains no more than $w - 1$ keys (value).

We describe how to construct a B-tree that obeys these principles.

6.2.3.1 *Example of construction of a B-tree*

Suppose we want to construct a B-tree of order 5 from the unordered set of kew

1 12 8 2 25 5 14 28 17 7 52 16 48 68 3 26 29 53 55 45

The first four items are ordered represented by the root, this is because a root has from two to $w = 5$ children and the number of keys in each non-leaf node is one less than the number of its children

1 2 8 12

When 25 arrives, pick the middle key to make a new root and the following $6, 14, 28$ get added to the leaf nodes, see Figure 6.9. We continue with the construction of the $B - tree$, see Figure 6.10. B-tree is commonly used in large databases. The name itself probably inspired by name of the inventor, "B" for Bayer's name or the place he worked, namely *Boieng*.

6.2.4 *kd-tree*

A requirement for searching by a tree is that the nodes of each level can be ordered in such a manner that a search in ascending order of the stored values can be performed. In vector spaces, the points are not ordered; for example, complex numbers can be viewed as a point or position vector in a two-dimensional Cartesian coordinate system, which is referred to

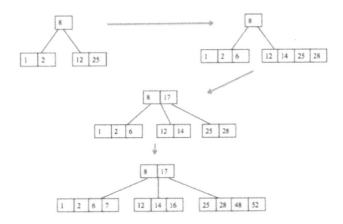

Fig. 6.9   The first four items are ordered represented by the root, this is because a root
has from two to $w = 5$ children and the number of keys in each non-leaf node is one less
than the number of its children $1, 2, 8, 12$. When 25 arrives, pick the middle key to make
a new root and the following $6, 14, 28$ get added to the leaf nodes. Adding 17 we split
the right leaf, then $7, 52, 16, 48$ get added to the leaf nodes.

as the complex plane. Because no natural linear ordering on the set of
complex numbers exists, they cannot be diagrammed as a line of elements.
The ordering of points requires a one-to-one mapping into a line (injective
mapping). The idea of a k-dimensional tree (kd-tree) is to hierarchically
decompose the space [Bentley (1975)]. In two-dimensional space, the point
set is split by a vertical line, in which half of the coordinate points are
positioned on the left side and half of the points are positioned on the right
side along the x-axis. Then, it is split by a vertical line, in which half
of the coordinate points are positioned upward and half of the coordinate
points are positioned downward along the y-axis. After the split, four cells
are present and the procedure is recursively repeated in each of these cells.
The recursion stops in the case that each point is represented by its own
cell. Each node in the tree is defined by the line that partitions the set of
points into left and right sets or upward and downward sets. The leaves
correspond to the points that are represented by a cell, as shown in Figure
6.11. During the search for a query represented by a two-dimensional vector, we traverse down the hierarchy until we find the cell that contains the
most similar object represented by a two-dimensional vector according to
a distance function, as shown in Figure 6.12. A three-dimensional kd-tree

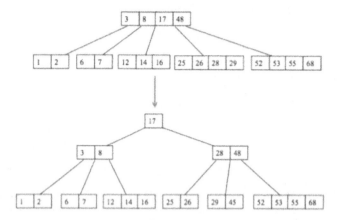

Fig. 6.10   Adding 68 causes us to split the right most leaf, promoting 48 to the root. Adding 3 causes us to split the left most leaf. As a onsequence 3 goes to the root and 26, 29, 53, 55 into the leaves. Finally adding 45 causes a split of a leave and promoting 28 to the root that is then split.

splits on the x, y and z-coordinates by generating eight cells (2^3) on the first level. An n-dimensional kd-tree recursively subdivides a set of points with alternating axis-aligned hyperplanes, which generate 2^n on the first level. Leaves in a kd-tree do not need to have the same depth (the tree does not need to be balanced). A kd-tree is a generalization of the binary search that divides the number of items to verify each iteration during the search for each dimension.

6.2.4.1   *Nearest neighbor search*

Searching the nearest neighbor for a query q in a n dimensional kd-tree is described as follows:

- Beginning with the root node, the algorithm recursively moves down the tree and continues on one side of the hyperplane regardless of whether the point is less than or greater than the corresponding value of the hyperplane dimension that splits the space into two cells. Each hyperplane is represented by one node with two children. The children represent other nodes or leaves.
- Once the algorithm reaches a leaf node, it determines the distance r_{max} of the query point q to the leaf node. The leaf node becomes

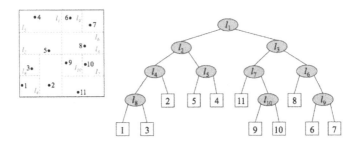

Fig. 6.11   In two-dimensional space, the point set is split by a vertical line, in which half of the coordinate points are positioned on the left side and half of the coordinate points are positioned on the right side along the x-axis. Then, it is split by a vertical line, in which half of the points are positioned upward and half of the points are positioned downward along the y-axis. After the split, four cells are present; in each of these cells the procedure is recursively repeated. The recursion stops in the case in which each point is represented by its own cell. Each node in the tree is defined by the line that partitions the set of points into left and right sets or upward and downward sets. The leaves correspond to the points that are each represented by a cell. In our example, 11 two-dimensional points are recursively split by ten lines $l_1, l_2, \cdots, l_{10}$.

the current solution.

- Then, the algorithm verifies whether any points on the other side of the splitting plane are closer to the search point. This verification is performed by verifying whether any other hyperplane is inside the hypersphere of radius r_{max} around the query point q.
- If the hypersphere of the radius r_{max} crosses the plane, be nearer points may exist on the other side of the plane; thus, the algorithm must move down the other branch of the tree. The distances to the other points are determined. If the distance is smaller than the new leaf node, it becomes the current solution and r_{max} is set to the current distance. The same recursive process is repeated.
- If the hypersphere of the radius r_{max} does not cross the plane, the algorithm terminates with the answer to the current solution node and r_{max}.

The nearest neighbor operation by the kd-tree is efficient in low-dimensional spaces with the dimension $n \leq 16$. In this case, the kd-tree uses $O(s \cdot n)$ space (for s data points). For randomly distributed s points, it takes $O(\log s)$ time to answer queries. In the worst case, the time is $O(s)$.

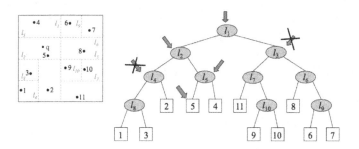

Fig. 6.12   The search for a query represented by a two-dimensional vector. We traverse down the hierarchy until we find the cell that contains the most similar object represented by a two-dimensional vector. The query vector q is compared by the line l_1 and the search continues in the left cell. Next, q is compared with the line l_2 and the search continues by the up cell. Then, q is compared with the line l_5 and the distance r_{max} to the point 5 is determined. The algorithm verifies whether any points may exist on the other side of the splitting plane, which is closer to the search point. This action is performed by verifying whether any other line is located inside the circle of radius r_{max} around the query point q, which is true in our case of line l_5. The distance to the point 6 is determined to be larger than r_{max}; thus, the nearest neighbor is the point 5.

6.2.4.2   *Range search*

The ϵ-similarity search defines a hypersphere of the radius ϵ around the query point q. Because kd-trees divide the space by hyperplanes, describing the range query by a n dimensional hyperrectangle, which is also referred to as a n-orthotope, instead of by an n dimensional hypersphere. A n-dimensional hypercube is an n-dimensional hyperrectangle with sides of equivalent length [Lee and Wong (1977)]. Because kd-trees divide the range of a domain in half at each level of the tree, they are useful for performing range searches by an n dimensional hyper rectangle; it is described as:

- Find all points in a query axis-aligned hyperrectangle.
- Check if point in node lies in given hyperrectangle.
- Recursively search each side of the hyperplane (if any can fall into the hyperrectangle).

For the two-dimensional case, we recursively search the left/bottom and the right/top. The range query time in this case is $O(\sqrt{s})$ assuming a balanced kd-tree (all leaves have the same depth). In two dimensions, a rectangle is described by four sides. For each side, we have to determine if the points of the range query are located inside or outside of the rectangle.

In a two-dimensional kd-tree, every node has two children that correspond to an outcome of the comparison of a vertical line and a horizontal line. We can consider a case of a vertical line. In a balanced kd-tree with s two-dimensional random points, we can assume that the points are arranged in a rectangle. A vertical (or horizontal) line has to compare $\sqrt{s}$ points to determine if the points are located on the left side or the right side (up or down in the case of a vertical line). Because a rectangle has four sides, we need $4 \cdot \sqrt{s}$ comparisons; it is at most

$$O(4 \cdot \sqrt{s}) = O(\sqrt{s}). \tag{6.19}$$

For three dimensions, the range query time is $O(s^{2/3})$ assuming a balanced kd-tree. A three-dimensional hyperrectangle is described by six Planes. For each plane, we have to determine if the points of the range query are located inside or outside of the rectangle. We consider the case of a vertical plane. In a balanced kd-tree with s three-dimensional random points, we can assume that the points are arranged in a hyperrectangle. A vertical plane has to compare $s^{2/3}$ points to determine if the points are located on the left side or the right side. Because a hyperrectangle has six planes, we need $6 \cdot s^{2/3}$ comparisons; it is at most

$$O(6 \cdot s^{2/3}) = O(s^{2/3}).$$

For n dimensions, the range query time is

$$O(s^{(n-1)/n}) = O(s^{(1-1/n)}) \tag{6.20}$$

assuming a balanced kd-tree.

6.2.4.3 *High dimensional space and kd-tree*

An increase in the number of dimensions has negative implications for the performance. It eventually reduces the search time to sequential scanning. In the worst case, the complexity of the nearest neighbor and boundary search in a kd-tree is $O(s)$, for high dimensions $O(s \cdot n)$.

Problems are caused by the fact that the volume of a hyperrectagle exponentially increases with increasing dimension. For the dimensionality, n the number of data points should be

$$s \gg 2^n.$$

Otherwise, nearly all points in the tree will be evaluated. Note that

$$s \gg 2^{256} = 1.15792 \times 10^{77}$$

points is required for a 256 dimensional vector, which is not possible. To understand how large this number, one should know that 6×10^{49} is the approximate number of atoms on Earth. We assume that kd-trees are efficient in low-dimensional spaces with the dimension $n \leq 16$ with

$$s \gg 2^{16} = 65536.$$

6.3 Metric Tree

The basic idea of metric indexes is to derive metrics from item properties to build a tree that can then be used to prune branches in processing queries. In metric indexes the keys in the trees represent regions which are subsets in the data space [Böhm *et al.* (2001)]. The n dimensional data space is recursively split by $n-1$ dimensional hyper-planes until the number of data items in a partition is below a certain threshold. Data is represented by vectors that are stored in nodes such that spatially adjacent vectors are stored in the same node. Each data vector is stored in exactly one node and there is no object duplication within a node. The nodes are organized hierarchically, each node points to a set of sub trees. Assigned to each node is a key represented by a region, which is a subset of the data space. Each key has an associated child, which is the root of a sub tree containing all nodes with regions that are contained in the key region of the proceeding key. However, unlike in the B-trees, where the keys are numbers which define intervals which do not overlap, key regions may overlap because the space has dimension greater one. This means that regions of nodes in different branches of the tree may overlap, which leads to high computing costs. Because of that, special heuristics are often used to avoid or to minimize the overlapping. Trees mainly differ by the definition of the region and the resulting search and building algorithms. The metric indexes tree can be used to prune branches in processing the queries because of the lower bounding property. The distance of a query point to each key region is greater than the distance to the key regions of its children.

6.3.1 *R-tree*

In R-trees, the key regions are minimum bounding rectangles (MBR) [Guttman (1984); Böhm *et al.* (2001)]. MBR is a multidimensional interval of the data space which is a minimal axis-parallel rectangle enclosing the complete point set with at least one data point. In the tree hierarchy, the

Intelligent Big Multimedia Databases

key MBR of a parent node contains the MBR keys of its children that are allowed to overlap (see Figure 6.13). A R-tree with W being the maximum

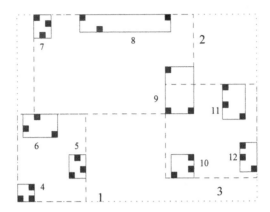

Fig. 6.13   In R-trees, key regions are minimum bounding rectangles. The children of the root (doted big rectangle) are represented by the region keys indicated by the numbers 1, 2, and 3 (dashed rectangles). The key region 1 has the children indicated by the numbers 4, 5, 6, which themselves have key regions representing the data (indicated by the black dots) and so on. A child can have more than one parent.

number of entries in one node a w being the minimum number of entries in a node with

$$2 \le w \le \frac{W}{2}$$

has the following properties:

- the root has at least two children unless it is a leaf;
- every parent node completely covers its children;
- a child MBR may be covered by more than one parent;
- a point query may follow multiple branches.
- every non-leaf node has between w and W children unless it is the root;
- every leaf node contains between w and W entries unless it is the root;
- R-tree is a perfectly balanced tree, all leaves appear on the same level.

Because a child MBR may be covered by more than one parent, more than one subtree under a visited node may be searched. The worst case performance is $O(s)$ for high dimensions $O(s \cdot n)$, however the average complexity for low dimensions (e.g. $n \leq 8$) is $O(\log_W(s))$.

6.3.1.1 *MBR*

The minimum bounding rectangles or smallest bounding or enclosing box is a term used in geometry. For a set of points in n dimensions, it refers to the box with the smallest measurement (area, volume, or hypervolume in higher dimensions) within which all points lie. The minimum bounding rectangles (MBRs) are axis-aligned, which indicates that the edges of the box are parallel to the (Cartesian) coordinate axes. Every face of any MBR contains at least one point of a object, as shown in Figure 6.14. A MBR in

Fig. 6.14   The minimum bounding rectangles (MBR) are axis-aligned, it means that the edges of the box are parallel to the (Cartesian) coordinate axes. Every face of any MBR contains at least one point of some object.

two dimensions is a rectangle with four vertices are A, B, C, and D with values

$$x_{low} < x_{high}, \quad y_{low} < y_{high}$$

the vertices are

$$A = (x_{low}, y_{low}), \quad B = (x_{low}, y_{high}), \quad C = (x_{high}, y_{low}), \quad D = (x_{high}, y_{high}).$$

A 2 dimensional MBR can be described by a four dimensional vector representing a point $\mathbf{R}$ with

$$\mathbf{R} = (x_{low}, x_{high}, y_{low}, , y_{high}).$$

A n dimensional MBR is described by a $2 \cdot n$ dimensional vector that represents a point $\mathbf{R}$; for each dimension, there is a *low* and a *high* value. With this representation, we can employ point access methods (PAM) that index points. Point access methods determine if an overlap exists between different points. The region description of a MBR comprises a lower bound and an upper bound. Among each pair of opposite edges of a MBR, only the edges located near the query point are considered for each dimension. Given the MBR definition, the lower bound is defined by the nearest corner that contains these edges and the upper bound is defined by the farthest corner that contains one of this edges.

6.3.1.2 *Range search*

In a range query, a search covers all points in the space whose Euclidian distance to the query point is smaller or equal to ϵ. A MBR that includes a sphere with the radius ϵ around the query point is determined. Then, the R-tree is recursively descended, excluding all branches whose MBR does not intersect with the query MBR. Because the regions may overlap at each level, the descended R-tree may include several branches. For a range query, the MBR that represents the query is mapped into the $2 \cdot n$ dimensional vector; and PAM can be employed to answer the query.

6.3.1.3 *Nearest neighbour search*

In nearest neighbor search algorithms, the upper bound on every surface is determined; the minimum is taken because only the nearer surface can contain the minimum. Two metrics are available for ordering the NN search. The minimum distance:

- $MINDIST(P, R)$ is the minimum distance between a point P and a rectangle R;
- If the point is inside the rectangle, $MINDIST = 0$;
- If the point is outside the rectangle, $MINDIST$ is the minimal possible distance from the point to any object in or on the perimeter of the rectangle.

Minimum over all dimensions distances from P to the *furthest* point of the *closest face*:

- $MINMAXDIST(P, R)$ is the minimum over all dimensions distances from P to the *furthest* point of the *closest face* of the R;
- it s the smallest possible upper bound of distances from the point P to the rectangle R;
- it guarantees that there is an object within the R at a distance to P less than or equal to it.

In Figure 6.15 example of $MINDIST$ and $MINMAXDIST$ are indicated.

It follows for an

$$MINDIST(P, R) \leq MINMAXDIST(P, R)$$

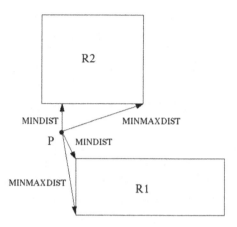

Fig. 6.15   Example of MINDIST and MINMAXDIST for a point P and rectangles $R1$ and $R2$.

Search ordering, MINDIST is optimistic and MINMAXDIST is pessimistic. Search pruning with d being a distance function (Euclidean) is done as:

- Downward pruning: An MBR R is discarded if there exists another R' such that $MINDIST(P, R) > MINMAXDIST(P, R)$
- Downward pruning: An object O is discarded if there exists an R such that $d(P, O) > MINIMAXDIST(P, R)$
- Upward pruning: An MBR R is discarded if an object O is found such that $MINDIST(P, R) > d(P, O)$.

6.3.1.4   *Algorithm for NN*

The Nearest Neighbour Search algorithm is given by:

(1) Initialize the nearest neighbor as empty (distance is set as infinite);
(2) Traverse down the tree from the root:
(3) Sort all newly its MBRs into a list by $MINDIST$ or $MINMAXDIST$;
(4) Apply search pruning to the list to remove unnecessary branches;
(5) Iterate the list until it is empty or a leaf node is reached;

   (a) For each iteration, apply the step 3 recursively to its children node;
   (b) For a leaf node compute each object's distance from the query point and update the nearest neighbor if a smaller distance is present;
   (c) When the list is empty, the nearest neighbor is returned.

6.3.2   *Construction*

An R-tree is a dynamic structure; thus, the goodness of the insertion algorithm is very important. The main difficulty of R-trees is the ability to construct an efficient tree that is balanced and for which the MBRs do not cover too much empty space and do not overlap too much. The three main operations are insertion, delation and splitting.

6.3.2.1   *Insertion*

Locate a place to insert a node by searching and insert. Insert into the subtree that requires the smallest enlargement of its bounding box.

6.3.2.2   *Deletion*

The node is not full. Reinsert other nodes to maintain balance.

6.3.2.3   *Split*

If a node is full, then a split needs to be performed. Because redistributing all objects of a node into two nodes has an exponential number of options, a heuristic needs to be employed. We present two heuristics: the quadratic method and the linear method. Both methods are heuristics that can be used to find a small area split. In the quadratic method, two objects that create as much empty space as possible are selected. In the linear method, the two objects that are farthest apart are selected. Two seeds with maximal separation are selected, then random rectangles are assigned to the selected seeds. The quadratic method provides a better quality of split, whereas the linear split is easier to implement.

6.3.3   *Variations*

In an SS-Tree, the page regions are spheres [Böhm *et al.* (2001)]. The average value of all points (centroid) is employed as the center of the sphere and the minimum radius is selected such that all objects are included in the sphere. Spheres do not enable an easy overlap-free split. In a tree hierarchy, the main spheres of a parent node contain the main spheres of its children, which are allowed to overlap. In a range query, the search is performed on all points in the space whose Euclidian distance to the query point is smaller or equal to ϵ.

The description of regions by spheres enables a rapid determination of a lower bound and an upper bound, which is the distance from the query point to the centroid minus the radius for the lower bound plus the radius for the upper bound value. According to Böhm, SS-trees outperform the R-trees [Böhm *et al.* (2001)].

Numerous tree structures, such as SR-trees, which can be regarded as a variation of the R-tree, such as the SS-tree, R*-trees, X-trees, TV-trees use different heuristics to minimize or prevent overlap of the main regions (for example MBRs).

6.3.4 *High-dimensional space*

Traditional tree-based methods employ the principle of hierarchical clustering of the data space, in which metric properties are used to construct a tree that can be used to prune branches while processing the queries. The performance of tree-based methods deteriorates with large dimensionality. To understand why these methods fail in high-dimensional spaces, let us assume that our tree has only the hierarchy space. We group the images into clusters represented by the cluster centers c_j. After clustering, k centroids

$$\mathbf{c}_1, \mathbf{c}_2 \cdots, \mathbf{c}_k$$

and k clusters

$$C_1, C_2 \cdots, C_k$$

are present with

$$C_j = \{\mathbf{x} | d_2(\mathbf{x}, \mathbf{c}_j) = \min_t d_2(\mathbf{x}, \mathbf{c}_t)\}. \tag{6.21}$$

Each cluster C_j contains the points that are closest to the centroid $\mathbf{c}_j$. During the categorization task of a given query vector $\mathbf{y}$, the most similar centroid $\mathbf{c}_i$ is determined representing the group of similar vectors. Does this simple model also work for query retrieval? Could we take advantage of the grouping of the vectors into clusters? The idea would be to determine the most similar centroid $\mathbf{c}_i$ which represents the most similar category. In the next step, we would search for the most similar vector according to the ϵ-similarity only in this cluster C_i. By doing so, we could save some considerable computation, see Figure 6.16. Suppose $l = \min_i d(\mathbf{y}, \mathbf{c}_i)$ is the distance to the closest centroid and r_{max} is the maximal radius of all the clusters. Only if $l \geq \epsilon \geq r_{max}$, we are guaranteed to determine ϵ similar vectors. Otherwise we have to analyze other clusters as well, Figures 6.17, 6.18 and Figure 6.19 indicate some counter examples for other cases

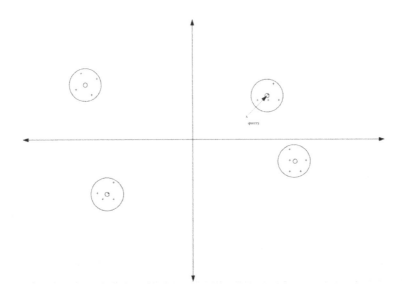

Fig. 6.16   The idea would be to determine the most similar centroid c_i which represents the most similar category. In the next step, we would search.

already present in dimension 2. When a cluster with a minimum distance l is determined, we know that the images in this cluster have a distance between $l + r_{max}$ and $l - r_{max}$. As a result, we have to analyze all clusters with $\{\forall i | d(\mathbf{y}, \mathbf{c}_i) < (l + r_{max})\}$. In the worst case, we have to analyze all clusters. The worst case occurs when the dimension of the vector space is high. The growth in the number of dimensions has negative implications in the performance of multidimensional index trees. These negative effects are named the "curse of dimensionality". Most problems are attributed to the fact that the volume of a minimum bounding rectangle with a constant radius or edge size increases exponentially with an increase in dimensions. For example, the volume of a high-dimensional cube approaches its surface with an increase in dimensions [Böhm *et al.* (2001)]. In high-dimensional spaces, a partition is only performed in a few dimensions and touches the boundary of the data space in most dimensions. A nearest-neighbor query in a high-dimensional space corresponds to a hyper-sphere with a large radius, which is larger than the extension of the data space in most dimensions [Böhm *et al.* (2001)]. The probability that the key regions (MBR boxes) in R-trees may overlap increases with an increase in the dimensions, which indicates that most regions of pages in different branches of the tree overlap.

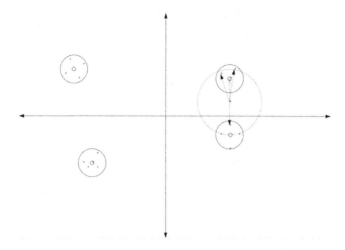

Fig. 6.17 If $l > r_{max}$ will we have all objects which are ϵ-similar?

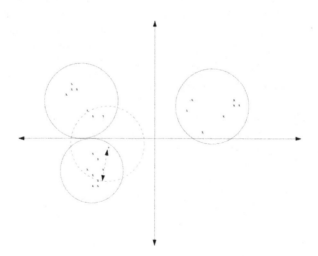

Fig. 6.18 If $l < r_{max}$ will we have all objects which are ϵ-similar?

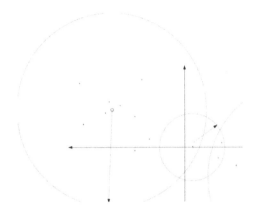

Fig. 6.19   If $l > \epsilon$ and $l < r_{max}$ will we have all objects which are ϵ-similar?

6.4   Space Filling Curves

Can we represent n-dim points by a B-tree? the n-dim vectors do not exhibit a natural linear ordering and cannot be diagrammed as a line of elements. A requirement for searching by a B-tree is that the nodes of each level can be ordered in such a manner that a search in ascending order of the stored values can be performed. A more precise question is how to map n-dimensional points onto 1-dimension. If the problem of the total order is overcome by this type of mapping, traditional one-dimensional indexing structures such as B-trees can be employed. Can we perform PCA? Have other ideas been explored? Assuming a finite granularity, we can map the corresponding n dimensional cells onto one-dimensional cells. For example we can assume finite granularity of a plane, such as 256×256 or 4×4, in two dimensions. With 4×4, 16 cells can be mapped on a line of 16 cells. How should we order the cells? We could order them using rows, as shown in Figure 6.20. This mapping provides acceptable results in the x dimension but does not perform well in y. A so called "snake curve" gives better results, but it is still bad preserving the distance in the y dimension, see Figure 6.21.

6.4.1   *Z-ordering*

The Z-ordering has few long jumps and it scopes the whole quadrant in the plane, see Figure 6.22. We can construct a mapping from a 1 dimensional

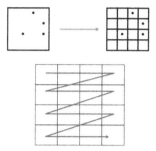

Fig. 6.20 In two dimensions we can assume finite granularity of a plane of 4 × 4 cells. Row-wise mapping of the cells from two dimensions into one dimension gives good results in the x dimension but is bad in y dimension.

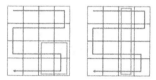

Fig. 6.21 A so called "snake curve" gives better results (see the first image and the square in which the error is small), but it is still bad preserving the distance in the y dimension (see the indicated rectangle over the y dimension).

Fig. 6.22 The Z-ordering has few long jumps and it scopes the whole quadrant in the plane.

interval to a n dimensional interval, for example $n = 2$. If the curve of this mapping passes through every point of the target space we call this a "space-filling curve". Z-ordering is a space filling curve and can be constructed recursively with increased finite granularity. In Figure 6.23 Z ordering of order-1 with 2 × 2 cells, of order-2 with 4 × 4 cells. and of order-3 with 8 × 8 cells are indicated. The curve is generated recursively, four Z or N shapes are connected to form a order-2 Z-ordering, see Figure 6.24. For

Fig. 6.23 Z ordering of order-1, of order-2 and of order-3.

Fig. 6.24   The curve is generated recursively, four Z or N shapes are connected to form a order-2 Z-ordering.

order-4 Z ordering, four order-2 Z-ordering are connected to form a order-3 Z-ordering. For order-$(n + 1)$ Z-ordering, four order-n Z-ordering are connected to form a order-$(n + 1)$ Z-ordering, see Figure 6.25. Z-ordering

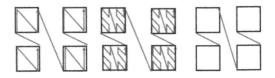

Fig. 6.25   For order-4 Z-ordering, four order-2 Z-ordering are connected to form a order-3 Z-ordering. For order-$(n + 1)$ Z-ordering, four order-n Z-ordering are connected to form a order-$(n + 1)$ Z-ordering.

is recursively constructed and self-similar, a shape Z or N appears similar at all scales of magnification. This property of self similarity at different scales is called fractal [Mandelbrot (1983)].

6.4.1.1   *Bit-shuffing*

How can we obtain the position z described by the two coordinates x and y on the curve

$$z = f(x, y) \tag{6.22}$$

with the mapping f being the Z-ordering. We could count but counting is expensive. A simpler method is to perform a bit-shuffing operation [Faloutsos and Roseman (1989); Moon *et al.* (2001)]. By the recursive construction of the Z-ordering of order n, the maximum number of values in each dimension is 2^n. Each coordinate can be represented by a binary code of length 2^n. For two dimensions, the coordinates are represented by binary code as $x = x_1x_2$, $y = y_1y_2$, in which the index 1 indicates the first digit and the index 2 indicates the second digit. The position z is given by the binary number

$$z = x_1y_1x_2y_2.$$

We interleave the bits of the two binary numbers into one string. For $x = x_1x_2x_3x_4$ and $y = y_1y_2y_3y_4$

$$z = x_1y_1x_2y_2x_3y_3x_4y_4.$$

For example with $x = 10$ and $y = 11$ $z = 1101 = 13$, see Figure 6.26. The

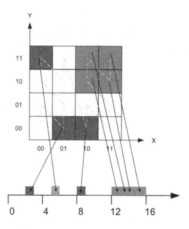

Fig. 6.26 The coordinates are represented by binary code as $x = x_1x_2$, $y = y_1y_2$ in which the index 1 indicate the first digit and the index 2 the second digit. The position z is given by the binary number $z = x_1y_1x_2y_2$. For example with $x = 10$ and $y = 11$ $z = 1101 = 13$

algorithm may be applied for higher dimensions d then 2. For d dimensional curves instead of two numbers t numbers are read and interleaved.

6.4.1.2 *Queries*

We can preform range queries using Z-ordering. The range queries are described by squares (or a rectangle). For example in the Figure 6.27 the query point is represented in the cell with the coordinates $x = 01$ and $y = 01$. The square is described by 9 cells with the positions on the Z-ordering

$$z_1 = 1; \ z_2 = 3; \ z_3 = 9; \ z_4 = 4; \ z_5 = 6;$$

$$z_6 = 12; \ z_7 = 5; \ z_8 = 7; \ z_9 = 13.$$

Then we sort the values representing the positions into

$$1, 3, 4, 5, 6, 7, 9, 12, 13$$

and get the following different ranges that are inside the square

$$Q_1 = [1], \ Q_2 = [3, 7], \ Q_3 = [9], \ Q_4 = [12, 13].$$

In the next step four range queries on the B-tree that represents the cor-

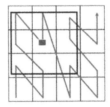

Fig. 6.27   Given the query in the cell with the coordinates $x = 01$ and $y = 01$, the range square is described by 9 cells.

responding Z-ordering are done. In our example the Z-ordering was of order-2, sixteen cells were represented. For order n $2^n \times 2^n$ cells can be represented. For a range query in two dimensional space with a range represented by a square of size $h \times h$ defined by a query $4 \times h - 4$ positions have to be determined (edges), then maximal $4 \times h - 4$ range queries have to be sorted (logarithmic complexity) and queried by a B-tree (logarithmic complexity). The number of range queries could be reduced further be eliminating long jumps between the cells.

6.4.1.3 *Limitations*

In higher dimensions, the square corresponds to a hypercube. Because the volume of a hypercube exponentially increases, the described approach to performing queries can only be employed in extremely low dimensions. An alternative approach for low dimensions is to divide the space into blocks and to group the data into blocks in order along a curve. The recursive method, in which space is partitioned during the construction of Z-ordering, can be represented by a tree. For two dimensions, this tree is a quad tree, a tree whose nodes are either leaves or have 4 children.

6.4.2 *Hilbert curve*

Hilbert space filling curve in 2 dimensions has less jumps then the Z-ordering [Hilbert (1891)], see Figure 6.28. Hilbert curve is a space filling

Fig. 6.28   Hilbert Space filling curve in 2 dimensions has less jumps then the Z-ordering.

curve and can be constructed recursively with increased finite granularity as the Z-ordering. In Figure 6.29 Hilbert curves of order-1 to order-6 with $2^6 \times 2^6$ cells are indicated. The curve is generated recursively, four shapes

Fig. 6.29   Hilbert curves of order-1 to order-6 with $2^6 \times 2^6$ cells.

are connected to form a order-2 Hilbert curve. The left bottom shape is rotated 90 degrees clockwise and the right shape is rotated 90 degrees counterclockwise. In the following four order-n Hilbert curves are connected to form a order-$(n+1)$ Hilbert curve with the bottom parts being rotated, see Figure 6.30.

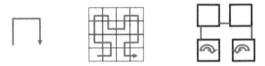

Fig. 6.30 The curve is generated recursively, four shapes are connected to form a order-2 Hilbert curve. The left bottom shape is rotated 90 degrees clockwise and the right shape is rotated 90 degrees counterclockwise. In the following four order-n Hilbert curves are connected to form a order-$(n + 1)$ Hilbert curve with the bottom parts being rotated.

6.4.2.1 *Bit-shuffing*

The mapping f that determines the position h on the Hilbert curve

$$h = f(x, y) \tag{6.23}$$

is based on the Gray code [Faloutsos and Roseman (1989); Moon *et al.* (2001)]. Gray code is a binary numeral system where two successive values differ in only one bit, see Table 6.1. For dimension two the coordinates are

Table 6.1 Gray code is a binary numeral system where two successive values differ in only one bit.

Decimal	Gray	Binary
0	000	000
1	001	001
2	011	010
3	010	011
4	110	100
5	111	101
6	101	110
7	100	111

represented by binary code as $x = x_1x_2$, $y = y_1y_2$ in which the index 1 indicate the first digit and the index 2 the second digit. The value of z is given by the binary number

$$z = x_1 y_1 x_2 y_2.$$

We interleave the bits of the two binary numbers (for two dimensions) into one string as before. Then we divide the string z into n 2 bit strings s_k for $k = 1, 2, \cdots, n$.

For $x = x_1 x_2 x_3 x_4$ and $y = y_1 y_2 y_3 y_4$ (order-4)

$$z = x_1 y_1 x_2 y_2 x_3 y_3 x_4 y_4 = z_1 z_2 z_3 z_4 z_5 z_6 z_7 z_8$$

$$s_1 = z_1 z_2, \; s_2 = z_3 z_4, \; s_3 = z_5 z_6, \; s_4 = z_7 z_8.$$

Each two bit substring s_k is interpreted as a Gray code, it is converted from the Gray code into a decimal number d_k according to the Table 6.2 and put into an array in the same order as the strings occurred. In the next

Table 6.2 Gray code for two bit string.

Decimal	Gray
0	00
1	01
2	11
3	10

step we correct the rotations that are done when recursively constructing the Hilbert curve,

- if the digit 0 is present in the array then switch every following occurrence of 1 in the array to 3 and every follow- ing occurrence of 3 in the array to 1;
- if the digit 3 is present in the array then switch every following occurrence of 0 in the array to 2 and every follow- ing occurrence of 2 in the array to 0.

Then, we convert each digit in the array to two-bit strings, concatenate all the strings in the same order and calculate the decimal value. For example, with $x = 10$ and $y = 11$ with $z = 1101$, we divide the string z into the 2 2 bit strings $s_1 = 11$ and $s_2 = 01$. The substrings s_1 and s_2 are interpreted as Gray code, which is converted from Gray code to a decimal number and placed into an array in the same order as the strings occurred, with $d_1 = 2$ and $d_2 = 1$. No switches are performed and the h that describes the position on the Hilbert curve becomes $h = 1001 = 9$, as shown in Figure 6.31.

Another example is $x = 11$ and $y = 01$ with $z = 1011$. We divide the string z into the 2 2 bit strings $s_1 = 10$ and $s_2 = 11$. The substring s_1 and s_2 are interpreted as Gray code, which is converted from Gray code to a decimal number and placed into an array in the same order as the strings, with $d_1 = 3$ and $d_2 = 2$. Because $d_1 = 3$, we switch $d_2 = 0$ and h, which describes the position on the Hilbert curve, becomes $h = 1100 = 12$.

With $x = 001$ and $y = 010$ with $z = 00110$, we divide the string z into the 3 2 bit strings $s_1 = 00$, $s_2 = 01$, $s_3 = 10$. The substrings are interpreted as Gray code, which is converted from Gray code to a decimal number and placed in an array in the same order as the strings, with $d_1 = 0$, $d_2 = 1$, $d_3 = 3$. Because $d_1 = 0$, we switch $d_2 = 3$, $d_3 = 1$ and h, which describes the position on the Hilbert curve, becomes $h = 001101 = 13$.

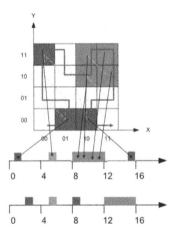

Fig. 6.31   We interleave the bits of the two binary numbers into one string as before. Then we divide the string z into n 2 bit strings s_k for $k = 1, 2, \cdots, n$. Each substring s_k is interpreted as a Gray code, it is converted from the Gray code into a decimal number d_k. We preform switches, then we convert each digit in the array to two-bit strings, concatenate all the strings in the same order and calculate the decimal value. For example with $x = 10$ and $y = 11$ with $z = 1101$, then we divide the string z into 2 2 bit strings $s_1 = 11$ and $s_2 = 01$. The substring s_1 and s_2 are interpreted as a Gray code, it is converted from the Gray code into a decimal number and put into an array in the same order as the strings occurred with $d_1 = 2$ and $d_2 = 1$. No switches are done and h describing the position on the Hilbert curve becomes $= 1001 = 9$. The line bellow indicate the corresponding positions of the Z-ordering.

6.4.2.2 *Queries*

The range queries are described by squares (or a rectangle). In the Figure 6.32 the query point is represented in the cell with the coordinates $x = 01$ and $y = 01$. The square is described by 9 cells with the positions on the Hilbert

$$h_1 = 2; \; h_2 = 3; \; h_3 = 13; \; h_4 = 4; \; h_5 = 7;$$

$$h_6 = 8; \; h_7 = 5; \; h_8 = 6; \; h_9 = 9.$$

Then we sort the values representing the positions into

$$2, 3, 4, 5, 6, 7, 8, 9, 13$$

and get the following different ranges

$$Q_1 = [2, 9], \; Q_2 = [13].$$

In the next step only two range queries on the B-tree that represents the

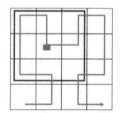

Fig. 6.32 Given the query in the cell with the coordinates $x = 01$ and $y = 01$, the range square is described by 9 cells.

corresponding Hilbert curve are executed. The number of range queries is reduced compared to Z-ordering because long jumps have between the cells have been eliminated. In our example instead of 4 queries 2 range queries are present. The number of range queries depends on the order of the space filling curve and is independent of the data set.

6.4.2.3 *Three dimensions*

In Figure 6.33 Z ordering in 3 dimensions of order-1, order-2 and of order-3 are indicated. The bit-shuffing algorithm as described for dimension two may be applied for higher dimensions d. The only change is that one reads and interleaves d numbers instead of two numbers. Hilbert curve in

(a)   (b)   (c)

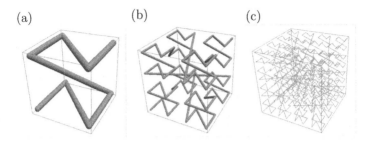

Fig. 6.33 Z ordering of (a) order-1, (b) of order-2 and of (c) order-3 in dimension three.

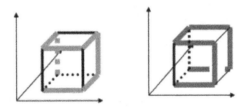

Fig. 6.34   Hilbert curve in 3 dimensions is not unique, there exists two different Hamiltonian paths on cube, two different order-1 curves.

3 dimensions is not unique, there exists two different Hamiltonian paths on cube, two different order-1 curves, see Figure 6.34. In Figure 6.35 the Hilbert curve n 3 dimensions of order-1, order-2 and of order-3 are indicated.

(a)   (b)   (c)

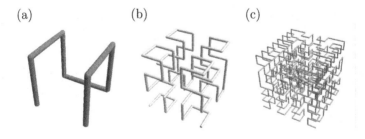

Fig. 6.35   Hilbert curve of (a) order-1, (b) of order-2 and of (c) order-3 in dimension three.

6.4.3 Fractals and the Hausdorff dimension

Giuseppe Peano (1858-1932) discovered a space-filling curve that passes through every point of a unit square [Peano (1890)]. His purpose was to construct a continuous mapping from the unit interval onto the unit square. He showed that a plane contains as many points as a line. Subsequently, David Hilbert (1862-1943) published a variation of Peano's construction, the Hilbert curve [Hilbert (1891)]. Space-filing curves are known as fractals. A fractal is a shape that is recursively constructed and self-similar. It is a shape that appears similar on all scales of magnification. We can define a fractal dimension by scaling and coping the self-similar shape. Felix Hausdorff 1868-1942) defined the fractal dimension, which is sometimes referred to as the Hausdorff dimension [Hausdorff (1919); Besicovitch (1929)]. With the scalar factor s and N being the number of shapes employed in the recursive construction, the following relation holds

$$N = s^D \tag{6.24}$$

where D is the Hausdorff dimension [Mandelbrot (1983)]. It follows that

$$D = \frac{\log(N)}{\log(s)} \tag{6.25}$$

A Hilbert curve that consists of $4 = N$ copies of itself each is twice ($s = 2$) as short as the whole, see Figure 6.36

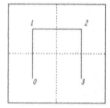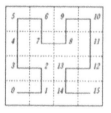

Fig. 6.36 A Hilbert curve that consists of $4 = N$ copies of itself each is twice ($s = 2$) as short as the whole.

$$D = 2 = \frac{\log(4)}{\log(2)} \tag{6.26}$$

the curve covers the whole of the square whose dimension is 2. The Hausdorff dimension may be not integer [Mandelbrot (1983)], for example for the Sierpinski triangle consists of $3 = N$ copies of itself each is twice ($s = 2$) as short as the whole (see Figure 6.37) with

(a)   (b)   (c)

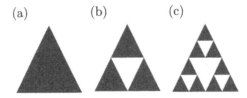

Fig. 6.37   Serpinski triangle consists of $3 = N$ copies of itself each is twice ($s = 2$) as short as the whole. (a) order-1, (b) of order-2 and of (c) order-3.

$$D = 1.58 = \frac{\log(3)}{\log(2)}. \tag{6.27}$$

6.4.3.1   *Felix Hausdorff*

Felix Hausdorff (November 8, 1868 - January 26, 1942) was a German mathematician who is considered to be one of the founders of modern topology, as shown in Figure 6.38. When the Nazis came to power, Hausdorff, who

Fig. 6.38   Felix Hausdorff (November 8, 1868 - January 26, 1942) was a German mathematician who is considered to be one of the founders of modern topology.

was Jewish, believed that he would be spared from persecution because he was a respected university professor. However, his abstract mathematics was denounced as useless and un-German. Although he was barred from publishing in Germany, Hausdorff continued to be an active research mathematician and published in Polish journals. When he could not avoid being sent to a concentration camp, Hausdorff committed suicide with his wife and sister-in-law on January 26, 1942 [Neuenschwander (1996)].

6.5   Conclusion

Traditional indexing trees can be described by two classes: trees derived from the kd-tree and trees composed of derivatives of the R-tree. Trees in the first class divide the data space along predefined hyper-planes regardless of the data distribution. The resulting regions are mutually disjoint and the majority of these regions do not represent any objects. With an increase in the dimension of space, we require numerous exponential objects to fill the space. The second class attempts to overcome this problem by dividing the data space according to the data distribution into overlapping regions, as described in the second section. The metric index trees efficiently operate when the number of dimensions is small. Space-filing curves indicate the relation between B-trees and metric trees. A space-filing curve defines several regions for range queries in dimensions, which requires B-trees to be queried several times.

Chapter 7

Approximative Indexing

The growth in the number of dimensions has negative implications in the performance of multidimensional index trees. These negative effects are named as the "curse of dimensionality." A nearest-neighbor query in a high dimensional space corresponds to a hyper-sphere with a huge radius which is mostly larger than the extension of the data space in most dimensions [Böhm et al. (2001)].

A solution to this problem consists of approximate queries which allow a relative error during retrieval. M-tree [Ciaccia and Patella (2002)] and A-tree [Sakurai et al. (2002)] with approximate queries perform retrieval in dimensions of several hundreds. A-tree uses approximated MBR instead of a the MBR of the R-tree. Approximate metric trees like NV-trees [Olafsson et al. (2008)] work with an acceptable error up to dimension 500. The most successful approximate indexing method is based on hash tables. Locality-sensitive hashing (LSH) [Andoni et al. (2006)] works fast and stable with dimensions around 100.

7.1 Curse of Dimensionality

The curse of dimensionality refers to various phenomena that arise when analyzing and organizing data in high-dimensional spaces. The volume of a hypercube exponentially increases; a hypercube graph in dimension n has 2^n vertices. For a hypercube with an edge of the size 2, the volume in dimension n is given by 2^n. If 100 points cover the one-dimensional unit interval $[0, 1]$ on a real line, considering the corresponding 10-dimensional unit hypercube, 100 points become isolated points in a vast empty space. The volume of a high-dimensional cube approaches its surface with an increase in dimension [Böhm et al. (2001)]. In high-dimensional spaces, a partition is only performed in a few dimensions, which touch the boundary of the data space in most dimensions. A hypercube corresponds to a sphere in l_∞ space; the volume v of a Euclidean ball of radius r in n-dimensional l_∞ space can be indicated by

$$v_n^\infty = (2 \cdot r)^n \tag{7.1}$$

Surprisingly the volume decreases for a sphere with fixed radius r in l_1 and l_2 space with the growing dimension. The volume v of a sphere with l_1 norm and with radius r in n-dimensional space is given by

$$v_n^1 = \frac{2^n}{n!} \cdot r^n, \tag{7.2}$$

suppose that r is fixed, then the volume v_n^1 approaches zero as n tends to infinity because

$$\lim_{n \to \infty} \frac{(2 \cdot r)^n}{n!} = 0. \tag{7.3}$$

On the other hand the radius r of a sphere with l_1 norm and with the volume v_n^1 in n-dimensional space is given by

$$r = \left(\frac{v_n^1 \cdot n!}{2^n} \right)^{1/n} = \frac{(v_n^1 \cdot n!)^{1/n}}{2}, \tag{7.4}$$

suppose that v_n^1 is fixed, then the radius r approaches infinity as n tends to infinity because

$$\lim_{n \to \infty} \frac{(v_n^1 \cdot n!)^{1/n}}{2} = \infty. \tag{7.5}$$

The same relation between the volume, the radius and the dimension are as well true for sphere with l_2 norm. Such a sphere with l_2 norm in dimension n is called a n ball, the volume can be indicated by explicit formulas

$$v_{2 \cdot n}^2 = \frac{\pi^n}{n!} \cdot r^{2 \cdot n}, \tag{7.6}$$

and

$$v_{2 \cdot n+1}^2 = \frac{2 \cdot n! \cdot (4 \cdot \pi)^n}{(2 \cdot n + 1)!} \cdot r^{2 \cdot n+1}.. \tag{7.7}$$

This relation have serious consequences for the ϵ-similarity in popular l_1 and l_2 spaces, in high dimensions the value of ϵ that describes the radius of the sphere is mostly larger than the extension of the data space in most dimensions [Böhm *et al.* (2001)].

7.2 Approximate Nearest Neighbor

Approximation enables calculations to be significantly accelerated compared with exact solutions in high-dimensional space. In some domains, heuristics are used to determine the feature that describes the multimedia data; obtaining an approximate nearest neighbor is an acceptable solution. The approximate nearest neighbor does not guarantee to return the actual nearest neighbor. The ϵ approximate nearest neighbor search is based on the ϵ similarity [Indyk and Motwani (1998); Indyk (2004)].

Let DB be a database of s multimedia objects $\mathbf{x}_k$ represented by vectors of dimension n in which the index k is an explicit key identifying each object with

$$\mathbf{x}_1, \mathbf{x}_2, \mathbf{x}_3, \cdots, \mathbf{x}_s.$$

The c ϵ-approximate nearest neighbor for a query vector $\mathbf{y}$ with the distance function d is defined as

- if there is a point $\mathbf{x}_k \in DB$ with $d(\mathbf{x}_k, \mathbf{y}) < \epsilon$,
- it returns $\mathbf{x}_q \in DB$ with $d(\mathbf{x}_q, \mathbf{y}) < c \cdot \epsilon$),

with $c \geq 1$.

7.3 Locality-Sensitive Hashing

The method uses a family of locality-sensitive hash functions to hash nearby objects in the high-dimensional space into the same bucket [Andoni *et al.* (2006)]. To perform a similarity search, the indexing method hashes a query object into a bucket, uses the data objects in the bucket as the candidate set of the results, and ranks the candidate objects using the distance measure of the similarity search. Several extensions of LSH, such as multi-probe LSH [Lv *et al.* (2007)], reduce the space requirements for hash tables.

Locality sensitive hashing is based on the idea of a hash function to hash the input items so that similar items are mapped to the same buckets with high probability. The family F of hash functions h are constructed with

$$h : R^n \to B \tag{7.8}$$

with two vectors mapped to the same bucket $b \in B$ with high probability

- if $d(\mathbf{x}_k, \mathbf{y}) < \epsilon$ then the probability $P_1 = Pr[h(\mathbf{x}_k) = h(\mathbf{y})]$ is high (not small);

- if $d(\mathbf{x}_k, \mathbf{y}) > c \cdot \epsilon$ then the probability $P_2 = Pr[h(\mathbf{x}_k) = h(\mathbf{y})]$ is small.

It means that $P_1 > P_2$. In this case the family F is called $(\epsilon, c \cdot \epsilon, P_1, P_2)$-sensitive [Indyk (2004); Andoni *et al.* (2006)].

7.3.0.2 *Hashing*

A hash function maps digital of arbitrary size to a fixed size M with M bins (discrete intervals, slots)

$$h(key) = bin \qquad (7.9)$$

M is the size of the hash table, the goal of a good hash function is the uniform spread of keys over hash buckets. A hash function in division hashing is defined as

$$h(x) = (a \cdot x + b) \bmod M \qquad (7.10)$$

with M being a prime number representing the size of the hash table.

7.3.1 *Binary Locality-sensitive hashing*

For a locality-sensitive hashing we define hash function h by choosing a set r random coordinates. For binary vectors of the dimension n we define hash function h by a simple projection P of some r random coordinates with the set I describing the chosen co-ordinates

$$P : B^n \to B^r \qquad (7.11)$$

For example with $n = 10$ and $r = 2$ with $I = \{2, 6\}$ for

$$\mathbf{x} = (0101110010),$$

then

$$h(\mathbf{x}) = (10).$$

The corresponding bin would to the decimal value plus one (the first bin corresponds to 0) and $M = 2^r$. For locals sensitive hashing

$$Pr[h(\mathbf{x}) = h(\mathbf{y})] = \theta(\mathbf{x}, \mathbf{y}). \qquad (7.12)$$

For binary vectors such a function $\theta()$ can be defined through the Hamming distance D. The Hamming distance is the number on which $\mathbf{x}$ and $\mathbf{y}$ differ, for binary vectors it corresponds to the Taxicab or Manhattan metric d_1. Then

$$Pr[h(\mathbf{x}) = h(\mathbf{y})] = \theta(\mathbf{x}, \mathbf{y}) = \left(1 - \frac{D(\mathbf{x}, \mathbf{y})}{n}\right)^{\kappa}. \qquad (7.13)$$

We can vary the probability by changing κ see Figure 7.1. The more similar there vectors are, the higher the probability that the projected values of the two vectors are equal.

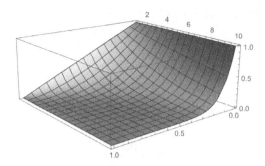

Fig. 7.1 We can vary the probability by changing κ, x-axis indicates the distance, y-axis the probability and the z-axis κ values from 1 to 10.

7.3.1.1 *Initialization algorithm*

- Choose several hash functions $h_1, \cdots, h_f$. For f random projections of r coordinates.
- Store each point $\mathbf{x}_k$ of the database DB in the bucket $h_i(\mathbf{x}_k)$ of the i-th hash array $i = 1, 2, \cdots, f$

7.3.1.2 *Query algorithm*

- In order to answer query $\mathbf{y}$;
- for each $i = 1, 2, \cdots, f$ retrieve points in a bucket et $h_i(\mathbf{y})$;
- return the closest point found. The bins in which the query vector is projected agree mostly with some projected vector $\mathbf{x}_k$.

7.3.1.3 *Partition into bands*

For $f \leq n$ orthogonal binary subspaces (sub hypercubes)

$$B^n = E_1 \oplus E_2 \oplus \ldots \oplus E_f \tag{7.14}$$

with

$$r = \frac{n}{f} \tag{7.15}$$

f is called band and r rows per band. The values f and r have to be determined by empirical experiments.

7.3.2 *Projection-based LSH*

For real vectors of the dimension n we define hash function h by a mapping onto a set of integers N

$$M : R^n \to N \tag{7.16}$$

with hash function based on the projection P onto one dimension represented by a vector $\mathbf{p}$

$$h(\mathbf{x}) = \left\lfloor \frac{\langle \mathbf{p} | \mathbf{x} \rangle + b}{w} \right\rfloor . \tag{7.17}$$

The entries of the vector $\mathbf{p}$ chosen independently from a stable distribution, for example normal distribution, b is a real number chosen uniformly from the range $[0, w]$ and

$$w \approx \epsilon.$$

The family F of hash functions is defined by $\mathbf{p}$ and b. For locals sensitive hashing

$$Pr[h(\mathbf{x}) = h(\mathbf{y})] = \theta(\mathbf{x}, \mathbf{y}) \tag{7.18}$$

and the function could the cos to the angle w between the vectors

$$\theta(\mathbf{x}, \mathbf{y}) = \cos \omega = \frac{\langle \mathbf{x} | \mathbf{y} \rangle}{\|\mathbf{x}\| \cdot \|\mathbf{y}\|}. \tag{7.19}$$

Related function is given by

$$\omega = \cos^{-1} \left(\frac{\langle \mathbf{x} | \mathbf{y} \rangle}{\|\mathbf{x}\| \cdot \|\mathbf{y}\|} \right) . \tag{7.20}$$

and

$$Pr[h(\mathbf{x}) = h(\mathbf{y})] = \theta(\mathbf{x}, \mathbf{y}) = 1 - \frac{\omega}{\pi}. \tag{7.21}$$

7.3.3 *Query complexity LSH*

Given a query vector $\mathbf{y}$, the algorithm iterates over the f hash functions h. It retrieves the data points that are hashed into the same bucket as $\mathbf{y}$. The process is stopped as soon as a point $\mathbf{x}_k$ within distance $c \cdot \epsilon$ from $\mathbf{y}$ is found [Indyk (2004)].

With the probabilities P_1 and P_2 with $c > 1$ and with s multimedia objects $\mathbf{x}_k$ represented by vectors of dimension n with

$$\rho = \frac{\log(P_1)}{\log(P_2)}, \tag{7.22}$$

for Hamming distance

$$\rho = \frac{\log(P_1)}{\log(P_2)} = \frac{1}{\log(c)}. \tag{7.23}$$

Then

$$f = s^\rho \tag{7.24}$$

and

$$g = \frac{\log(s)}{1/\log(P_2)} \tag{7.25}$$

the query time is given by

$$O(s^\rho \cdot (g + n)). \tag{7.26}$$

7.4 Johnson-Lindenstrauss Lemma

The Johnson-Lindenstrauss lemma [W. Johnson (1984)] states that if s points in vector space of dimension n are projected onto a randomly selected subspace of suitably high dimensions m, then the Euclidean distance between the points are approximately preserved. For

$$0 < \epsilon < 1$$

and a set of s vectors of the dimension n and dimension m with

$$m > 8 \cdot \frac{\log(s)}{\epsilon^2} \tag{7.27}$$

and a linear mapping

$$f : R^n \to R^m \tag{7.28}$$

exists such that that for the Euclidean metric

$$(1 - \epsilon) \cdot \|\mathbf{x} - \mathbf{y}\|^2 \le \|f(\mathbf{x}) - f(\mathbf{y})\|^2 \le (1 + \epsilon) \cdot \|\mathbf{x} - \mathbf{y}\|^2. \tag{7.29}$$

The dimension m of the subspace depends on s and on ϵ (but not on n). For $s = 10000$ and a big $\epsilon = .99$ the resulting dimension is $m = 75$. But for or $s = 10000$ and $\epsilon = .01$ the resulting dimension is $m = 736827$. In Figure 7.2 we see the relation of ϵ for a fixed $s = 10000$ and in Figure 7.3 we see that the dimension is mostly dependent on ϵ. It is stated that the Johonson-Lindenstrauss lemma is only applicable for very small set of points, however for $s = 100$ and $\epsilon = 0.5$ the dimension is still big, $m = 147$, see Figure 7.4. Because of the "curse of dimensionality" even small ϵ values do not guarantee that we fined a good approximate nearest neighbour, we need to search for an alternative method.

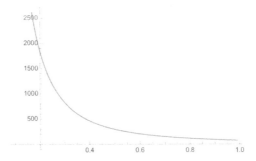

Fig. 7.2   Fixed $s = 10000$ with $0.1 \leq \epsilon \leq 0.99$ on the x-axis, y-axis indicates the dimension m.

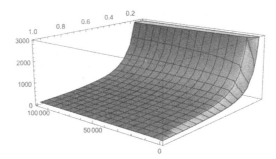

Fig. 7.3   With $100 \leq s \leq 100000$ on the x-axis and with $0.1 \leq \epsilon \leq 0.99$ on the z-axis, y-axis indicates the dimension m.

7.5   Product Quantization

Product quantization for nearest neighbor search [Jegou *et al.* (2011)] works with an acceptable error up to dimension 1000. The vector $\mathbf{x}$ of dimension m is split into f distinct sub-vectors of dimension $p = dim(m/f)$. The sub-vectors are quantized using f quantiziers:

$$\mathbf{x} = \underbrace{x_1, , x_2, \cdots , x_p}_{u_1(\mathbf{x})}, \cdots , \underbrace{x_{m-p+1}, \cdots , x_m}_{u_f(\mathbf{x})} \tag{7.30}$$

$$u_t(x) \in x | t \in \{1..f\}$$

We group the sub-vectors of dimension $p = dim(m/f)$ into clusters represented by the cluster centres c_j of dimension p. After the clustering cluster

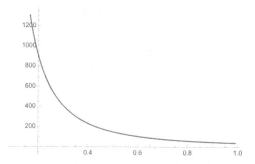

Fig. 7.4 Fixed $s = 100$ with $0.1 \leq \epsilon \leq 0.99$ on the x-axis, y-axis indicates the dimension m.

centres $c_1, c_2, c_3, ..., c_k$ with clusters $C_1, C_2, C_3, ..., C_k$ are present with

$$C_j = \{u_t(x) | d(u_t(x), c_j) = \min_i d(u_t(x), c_i)\} \qquad (7.31)$$

$$c_j = \{\frac{1}{|C_j|} \sum_{u_t(x) \in C_j} u_t(x)\}. \qquad (7.32)$$

We assume that all sub-quantizers have the same number k of clusters and represent vectors by the corresponding cluster centres:

$$U(\mathbf{x}) = \underbrace{c_{i1}, c_{i2}, \cdots, c_{ip}}_{u_1(x) = c_{1(x)} = c_i}, \cdots, \underbrace{c_{j1}, \cdots, c_{jp}}_{u_f(x) = c_{f(x)} = c_j} \qquad (7.33)$$

To a query vector y we determine the most similar vector x of the database using the qunatizied codes and the Euclidean distance function d.

$$d(U(\mathbf{x}), U(\mathbf{y})) = \sqrt{\sum_{t=1}^{f} d(u_t(\mathbf{x}), (u_t(\mathbf{y}))^2} = \sqrt{\sum_{t=1}^{f} d(c_{t(x)}, c_{t(y)})^2} \qquad (7.34)$$

By using $d(U(\mathbf{x}), U(\mathbf{y}))$ instead of $d(\mathbf{x}, \mathbf{y})$ an estimation *error* is produced:

$$d(U(\mathbf{x}), U(\mathbf{y})) + error = d(\mathbf{x}, \mathbf{y}) \qquad (7.35)$$

To speed up the computation of $d(U(\mathbf{x}), U(\mathbf{y}))$ all the possible $d(c_{t(x)}, c_{t(y)})^2$ are pre-computed and stored in a look-up table. The size of the look-up table depends on the number k, it is k^2. The bigger the value of k, the slower the computations due to the size of the look-up table. However the bigger the value of k the smaller is the estimation error. For example an grey image of the dimension 12288 is split into 3072 distinct sub-vectors of dimension $4 = dim(12288/3072)$, each sub-vector corresponds to a squared mask M of a size 2×2, see Figure 7.5 and 7.6.

Fig. 7.5   Examples of of squared masks M of a size 2×2.

(a)  (b)

Fig. 7.6   Grey image (a) and its quantized representation (b).

7.6   Conclusion

LSH is simple and easy. A limitation of approximative indexing, such as LSH, is the dimension of the data, which is limited to the order of several hundreds. They do not work in an extreme high-dimensional space (order of several thousands) and they do not perform exact queries.

Chapter 8

High Dimensional Indexing

Traditional indexing of multimedia data leads to dilemma. Either the number of features has to be reduced or the quality of the results in unsatisfactory, or approximate queries is preformed leading to a relative error during retrieval. The promise of the recently introduced subspace-tree is the logarithmic retrieval complexity of extremely high dimensional features. The subspace-tree indicates that the conjecture "the curse of dimensionality" could be false. The search in such a structure starts at the subspace with the lowest dimension. In this subspace, the set of all possible similar objects is determined. In the next subspace, additional metric information corresponding to a higher dimension is used to reduce this set. This process is then repeated. The theoretical estimation of temporal complexity of the subspace tree is logarithmic for the Gaussian (Normal) distribution of the distances between the data points.

8.1 Exact Search

While there are relatively efficient approximate similarity search algorithms it is widely belived that the exact search suffers from dimensionality [Pestov (2012)]. Thus, it seems that solving the problem in the most general case for an arbitrary dataset is impossible. In approximate indexing, the data points that may be lost as some distances are distorted. Approximate indexing [Indyk and Motwani (1998)], [Indyk (2004)] seems to be in some sense free from the curse of dimensionality, [Pestov (2012)].

In this chapter we described exact indexing for a vector space V and a distance function d for high dimensions. Exact indexing is based on exact similarity search, and no data points are lost during range queries. For a range query vector $\mathbf{y}$ from a collection of s vectors. Let DB be a database of s multimedia objects $\mathbf{x}_k$ represented by vectors of dimension n in which the index k is an explicit key identifying each object,

$$\{\mathbf{x}_k \in DB \mid k \in \{1..s\}\}.$$

with

$$\mathbf{x}_1, \mathbf{x}_2, \mathbf{x}_3, \cdots, \mathbf{x}_s.$$

The ϵ-similarity is defined for a range queries. For a vector $\mathbf{y}$ *all* vectors $\mathbf{x}_j$ are ϵ-similar to $\mathbf{y}$ according to the distance function d with

$$d(\mathbf{x}_j, \mathbf{y}) < \epsilon. \tag{8.1}$$

8.2 GEMINI

The idea behind the generic multimedia indexing (GEMINI) [Faloutsos *et al.* (1994); Faloutsos (1999)] approaches is to find a feature extraction function that maps the high dimensional objects into a low dimensional space. In this low dimensional space, a so-called 'quick-and-dirty' test can discard the non-qualifying objects. Objects that are very dissimilar in the feature space are expected to be very dissimilar in the original space (see Figure 8.1).

Ideally, the feature map should preserve the exact distances, but this is only possible if both spaces have the same dimension. However, if the distances in the feature space are always smaller or equal than the distances in the original space, a bound which is valid in both spaces can be determined. The distance of similar objects is smaller or equal to ϵ in the original space and, consequently, it is smaller or equal to ϵ in the feature space as well. No object in the feature space will be missed (false dismissals) in the feature space. However, there will be some objects that are not similar in the original space (false hints/alarms). That means that we are guaranteed to have selected all the objects we wanted plus some additional false hits in the feature space. In the second step, false hits have to be filtered from the set of the selected objects through comparison in the original space. The size of the collection in the feature space depends on ϵ and the proportion between both spaces may reach the size of the entire database if the feature space is not carefully chosen.

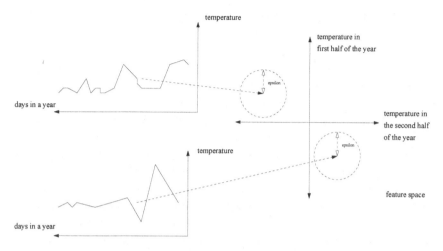

Fig. 8.1   Feature extraction function which maps the high dimensional objects into a low dimensional space. The temperature in a city measured in days is mapped into the temperature of the first half of the year and the second half of the year. The distance between similar objects should be smaller or equal to ϵ. This tolerance is represented by a sphere with radius ϵ in the feature space.

8.2.1   *1-Lipschitz property*

Distance-based exact indexing is based on the 1-Lipschitz property [Pestov (2012)]. A mapping function $F()$ maps two vectors $\mathbf{x}$ and $\mathbf{y}$ into a lower dimensional space, where d is a metric in the original space and $d_{feature}$ is a metric in the feature space that satisfies the 1-Lipschitz[1] property

$$d_{feature}(F(\mathbf{x}), F(\mathbf{y})) \leq d(\mathbf{x}, \mathbf{y}). \tag{8.2}$$

Using the 1-Lipschitz property, a bound that is valid in both spaces can be determined. The distance from similar vectors to a query vector $\mathbf{y}$ is smaller or equal in the original space and, consequently, is smaller or equal in the lower dimensional space as well. During the computation, all the points below the bound are discarded. In the second step, the wrong candidates are filtered by comparisons in the original space. This equation is also known as the lower bounding lemma [Faloutsos *et al.* (1994)], [Faloutsos (1999)];

Lemma 8.1. *Let O_1 and O_2 be two objects; $F()$, the mapping of objects into f dimensional space should satisfy the following formula for all objects,*

---

[1]k-Lipschitz property for a constant value k is given by $d_{feature}(F(\mathbf{x}), F(\mathbf{y})) \leq k \cdot d(\mathbf{x}, \mathbf{y})$, however in our case k is always 1.

where d is a distance function in the original space and $d_{feature}$, in the feature subspace:

$$d_{feature}(F(O_1), F(O_2)) \leq d(O_1, O_2). \tag{8.3}$$

In the first step, in the GEMINI approach, the distance function has to be defined. The second step consists in finding the feature extraction function $F()$ that satisfies the bounding lemma and determining it. $F()$ has to capture most of the characteristics of the objects in a low dimensional feature space. In most cases, the distance functions used in the original space and in the feature space are equal. Given Parseval's theorem, which states that the Discrete Fourier Transform (DFT) preserves Euclidian distances between signals, the DTF which keeps the first coefficients of the transform is an example of a feature function $F()$ [Faloutsos *et al.* (1994)], [Faloutsos (1999)]. Accordingly, one can use any orthonormal transform because they all preserve the distance between the original and the transformed space. One can also use data dependent transforms as feature functions $F()$, such as the Karhunen Loeve transform. However, they have to be recalculated as soon as new data arrives [Faloutsos *et al.* (1994)].

8.2.1.1 *Color histogram example*

For an efficient retrieval of images based on their 3-band RGB (Red, Green, Blue) color histogram an efficient approximation to the histogram color distance is required. This is achieved by the average color of an image. The average color of an image $\mathbf{x} = (R_{avg}, G_{avg}, B_{avg})^T$ is defined with

$$R_{avg} = \sum_{p=1}^{N} R(p),$$

$$G_{avg} = \sum_{p=1}^{N} G(p),$$

$$B_{avg} = \sum_{p=1}^{N} B(p).$$

N represents the pixels in the image, $R(p)$, $G(p)$, $B(p)$ are the red, green and blue components (range $0-255$) of the pth pixels. The distance between two average color is computed using the Euclidian distance function. By the "Quadratic Distance Bounding" theorem it is guaranteed that the distance between vectors representing histograms is bigger or equal as the distance between histograms of average color images. The proof of the "Quadratic Distance Bounding" theorem is based upon the unconstrained minimization problem using Langrange multipliers [Faloutsos *et al.* (1994)].

8.2.2 *Lower bounding approach*

We developed the subspace tree based on the analysis of the GEMINI approach. Let DB be a database of s multimedia objects $\mathbf{x}_k$ represented by vectors of dimension n in which the index k is an explicit key identifying each object,

$$\{\mathbf{x}_k \in DB \mid k \in \{1..s\}\}.$$

The set DB can be ordered according to a given multimedia object $\mathbf{y}$ using a distance function d [Wichert (2008)]. This is done by a monotone increasing sequence corresponding to the increasing distance of $\mathbf{y}$ to $\mathbf{x}_k$ with an explicit key that identifies each object indicated by the index k,

$$d[\mathbf{y}]_t := \{d(\mathbf{x}_k, \mathbf{y}) \mid \forall t \in \{1..s\} : d[\mathbf{y}]_t \leq d[\mathbf{y}]_{t+1}\}$$

if $\mathbf{y} \in DB$, then $d[\mathbf{y}]_1 := 0$. The set of similar multimedia objects in correspondence to $\mathbf{y}$, $DB[\mathbf{y}]_\epsilon$, is the subset of DB, $DB[\mathbf{y}]_\epsilon \subseteq DB$ with size $\sigma = |DB[\mathbf{y}]_\epsilon|$, $\sigma \leq s$:

$$DB[\mathbf{y}]_\epsilon := \{\mathbf{x}_k \in DB \mid d(\mathbf{x}_k, \mathbf{y}) \leq \epsilon\}.$$

8.2.2.1 *Scaled RGB images example*

We combine the color information and its spatial distribution through simple image matching in high-dimensional space. We scale the digital images to a fixed size and map them into a 3-band RGB (Red, Green, Blue) representation. With this transformation, we are able to represent the images as vectors and to compute the Euclidian distance between any pair. So the used features are the scaled RGB images themselves, representing the color autocorrelogram and layout information [Wichert (2008)]. Two images $\mathbf{x}$ and $\mathbf{y}$ are similar if their distance is smaller or equal to ϵ, $d(\mathbf{x}, \mathbf{y}) \leq \epsilon$. The result of a range query computed by this method is a set of images that have spatial color characteristics that are similar to the query image. Figure 8.2 shows two images with minimum Euclidian distance to two other query images, which were not present in the test database. In Figure 8.3 we see the image test database DB ordered relatively to a given image $\mathbf{y}$ using the Euclidian distance function d.

Fig. 8.2   For two query color images representing land and sea the images with the most similar color characteristics are shown.

8.2.2.2   *Feature space*

All the multimedia objects of the DB are mapped with $F()$, the mapping which satisfies the lower bounding lemma in f dimensional space,

$$\{F(\mathbf{x}_k) \in F(DB) \mid k \in \{1..s\}\}.$$

The set $F(DB)$ can be ordered in relation to a given multimedia object $F(\mathbf{y})$ and a distance function $d_{feature}$. This is done by a monotone increasing sequence corresponding to the increasing distance of $F(\mathbf{y})$ to $F(\mathbf{x}_k)$, with an explicit key identifying each object indicated by the index k,

$$d[F(\mathbf{y})]_t := \{d_{feature}(F(\mathbf{x}_k), F(\mathbf{y})) \mid \forall t \in \{1..s\} : d[F(\mathbf{y})]_t \le d[F(\mathbf{y})]_{t+1}\}$$

The set of similar multimedia objects in correspondence to $F(\mathbf{y})$, $F(DB[\mathbf{y}])_\epsilon$ is the subset of $F(DB)$, $F(DB[\mathbf{y}])_\epsilon \subseteq F(DB)$ with size $\sigma_F := |F(DB[\mathbf{y}])_\epsilon|$, $\sigma \le \sigma_F \le s$:

$$F(DB[\mathbf{y}])_\epsilon := \{F(\mathbf{x}_k) \in F(DB) \mid d_{feature}(F(\mathbf{x}_k), F(\mathbf{y})) \le \epsilon\}.$$

Corollary 8.1.

     An ϵ only exists if $min^*(d[\boldsymbol{y}]_n) < d[F(\boldsymbol{y})]_s$ and is chosen from the interval $[min^*(d[\boldsymbol{y}]_n), d[F(\boldsymbol{y})]_s]$ where

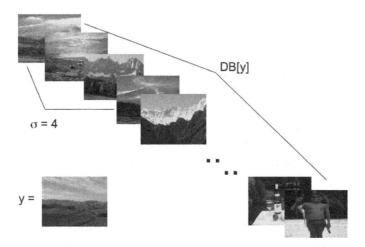

Fig. 8.3 Ordered image test database DB to a given image **y** using the Euclidian distance function d. The size of the set of similar multimedia objects in correspondence to **y** is $4 = \sigma = |DB[\mathbf{y}]_\epsilon|$. The top level image is the most similar corresponding to the distance $d[\mathbf{y}]_1$. The bottom image is the most dissimilar corresponding to $d[\mathbf{y}]_s$.

$$min^*(d[\boldsymbol{y}]_n) = \begin{cases} d[\boldsymbol{y}]_1 \ if \ d[\boldsymbol{y}]_1 \neq 0 \\ d[\boldsymbol{y}]_2 \ if \ d[\boldsymbol{y}]_1 = 0. \end{cases}$$

To determine $DB[\mathbf{y}]_\epsilon$ through linear search, we need $s \cdot n$ computing steps, assuming that computation of distance between two n-dimensional vectors requires n computing steps [Wichert (2008)]. To determine $DB[\mathbf{y}]_\epsilon$ when $F(DB[\mathbf{y}])_\epsilon$ is present, we need $\sigma_F \cdot n$ steps; the false hits are separated from the selected objects through comparison in the original space. If no metric tree is used to index the feature space, the savings used result from the size of $F(DB[\mathbf{y}])_\epsilon$ in proportion to the dimensions of both spaces $\frac{f}{n}$.

Corollary 8.2. *The computing time of $DB[\boldsymbol{y}]_\epsilon$ is saved comparatively to linear matching in the original space if:*

$$s \cdot n > \sigma_F \cdot n + s \cdot f \tag{8.4}$$

$$\left\lfloor s \cdot \left(1 - \frac{f}{n}\right) \right\rfloor > \sigma_F. \tag{8.5}$$

8.2.2.3 *1-Lipschitz property and the curse of dimensionality*

The application of the 1-Lipschitz property as used in metric trees and pivot tables does not resolve the curse of dimensionality, as shown in [Pestov (2011)]. For high-dimensional spaces, the functions that obey the 1-Lipschitz property discard fewer points as the number of dimensions grows [Pestov (2011)]. The number of points discarded drops as fast as the number of dimensions grows. As stated in [Pestov (2012)], every 1-Lipschitz function concentrates sharply near its mean (or median) value, which leads to a degradation of the method's performance.

8.2.3 *Projection operators*

V is an n-dimensional vector space and $F()$ is a linear mapping that obeys the lower bound lemma from the vector space V into an f-dimensional subspace U. In the GEMINI approach the feature space does not need to be a subspace. Here we can map the computed metric distance between objects in the f-dimensional subspace U into the m-dimensional space V which contains the subspace U. In this case, the lower bounding lemma is extended [Wichert *et al.* (2010)];

Lemma 8.2. *Let O_1 and O_2 be two objects; $F()$, the mapping of objects into f dimensional subspace U should satisfy the following formula for all objects, where d is a distance function in the space V and d_U in the subspace U:*

$$d_U(F(O_1), F(O_2)) \leq d(F(O_1), F(O_2)) \leq d(O_1, O_2). \tag{8.6}$$

A mapping that reduces the dimensionality of a vector space can be represented by a projection operator in a Hilbert space, which extends the two or three dimensional Euclidean space to spaces with any finite or infinite number of dimensions. If W is a subspace of V, then the orthogonal complement of W is also a subspace of V. The orthogonal complement $W^\perp$ is the set of vectors

$$W^\perp = \{\mathbf{y} \in V | \langle \mathbf{y} | \mathbf{x} \rangle = 0 \ \ \mathbf{x} \in V\} \tag{8.7}$$

and

$$V = W \oplus W^\perp. \tag{8.8}$$

Each vector $\mathbf{x} \in V$ can be represented as $\mathbf{x} = \mathbf{x}_W + \mathbf{x}_{W^\perp}$ with $\mathbf{x}_W \in W$ and $\mathbf{x}_{W^\perp} \in W^\perp$. The mapping $P \cdot \mathbf{x} = \mathbf{x}_W$ is an orthogonal projection.

Such a projection is always a linear transformation and can be represented by a projection matrix P. The matrix is self-adjoint with $P = P^2$. An orthogonal projection can never increase a norm

$$\|P \cdot \mathbf{x}\|^2 = \|\mathbf{x}_W\|^2 \leq \|\mathbf{x}_W\|^2 + \|\mathbf{x}_{W^\perp}\|^2 = \|\mathbf{x}_W + \mathbf{x}_{W^\perp}\|^2 = \|\mathbf{x}\|^2. \quad (8.9)$$

Using the triangle inequality

$$\|\mathbf{x} + \mathbf{y}\| \leq \|\mathbf{x}\| + \|\mathbf{y}\| \quad (8.10)$$

setting

$$\|\mathbf{x}\| = \|\mathbf{y} + (\mathbf{x} - \mathbf{y})\| \leq \|\mathbf{y}\| + \|\mathbf{x} - \mathbf{y}\| \quad (8.11)$$

the tighten triangle inequality

$$\|\mathbf{x}\| - \|\mathbf{y}\| \leq \|\mathbf{x} - \mathbf{y}\|. \quad (8.12)$$

follows. From the fact that the orthogonal projection can never increase the norm and the tightened triangle inequality, any orthogonal projection operator has the 1-Lipschitz property

$$\|\|P \cdot \mathbf{x}\| - \|P \cdot \mathbf{y}\|\| \leq \|P \cdot \mathbf{x} - P \cdot \mathbf{y}\| = \|P \cdot (\mathbf{x} - \mathbf{y})\| \leq \|\mathbf{x} - \mathbf{y}\|. \quad (8.13)$$

It follows that any projection satisfies the 1-Lipschitz property, which means that the lower bounding postulate [Faloutsos *et al.* (1994)],[Faloutsos (1999)] and any orthogonal projection are satisfied. For example, the "Quadratic Distance Bounding" theorem is satisfied [Faloutsos *et al.* (1994)]. There is no need for a more complicated proof based upon the unconstrained minimization problem using Lagrange multipliers [Faloutsos *et al.* (1994)].

8.2.4 *Projection onto one-dimensional subspace*

For $\|\mathbf{p}\| = 1$, $\mathbf{p} \cdot \mathbf{p}^\top$ is an orthogonal projection onto a one-dimensional space generated by $\mathbf{p}$ [Wichert and Moreira (2015)]. For example for the vector of length m

$$\mathbf{p} = \left(\frac{1}{\sqrt{m}}, \frac{1}{\sqrt{m}}, \cdots, \frac{1}{\sqrt{m}} \right) \quad (8.14)$$

the orthogonal projection from R^m onto one-dimensional space R is

$$P = \mathbf{p} \cdot \mathbf{p}^\top = \begin{pmatrix} \frac{1}{m} & \frac{1}{m} & \cdots & \frac{1}{m} \\ \frac{1}{m} & \frac{1}{m} & \cdots & \frac{1}{m} \\ \vdots & \vdots & \ddots & \vdots \\ \frac{1}{m} & \frac{1}{m} & \cdots & \frac{1}{m} \end{pmatrix}. \quad (8.15)$$

For $f \leq n$ orthogonal subspaces

$$R^n = E_1 \oplus E_2 \oplus \ldots \oplus E_f \qquad (8.16)$$

of the vector space R^n we can define a projection $P : R^n \mapsto R^f$ as a sum of f projections onto one dimensional space

$$P = \mathbf{p}_1 \cdot \mathbf{p}_1^\top + \mathbf{p}_2 \cdot \mathbf{p}_2^\top \ldots + \mathbf{p}_f \cdot \mathbf{p}_f^\top \qquad (8.17)$$

with $\mathbf{p}_i \cdot \mathbf{p}_i^\top : E_i \mapsto R$ and $\|\mathbf{p}_i\| = 1$. The 1-Lipschitz property of the projection from the subspace E_i the one dimensional space R is

$$\left| \|\mathbf{p}_i \cdot \mathbf{p}_i^\top \cdot \mathbf{x}\| - \|\mathbf{p}_i \cdot \mathbf{p}_i^\top \cdot \mathbf{y}\| \right| \leq |\|\mathbf{x}\| - \|\mathbf{y}\|| \leq \|\mathbf{x} - \mathbf{y}\|. \qquad (8.18)$$

The projection P, represented by Equation 8.17, should distort the distances between the vector space R^n and R^f as little as possible. As a consequence, the distortion for each subspace E_i should be minimized. Because of the 1-Lipschitz property for the one-dimensional space, according to the Equation 8.18, we need to minimize the distance in the one-dimensional space between the length of the vector and the length of its projected counterpart

$$\left| \|\mathbf{p}_i \cdot \mathbf{p}_i^\top \cdot \mathbf{x}\| - \|\mathbf{x}\| \right|. \qquad (8.19)$$

Suppose the dimensionality of the subspace E_i is m. We define the vector **a** as

$$\mathbf{a} = \mathbf{p}_i \cdot \mathbf{p}_i^\top \cdot \mathbf{x}. \qquad (8.20)$$

It follows that

$$a = \sqrt{m} \cdot \alpha = \|\mathbf{a}\| = \|\mathbf{p}_i \cdot \mathbf{p}_i^\top \cdot \mathbf{x}\| \qquad (8.21)$$

and with

$$a_1 = a_2 = \ldots = a_k = \ldots = a_m = \alpha$$

$$\mathbf{a} = (a_1, a_2, ..a_k, .., a_m). \qquad (8.22)$$

With a being the length of the projected vector we preform the following operation

$$\min\{|a - \|\mathbf{x}\||\}. \qquad (8.23)$$

From the tighten triangle inequality, it follows that

$$\min\{a - \|\mathbf{x}\|\} \leq \min\{\|\mathbf{a} - \mathbf{x}\|\} \qquad (8.24)$$

according to the Euclidean distance function. To minimize the Euclidean metric $\|\mathbf{a} - \mathbf{x}\|$, how do we choose the value of α [Wichert and Verissimo (2012); Wichert and Moreira (2015)]? It follows that

$$\min_{\alpha} \left(\sqrt{(x_1 - \alpha)^2 + (x_2 - \alpha)^2 + ... + (x_m - \alpha)^2} \right) \qquad (8.25)$$

$$0 = \frac{\partial d(\mathbf{x}, \mathbf{a})}{\partial \alpha} = \frac{m \cdot \alpha - \left(\sum_{i=1}^{m} x_i\right)}{\sqrt{m \cdot \alpha^2 + \sum_{i=1}^{m} x_i^2 - 2 \cdot \alpha \cdot \left(\sum_{i=1}^{m} x_i\right)}} \qquad (8.26)$$

with the solution

$$\alpha = \frac{\sum_{i=1}^{m} x_i}{m} \qquad (8.27)$$

which is the mean value of the vector $\mathbf{x}$. It follows

$$a = \sqrt{m} \cdot \alpha = \sqrt{m} \cdot \frac{\sum_{i=1}^{m} x_i}{m} = \|\mathbf{p}_i \cdot \mathbf{p}_i^\top \cdot \mathbf{x}\| \qquad (8.28)$$

with the corresponding projection matrix P_i

$$P_i = \mathbf{p}_i \cdot \mathbf{p}_i^\top = \begin{pmatrix} \frac{1}{m} & \frac{1}{m} & \cdots & \frac{1}{m} \\ \frac{1}{m} & \frac{1}{m} & \cdots & \frac{1}{m} \\ \vdots & \vdots & \ddots & \vdots \\ \frac{1}{m} & \frac{1}{m} & \cdots & \frac{1}{m} \end{pmatrix}. \qquad (8.29)$$

P_i is generated by the normalised vector $\mathbf{p}_i$

$$\mathbf{p}_i = \left(\frac{1}{\sqrt{m}}, \frac{1}{\sqrt{m}}, \cdots, \frac{1}{\sqrt{m}} \right). \qquad (8.30)$$

which indicates the direction of the m-secting line, which is a continuous map from a one-dimensional space to an m-dimensional space given by

$$\begin{aligned} x_1 &= x_1 \\ x_2 &= x_1 \\ x_3 &= x_1 \\ &\vdots \\ x_m &= x_1 \end{aligned} \qquad (8.31)$$

For $m = 2$, this equation is the bisecting line with $x_1 = x_2$ or, represented as a curve,

$$\begin{aligned} x_1 &= x_1 \\ x_2 &= x_1 \end{aligned} \qquad (8.32)$$

which, for uncorrelated data P_i, is the best projection onto one dimension, as indicated in next section. The projection can be computed efficiently without needing matrix operations as the mean value of the vector multiplied with the square root of its dimensionality.

$$\sqrt{m} \cdot \frac{\sum_{i=1}^{m} x_i}{m} = \left\| \begin{pmatrix} \frac{\sum_{i=1}^{m} x_i}{m} \\ \frac{\sum_{i=1}^{m} x_i}{m} \\ \vdots \\ \frac{\sum_{i=1}^{m} x_i}{m} \end{pmatrix} \right\| = \left\| \begin{pmatrix} \frac{1}{m} & \frac{1}{m} & \cdots & \frac{1}{m} \\ \frac{1}{m} & \frac{1}{m} & \cdots & \frac{1}{m} \\ \vdots & \vdots & \ddots & \vdots \\ \frac{1}{m} & \frac{1}{m} & \cdots & \frac{1}{m} \end{pmatrix} \cdot \begin{pmatrix} x_1 \\ x_2 \\ \vdots \\ x_m \end{pmatrix} \right\|. \quad (8.33)$$

A projection

$$P : R^n \mapsto R^f \quad (8.34)$$

given the decomposition into f orthogonal spaces according to Equation 8.16 is composed of a sum of f projections onto a one-dimensional space. Each projection is a projection on an m-secting line with

$$P_i : R^m \mapsto R. \quad (8.35)$$

The method works with the space split in any way. For simplicity, we assume that the n-dimensional space is split into f equal-dimensional subspaces. In this case, the projections are efficiently computed as the mean value of each sub-vector. The corresponding mean values are multiplied with the constant

$$c = \sqrt{m} = \sqrt{\frac{n}{f}}. \quad (8.36)$$

The selection of the division can be determined by empirical experiments in which we relate m to n with the constraint that n is divisible by m.

8.2.4.1 *Example 1*

For example the orthogonal projection of points $\mathbf{x} = (x_1, x_2) \in \mathbf{R}^2$ on the bisecting line $U = \{(x_1, x_2) \in \mathbf{R}^2 | x_1 = x_2\} = \{(x_1, x_1) = \mathbf{R}^1\}$ corresponds to the mean value of the projected points. It can be represented by the projection matrix with

$$P = \begin{pmatrix} \frac{1}{2} & \frac{1}{2} \\ \frac{1}{2} & \frac{1}{2} \end{pmatrix}$$

and the orthonormalbasis of U is $\mathbf{x}_1 = (\frac{1}{\sqrt{2}}, \frac{1}{\sqrt{2}})$. The point $\mathbf{a} = (2, 4)$ is mapped into $P(\mathbf{a}) = 3$, and $\mathbf{b} = (7, 5)$ into $P(\mathbf{b}) = 6$. The distance in U is $d_u(P(\mathbf{a}), P(\mathbf{b})) = \sqrt{|6 - 3|^2}$, $c = \sqrt{2}$, so the distance in $\mathbf{R}^2$ is $d(P(\mathbf{a}), P(\mathbf{b})) = 3 \cdot \sqrt{2} \leq d(\mathbf{a}, \mathbf{b}) = \sqrt{26}$ (see Figure 8.4).

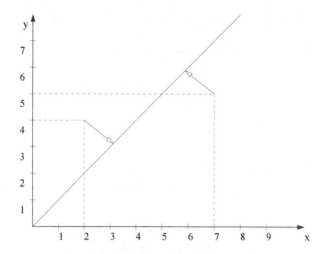

Fig. 8.4 For example, the orthogonal projection of points $\mathbf{x} = (x_1, x_2) \in \mathbf{R}^2$ on the bisecting line $U = \{(x_1, x_2) \in \mathbf{R}^2 | x_1 = x_2\} = \{(x_1, x_1) = \mathbf{R}^1\}$ corresponds to the mean value of the projected points. $\mathbf{a} = (2, 4)$ is mapped into $P(\mathbf{a}) = 3$, and $\mathbf{b} = (7, 5)$ into $P(\mathbf{b}) = 6$.

8.2.4.2 *Example 2*

For 3-band RGB (Red, Green, Blue) color images with 24 bits pixel depth, 8 bits per primary color with 256 values, the average color of an image $\mathbf{x} = (R_{avg}, G_{avg}, B_{avg})^T$ corresponds to an orthogonal projection. Because of that, the equation $d_{avg}(F_{avg}(\mathbf{x}_1), F_{avg}(\mathbf{x}_2)) \leq d(\mathbf{x}_1, \mathbf{x}_2)$ which is guaranteed by "Quadratic Distance Bounding" theorem is also guaranteed by the orthogonal projection, even the more efficient equation

$$d_{avg}(F_{avg}(\mathbf{x}_1), F_{avg}(\mathbf{x}_2)) \leq d(F_{avg}(\mathbf{x}_1), F_{avg}(\mathbf{x}_2)) \leq d(\mathbf{x}_1, \mathbf{x}_2) \qquad (8.37)$$

is valid with

$$c = \sqrt{\frac{3 \cdot 256}{3}} = 16 \qquad (8.38)$$

and

$$d(F_{avg}(\mathbf{x}_1), F_{avg}(\mathbf{x}_2)) = 16 \cdot d_{avg}(F_{avg}(\mathbf{x}_1), F_{avg}(\mathbf{x}_2)). \qquad (8.39)$$

8.2.4.3 *Example 3*

In this example we apply the decomposition of orthogonal subspaces. A lower resolution of an image corresponds to an orthogonal projection in rectangular windows, which define sub-images of an image. The image is tiled with rectangular windows W of size $j \times k$ in which the mean value is computed (averaging filter). The arithmetic mean value computation in a window corresponds to an orthogonal projection of these values onto a bisecting line. The size of the image is size 240×180 the size of the window is 6×6 and the lower resolution image is of the size 40×30 (see Figure 8.5). We defined $1200 = 40 \times 30$ orthogonal subspaces

$$R^{43200} = E_1 \oplus E_2 \oplus \ldots \oplus E_{1200} \tag{8.40}$$

of the vector space $R^{43200=240 \times 120}$ as a projection $P : R^{n=43200} \mapsto R^{f=1200}$ as a sum of 1200 projections onto one dimensional space. Each subspace E_i described by the rectangular window W and has the dimension $6 \times 6 = 36 = m$.

(a)

(b)

Fig. 8.5   (a) Image of an elephant, with the size 240×180. (b) Image of the elephant, resolution 40×30.

8.2.5 l_p *norm dependency*

Some applications require distance functions that differ from the Euclidian distance function. In addition to the Euclidean distance function, the

Manhattan distance and the Chebyshev distance function are commonly used. In the following, we generalize the Euclidean norm to the l_p norm that induces a corresponding metric [Wichert and Moreira (2015)]. The l_p norm is defined as the following (for $p = 2$ it is the Euclidean norm) [Wichert and Moreira (2015)]:

$$\|\mathbf{x}\|_p = (|x_1|^p + |x_2|^p + \cdots + |x_m|^p)^{\frac{1}{p}} \qquad (8.41)$$

l_p norms are equivalent and the following relation holds for $0 < q < p$

$$\|\mathbf{x}\|_p \le \|\mathbf{x}\|_q \le m^{\frac{1}{q}-\frac{1}{p}} \cdot \|\mathbf{x}\|_p \qquad (8.42)$$

and

$$m^{\frac{1}{p}-\frac{1}{q}} \cdot \|\mathbf{x}\|_q \le \|\mathbf{x}\|_p \le \|\mathbf{x}\|_q. \qquad (8.43)$$

The tighten triangle inequality is valid in any l_p norm due to the definition of norm. Because the l_p norms are equivalent the following equation is valid as well for any l_p norm

$$\|P \cdot \mathbf{x}\|_p - \|P \cdot \mathbf{y}\|_p \le \|P \cdot \mathbf{x} - P \cdot \mathbf{y}\|_p = \|P \cdot (\mathbf{x} - \mathbf{y})\|_p \le \|\mathbf{x} - \mathbf{y}\|_p \quad (8.44)$$

and

$$\|P \cdot \mathbf{x}\|_p \le \|\mathbf{x}\|_p. \qquad (8.45)$$

The linear projection operator P has the 1-Lipschitz property in any l_p norm and

$$m^{\frac{1}{p}} \cdot \frac{\sum_{i=1}^m x_i}{m} = \left\| \begin{pmatrix} \frac{\sum_{i=1}^m x_i}{m} \\ \frac{\sum_{i=1}^m x_i}{m} \\ \vdots \\ \frac{\sum_{i=1}^m x_i}{m} \end{pmatrix} \right\|_p = \left\| \begin{pmatrix} \frac{1}{m} & \frac{1}{m} & \cdots & \frac{1}{m} \\ \frac{1}{m} & \frac{1}{m} & \cdots & \frac{1}{m} \\ \vdots & \vdots & \ddots & \vdots \\ \frac{1}{m} & \frac{1}{m} & \cdots & \frac{1}{m} \end{pmatrix} \cdot \begin{pmatrix} x_1 \\ x_2 \\ \vdots \\ x_m \end{pmatrix} \right\|_p. \quad (8.46)$$

The projection P can be computed efficiently without needing a matrix operation as the mean value of the vector multiplied with the constant $c = m^{\frac{1}{p}}$. For the dimension m, for the l_1 norm, $c = m$, for the l_2 norm, $c = \sqrt{m}$, and for the l_∞ norm, $c = 1$. A lower l_p norm corresponds to a higher constant $m \ge c \ge 1$ and less information loss. We cannot gain any advantage of the 1-Lipschitz property using the different l_p norms. The behavior of the constant c is related to the equivalence of the norms relation. For example, the l_1 and l_2 relation is

$$\|\mathbf{x}\|_2 \le \|\mathbf{x}\|_1 \le \sqrt{m} \cdot \|\mathbf{x}\|_2. \qquad (8.47)$$

The lower bounding lemma is extended;

Lemma 8.3. *(Lower bounding) Let O_1 and O_2 be two vectors; if $V = \mathbf{R}^m$ is a vector space and U is an f-dimensional subspace obtained by a projection and a distance function $d = l_p$, then*

$$d(U(O_1), U(O_2)) = \left(\frac{m}{f}\right)^{\frac{1}{p}} \cdot d_U(U(O_1), U(O_2)) \leq d(O_1, O_2). \quad (8.48)$$

For a distance function $d = l_p$ we can map the computed metric distance d_U between objects in the f-dimensional orthogonal subspace U into the m-dimensional space V which contains the orthogonal subspace U by just multiplying the distance d_U by a constant

$$c = \left(\frac{m}{f}\right)^{\frac{1}{p}}.$$

8.2.5.1 *Other mappings*

For $\|\mathbf{q}\|_p = 1$ with $Q = \mathbf{q}^\top \cdot \mathbf{q}$ is a mapping onto one dimensional space generated by $\mathbf{q}$. It is not a projection for $p > 2$ because the matrix is not self-adjoint with $Q = Q^2$. The mapping on the m-secting line. the operator can be understood as

$$Q = \mathbf{q}^\top \cdot \mathbf{q} = \begin{pmatrix} \frac{1}{m^{\frac{2}{p}}} & \frac{1}{m^{\frac{2}{p}}} & \cdots & \frac{1}{m^{\frac{2}{p}}} \\ \frac{1}{m^{\frac{2}{p}}} & \frac{1}{m^{\frac{2}{p}}} & \cdots & \frac{1}{m^{\frac{2}{p}}} \\ \vdots & \vdots & \ddots & \vdots \\ \frac{1}{m^{\frac{2}{p}}} & \frac{1}{m^{\frac{2}{p}}} & \cdots & \frac{1}{m^{\frac{2}{p}}} \end{pmatrix}. \quad (8.49)$$

Q is generated by the l_p normalized vector $\mathbf{q}$ indicating the direction of the m-secting line.

$$\mathbf{q}^\top = \left(\frac{1}{m^{\frac{1}{p}}}, \frac{1}{m^{\frac{1}{p}}}, \cdots, \frac{1}{m^{\frac{1}{p}}}\right). \quad (8.50)$$

The mapping can be computed efficiently without requiring matrix operations as the mean value of the vector multiplied with the constant $d = m^{\frac{p-1}{p}}$.

$$m^{\frac{p-1}{p}} \cdot \frac{\sum_{i=1}^m x_i}{m} = \left\| \begin{pmatrix} \frac{\sum_{i=1}^m x_i}{m^{\frac{2}{p}}} \\ \frac{\sum_{i=1}^m x_i}{m^{\frac{2}{p}}} \\ \vdots \\ \frac{\sum_{i=1}^m x_i}{m^{\frac{2}{p}}} \end{pmatrix} \right\|_p = \left\| \begin{pmatrix} \frac{1}{m^{\frac{2}{p}}} & \frac{1}{m^{\frac{2}{p}}} & \cdots & \frac{1}{m^{\frac{2}{p}}} \\ \frac{1}{m^{\frac{2}{p}}} & \frac{1}{m^{\frac{2}{p}}} & \cdots & \frac{1}{m^{\frac{2}{p}}} \\ \vdots & \vdots & \ddots & \vdots \\ \frac{1}{m^{\frac{2}{p}}} & \frac{1}{m^{\frac{2}{p}}} & \cdots & \frac{1}{m^{\frac{2}{p}}} \end{pmatrix} \cdot \begin{pmatrix} x_1 \\ x_2 \\ \vdots \\ x_m \end{pmatrix} \right\|_p. \quad (8.51)$$

However this mapping can increase a norm. For the norm l_p the induced matrix norm is

$$\|Q\|_p = \max_{\|x_-p\|} \|Q \cdot \mathbf{x}\|_p \qquad (8.52)$$

and for $\mathbf{x} = \mathbf{q}$

$$\|Q\|_p = m^{\frac{p-2}{p}}. \qquad (8.53)$$

It follows that for $p > 2$

$$\|Q \cdot \mathbf{x}\|_p > \|\mathbf{x}\|_p \qquad (8.54)$$

the norm is increased. Only for $p \leq 2$ the norm is not increased with l_2 the projection P and l_1 the simple mean value [Wichert and Moreira (2015)].

8.2.6 *Limitations*

A projection, $P : R^n \mapsto R^f$, maps two vectors, $\mathbf{x}$ and $\mathbf{y}$, into a lower-dimensional space and satisfies the 1-Lipschitz property:

$$\|P \cdot \mathbf{x} - P \cdot \mathbf{y}\|_p \leq \|\mathbf{x} - \mathbf{y}\|_p. \qquad (8.55)$$

Using the 1-Lipschitz property, a bound that is valid in both spaces can be determined. The distance of similar vectors to a query vector $\mathbf{y}$ is smaller or equal in the original space of dimensionality n, and, consequently, it is also smaller or equal in the lower-dimensional space of the dimensionality f. During the computation, all the points below the bound are discarded. In the second step, the wrong candidates are filtered by comparisons in the original space. The number of points discarded drops as fast as the relation between the dimensionalities $\frac{n}{f}$ grows. Depending on the correlation between the dimensionalities, the 1-Lipschitz property is only useful if the relation is sufficiently small with

$$\frac{n}{f} \leq d \qquad (8.56)$$

where d varies between $2 \leq d \leq 16$ in relation to the data set. However, high-dimensional indexing requires that the mapping $F : R^n \mapsto R^d$ with $n \gg d$ satisfies the 1-Lipschitz property. For such a function, only a tiny fraction of the points of a given set are below the bound. Thus, the majority of the points have to be filtered by comparisons in the original space. Therefore, no speed up, compared to the use of a simple list matching, can be achieved, as proclaimed by the conjecture "the curse of dimensionality". If at least some points of a given set are below the bound, there is a way to build a recursive function that achieves a considerable speed up using a simple list matching. Motivated by the divide and conquer principle and the tree structure, one can build such a function recursively, indicating that the "the curse of dimensionality" conjecture is *wrong* for some data sets. It is well known that, for a dimensionality d ($2 \leq d \leq 16$), metric index trees operate efficiently. Thus, in the next step we define an efficient indexing structure that builds on the mapping $P : R^n \mapsto R^d$ that satisfies the 1-Lipschitz property, with P being a projection [Wichert and Moreira (2015)].

8.3 Subspace Tree

We can define a sequence of subspaces $U_0, U_1, U_2, \ldots, U_t$ with $V = U_0$ in which each subspace is a subspace of another space

$$U_0 \supset U_1 \supset U_2 \supset \ldots \supset U_t$$

and with $dim(U_r)$ indicating the dimension of the subspace U_r

$$dim(U_0) > dim(U_1) > dim(U_2) \ldots > dim(U_t).$$

8.3.0.1 *Example*

An example of a sequence of subspaces is the sequence of real vector subspaces

$$\mathbf{R^n} \supset \mathbf{R^{n-1}} \supset \mathbf{R^{n-2}} \supset \ldots \supset \mathbf{R^1}$$

formed by the mapping from one subspace to another which always sets the last coordinate ($\neq 0$) to 0. In this case, the distance functions used in the original space and in the subspace are equal [Wichert (2008); Wichert *et al.* (2010)].

8.3.1 *Subspaces*

With

$$\{\mathbf{x}_k \in DB \mid k \in \{1..s\}\}$$

all s multimedia objects of DB are in space $V = U_0$, which is represented by $V(DB) = U_0(DB)$. The DB mapped by $F_{0,1}()$ from space U_0 to its subspace U_1 is indicated by $U_1(DB)$. A subspace U_r can be mapped from different spaces by different functions $\{F_{l,r}()|U_l \to U_r, l < r\}$ in contrast to the universal GEMINI approach [Faloutsos *et al.* (1994)], in which the mapped *DB* only depends on the function $F()$. Because of this a notation is used which does not depends on the mapped function, but on the subspace U_r itself,

$$\{U_r(\mathbf{x}_k) \in U_r(DB) \mid k \in \{1..s\}\}. \tag{8.57}$$

The set $U_r(DB)$ can be ordered in relation to a given multimedia object $U_r(\mathbf{y})$ and a distance function $d = l_p$. This is done by a monotone increasing sequence corresponding to the increasing distance of $U_r(\mathbf{y})$ to $U_r(\mathbf{x}_k)$, with an explicit key identifying each object indicated by the index k,

$$d[U_r(\mathbf{y})]_t := \{d(U_r(\mathbf{x}_k), U_r(\mathbf{y})) \mid \forall t \in \{1..s\} : d[U_r(\mathbf{y})]_t \le d[U_r(\mathbf{y})]_{t+1}\}. \tag{8.58}$$

We will use the same distance function for all subspaces, in most cases it will be the Euclidean distance function $d = l_2$. The set of similar multimedia objects in correspondence to $U_r(\mathbf{y})$, $U_r(DB[\mathbf{y}])_\epsilon$ is the subset of $U_r(DB)$,

$$U_r(DB[\mathbf{y}])_\epsilon := \{U_r(\mathbf{x}_k) \in U_r(DB) \mid d(U_r(\mathbf{x}_k), U_r(\mathbf{y})) \le \epsilon\}.$$

For each subspace U_r, the number of points below the bound ϵ is indicated by the value σ_r

$$\sigma_r := |U_r(DB[\mathbf{y}])_\epsilon,$$

it follows that

$$\sigma_0 < \sigma_1 < \ldots < \sigma_t < s \tag{8.59}$$

where s is the size of the data set.

8.3.1.1 *Projections*

We define a family of projections for the sequence of subspaces with the following

$$P_1 : U_0 \mapsto U_1; P_2 : U_1 \mapsto U_2; \ldots; P_t : U_{t-1} \mapsto U_t. \tag{8.60}$$

and the relation between neighbouring subspaces is sufficiently small $d \le 16$ with

$$\frac{dim(U_0)}{dim(U_1)} \le d, \frac{dim(U_1)}{dim(U_2)} \le d, \ldots \frac{dim(U_{t-1})}{dim(U_t)} \le d. \tag{8.61}$$

The family of projections defines the sequence of subspaces. Given a bound ϵ and a query vector $\mathbf{y}$ for each subspace including the original space U_0, certain points are below the bound. For each subspace U_r, the number of points below the bound ϵ is indicated by the value σ_r. where s is the size of the data set. The resulting computing cost given a bound ϵ and a query vector $\mathbf{y}$ is

$$cost_s = \sum_{i=1}^{t} \sigma_i \cdot dim(U_{i-1}) + s \cdot dim(U_t). \tag{8.62}$$

8.3.1.2 *Computational procedure*

The algorithm to determine all ϵ-similar objects is composed of two loops. The first loop iterates over the elements of the database DB, and the second iterates over their representation. We can easily parallelize the algorithm over the first loop; different parts of the database can be processed by different processors, kernels, or computers.

Algorithm to determine NN

forall $\{\mathbf{x}_k \in DB | i \in \{1..s\}\}$
$\quad\{$
$\quad\quad for(r = t; r \neq 0, r - -)$
$\quad\quad\quad\{$
$\quad\quad\quad\quad load(U_r(\mathbf{x})_k);$
$\quad\quad\quad\quad$ /* 1-Lipschitz property */
$\quad\quad\quad\quad if\ (\|U_r(\mathbf{x})_k - U_r(\mathbf{y}))\|_p >= \epsilon)$
$\quad\quad\quad\quad\quad break ::;$
$\quad\quad\quad\quad\quad if\ (r = 0)\ print\ \mathbf{x}_k\ is\ NN\ of\ \mathbf{y}$
$\quad\quad\quad\}$
$\quad\}$

Each call of the 1-Lipschitz property costs $dim(U_r)$. The cost according to Equation 8.62 correspond to the number of 1-Lipschitz property calls, corresponding to the value σ_k. The cost of list matching is

$$cost_l = s \cdot dim(U_0) \tag{8.63}$$

The saving $cost_s < cost_l$ is related to the bound ϵ. Empirical experiments suggest that $cost_s \ll cost_l$ for a bound with $\sigma_0 < d$.

8.3.2 *Content-based image retrieval by image pyramid*

The database consists of 9.876 web-crawled color images of size 128×96, it was used in the SIMPLIcity project [Wang *et al.* (2001)]. The images were scaled to the size of 128×96 through a bilinear method resulting in a 12288-dimensional vector space. Each color is represented by 8 bits [Wichert (2008)]. Each of the tree bands of size 128×96 is tiled with rectangular windows W of size 4×4. We apply the orthogonal projection P. The resulting family of projections,

$$P_1 : U_0 \mapsto U_1; P_2 : U_1 \mapsto P_2; P_3 : U_2 \mapsto U_3 \tag{8.64}$$

defines the dimensionalities of the subspaces for each band

$$dim(U_0) = 12288 > dim(U_1) = 768$$
$$> dim(U_2) = 48 = 8 \times 6 > dim(U_3) = 12 = 4 \times 3.$$

For an orthogonal projection, the sequence of subspaces $U_0 \supset U_1 \supset U_2 \supset U_3$ corresponds to the "image pyramid" [Burt and Adelson (1983)], [Gonzales and Woods (2001)], which has a base that contains an image with a high-resolution and an apex that is the low-resolution approximation of the image. In Table 8.1, we indicate the mean costs for a disjunct sample of $S \subseteq DB$ with size $|S| = 400$ according to Equation 8.62 compared to a simple list matching for different l_p norms. A lower l_p norm corresponds to a higher constant and results in lower costs (the l_1 norm gives the best results). The list matching costs are

$$cost_l = s \cdot dim(U_0) = 9876 \cdot (12288 \cdot 3) \tag{8.65}$$

The multiplication with 3 corresponds to the 3-bands (Red, Green, Blue). In Figure 8.7 we relate the mean computation costs (divided by three)

Table 8.1   The ratio of list matching to the mean computation costs according to Equation 8.62. The mean computation cos were determined over a disjunct sample of $S \subseteq DB$ with size $|S| = 400$ for the three bands.

l_p	ϵ for ≈ 52 NN	cost	ratio
l_1	1240000	8571752	42.47
l_2	8500	10386043	35.05
l_4	825	12464281	29.32
l_∞	161	39639239	9.19

to the number of the most similar images which should be retrieved to a given query image. To estimate ϵ and its dependency on σ_r, we define a mean sequence $d[U_r(DB)]_t$ which describes the characteristics of an image database in our system:

$$d[U_r(DB)]_t := \sum_{k=1}^{|S|} \frac{d[U_r(\mathbf{x}_k)]_t}{|S|}. \tag{8.66}$$

As can be seen in Figure 8.8 $d[U_r(DB)]_t$ (with $|S| = 1000$) can be used for an estimation of the value of ϵ, for example, the maximum possible value. We can determine mean distance $d[U_r(DB)]_t$ for a given t. We can not determine t from a given mean distance value using $d[U_r(DB)]_t$, because $d[U_r(DB)]_t$ was computed over mean values over distances, and not over the mean value of k σ_r representing $\overline{\sigma}_r$. $d[U_k(DB)]_t$ can be used for an estimation of the value of ϵ, for example, the maximum possible value.

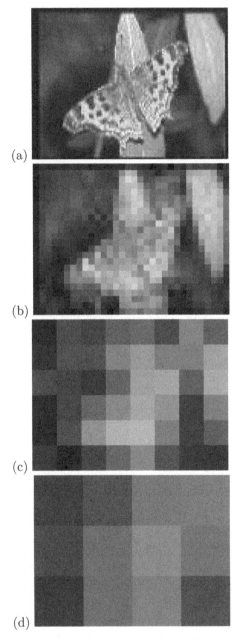

Fig. 8.6   (a) Image of a butterfly, with the size 128 × 96. (b) Image of the butterfly, resolution 32 × 24. (c) Image of the butterfly, resolution 8 × 6. (d) The image of the butterfly, resolution 4 × 3.

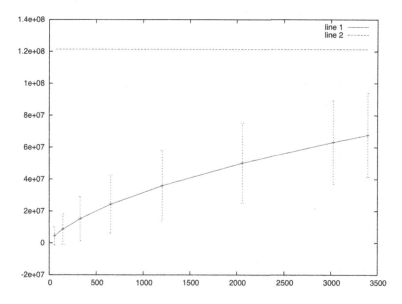

Fig. 8.7   Line indicates the constant list matching costs divided by three (12288). Line 2 indicates the mean computing costs using the subspace tree divided by three. The error bars indicate the standard deviation. The x-axis indicates the number of the most similar images which are retrieved and the y-axis, the computing costs in time according to Equation 8.62.

8.3.3   *The first principal component*

The covariance matrix represents the tendency of two dimensions varying in the same direction as indicated by the data points. The Karhunen-Loève transform rotates the coordinate system in such a way that the new covariance matrix will be diagonal. Therefore, each dimension will be uncorrelated. The transformation is described by an orthonormal matrix, which is composed of the normalized eigenvectors of the covariance matrix. The squares of the eigenvalues represent the variances along the eigenvectors. If we use PCA iteratively on images instead of sub-sampling, will we achieve high effectiveness? With PCA applied to the whole space R^n with $F : R^n \mapsto R^f$ with $n \gg 16$ only a tiny fraction of the points of a given set are below the bound, the results are unsatisfactory [Wichert and Verissimo (2012)]. With the decomposition for $f \leq n$ orthogonal subspaces

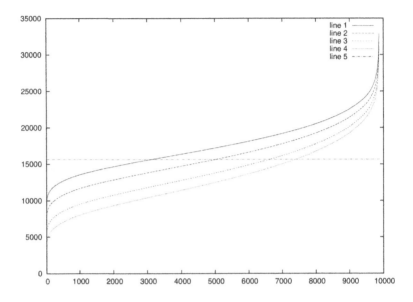

Fig. 8.8   Characteristics of $d[U_0(DB)]_t$ = line 1, $d[U_1(DB)]_t$ = line 2, $d[U_2(DB)]_n t$ line 3 and $d[U_3(DB)]_t$ = line 4 in the original space U_0, and the maximal value of ϵ is represented by line 5 (with $|S| = 1000$).

$$R^n = E_1 \oplus E_2 \oplus \ldots \oplus E_f \qquad (8.67)$$

of the vector space R^n and with the assumption that each subspace E_i has the dimension m we will compute a covariance matrix for each subspace [Wichert and Moreira (2015)]. With a covariance matrix of dimension $m \times m$ the first principal component corresponds to the normalized eigenvector $\mathbf{z}$ with the highest variance. $\|\mathbf{z}\| = 1$ with $Z = \mathbf{z} \cdot \mathbf{z}^\top$ is the best projection onto one-dimensional space because, in a Hillbert space, the first principal component passes through the mean and minimizes the sum of squares of the distances of the points from the line. It follows that

$$\|\mathbf{x}\| \geq \|P \cdot \mathbf{x}\| \geq \|Z \cdot \mathbf{x}\|. \qquad (8.68)$$

For uncorrelated data, $Z = P$ represents the projection on the m-secting line. For correlated data contrary to the projection on the m-secting line, all the components of the vector $\mathbf{z}$ do not need to be equal, and the projection cannot be computed efficiently. For a vector $\mathbf{o}$ of length $\sqrt{m}$ in the direction of the m-secting line where P is the projection on the m-secting line,

$$\mathbf{o} = \underbrace{(1, 1, 1, \cdots, 1)}_{m} \tag{8.69}$$

it follows that

$$\sqrt{m} = \|\mathbf{o}\| = \|P \cdot \mathbf{o}\| \geq \|Z \cdot \mathbf{o}\| \geq 1. \tag{8.70}$$

The value

$$\sqrt{m} - \|Z \cdot \mathbf{o}\| \tag{8.71}$$

indicates the diversion from the m-secting line with value 0 corresponding to uncorrelated data and $\sqrt{m} - 1$ one dimension data with

$$\sqrt{m} - 1 \geq \sqrt{m} - \|Z \cdot \mathbf{o}\| \geq 0. \tag{8.72}$$

For a given decomposition into f orthogonal spaces according to the Equation 8.67 the data points are mapped into corresponding subspaces E_i. For each subspace E_i the covariance matrix C_i is computed. In the next step for each covariance matrix C_i the first principal component with the highest variance is determined. It is represented by the normalised eigenvector $\mathbf{z}_i$. Each projection

$$Z_i = \mathbf{z}_i \cdot \mathbf{z}_i^\top \tag{8.73}$$

is a projection onto the first principal component with $Z_i : R^m \mapsto R$. An adaptive projection $A : R^n \mapsto R^f$, given the decomposition into f orthogonal spaces according to the Equation 8.67, is composed of a sum of f projections Z_i onto a one-dimensional space.

$$A = \mathbf{z}_1 \cdot \mathbf{z}_1^\top + \mathbf{z}_2 \cdot \mathbf{z}_2^\top \ldots + \mathbf{z}_f \cdot \mathbf{z}_f^\top. \tag{8.74}$$

The method works under any splitting of the space, such as the projection $P : R^n \mapsto R^f$.

8.3.4 *Examples*

We apply computational procedure on high-dimensional data set of 100000 vectors of dimensionality 960. The vectors represent the GIST global descriptor of an image and are composed by concatenated orientation image histograms [Jegou et al. (2011)]. The vector $\mathbf{x}$ of dimensionality 960 is split into 480 distinct sub-vectors of dimensionality 2. The data points are described by 480 covariance matrices C_i for each subspace. For all points, the covariance matrices are computed iteratively.

$$\mathbf{x} = \underbrace{x_1, x_2}_{C_1}, \underbrace{x_3, x_4}_{C_2}, \cdots \cdots, \underbrace{x_{479}, x_{959}}_{C_{480}} . \tag{8.75}$$

The resulting 480 projections, $\mathbf{z}_i \cdot \mathbf{z}_i^\top$, define the adaptive projection A : $R^{960} \mapsto R^{480}$. We apply the adaptive projection and the determination of the adaptive projection recursively. The resulting family of projections,

$$A_1 : U_0 \mapsto U_1; A_2 : U_1 \mapsto U_2; \ldots; A_7 : U_6 \mapsto U_7 \tag{8.76}$$

defines the dimensionalities of the subspaces.

$dim(U_0) = 960 > dim(U_1) = 480 > dim(U_2) = 240 > dim(U_3) = 120$
$> dim(U_4) = 60 > dim(U_5) = 30 > dim(U_6) = 10 > dim(U_7) = 5.$

In Table 8.2, we indicate the mean costs according to Equation 8.62 using the l_2 norm. For an orthogonal projection, the sequence of subspaces

Table 8.2 Mean ratio of list matching to the mean computation costs according to Equation 8.62. The values were determined over a disjunct sample of $S \subseteq DB$ with size $|S| = 400$. The adaptive projection gives only a slight improvement. The diversion from the m-secting line according to Equation 8.71 is always $\ll 0.0001$.

projection	ϵ for ≈ 52 NN	mean cost	ratio
orthogonal	6300	4584277	21.38
adaptive	6300	4393127	22.31

$U_0 \supset U_1 \supset U_2 \supset U_3$ corresponds to the "image pyramid" [Burt and Adelson (1983)], [Gonzales and Woods (2001)], which has a base that contains an image with a high-resolution and an apex that is the low-resolution approximation of the image. Each of the tree bands of size 128×96 is tiled with rectangular windows W of size 4×4. The data points are described by 32×24 covariance matrices C_i for each subspace, for each band. The resulting $768 = 32 \times 24$ projections $\mathbf{z}_i \cdot \mathbf{z}_i^\top$ define the adaptive projection $A : R^{12288} \mapsto R^{768}$ for each band (Red, Green, Blue). We apply the adaptive projection and the determination of the adaptive projection recursively. The resulting family of projections,

$$A_1 : U_0 \mapsto U_1; A_2 : U_1 \mapsto U_2; A_3 : U_2 \mapsto U_3 \tag{8.77}$$

defines the dimensionalities of the subspaces for each band

$dim(U_0) = 12288 > dim(U_1) = 768$
$> dim(U_2) = 48 > dim(U_3) = 12.$

In Table 8.3, we indicate the mean costs according to Equation 8.62 (divided by three) using the l_2 norm.

Table 8.3 Mean ratio of list matching to the mean computation costs according to Equation 8.62. The values were determined over a disjunct sample of $S \subseteq DB$ with size $|S| = 400$ for the three bands. The diversion from the m-secting line, according to Equation 8.71, is always $\ll 0.0001$.

projection	ϵ for ≈ 52 NN	cost	ratio
adaptive	8500	10343766	35.20
orthogonal	8500	10386043	35.05

8.3.5 *Hierarchies*

Different hierarchies lead to different computing costs for the same problem. What is the size of the hierarchy in order for the computing costs to be as low as possible? We determine the mean image pyramid of the image

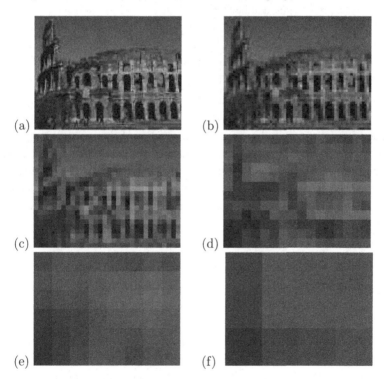

Fig. 8.9 Mean image pyramid of the "test" image databases. (a) Image of Colosseum, with the size 128 × 96. b) Image of the Colosseum, resolution 64 × 48. (c) Image of the Colosseum, resolution 32 × 24. (d) Image of the Colosseum, resolution 16 × 12. (e) Image of the Colosseum, resolution 8 × 6. (f) Image of the Colosseum, resolution 4 × 3.

databases (size $128 \cdot 96$) of 1000 images, the sequence of subspaces $U_0 \supset U_1 \supset U_2 \supset U_3 \supset U_4 \supset U_5$ correspond to different resolutions of the images (see Figure 8.9). The dimensions of the resulting subspaces are

$$dim(U_0) = 12288 > dim(U_1) = 3072 > dim(U_2) = 768 > dim(U_3) = 192$$

$$dim(U_3) = 192 > dim(U_4) = 48 > dim(U_5) = 12$$

multiplied by factor 3 for color images. In the next step we determined the combinations which lead to the lowest costs (see Table 8.4) and indicated the corresponding mean computing costs (see, Figure 8.10) [Wichert *et al.* (2010)].

Table 8.4   Best combination of subspaces. Presence of a subspace is indicated by '*'

sub space	1	2	3	4	5
U_1		*	*	*	*
U_2	*		*	*	*
U_3		*		*	*
U_4			*		*
U_5				*	*

The computing costs decrease as the number of spaces increase as indicated by Figure 8.10. However, the decrease of the computing costs becomes finally minimal when the computational overhead such as the time needed to access the corresponding data, becomes finally bigger than the achieved saving. Actually, the subspace tree is related to a search tree as indicated in the following.

8.3.6   Tree isomorphy

The isomorphy to a tree results from the assumption that the value of σ_r is reciprocal to the preceding dimensionality [Wichert *et al.* (2010)]. Therefore, a bigger dimensionality $dim(U_{r+1})$ results in a smaller value σ_r, and vice versa. We can express this relation by

$$const \cdot \sigma_r = \frac{1}{dim(U_{r+1})} \tag{8.78}$$

and

$$\sigma_r = \frac{1}{const \cdot dim(U_{r+1})} \tag{8.79}$$

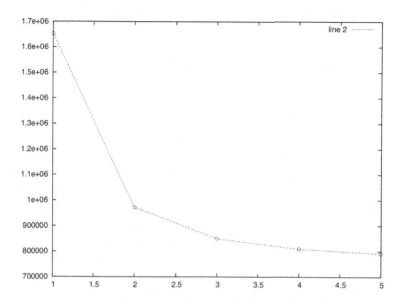

Fig. 8.10 Mean computing cost according to the Equation 8.62 divided by three depend on the number of used subspaces to retrieve ≈ 24 images. The number of subspaces are represented by the abscissa, beginning with one subspace and ending with five subspaces. The improvement over list matching with one subspace is 7 times less computational steps and with five subspaces 14 times less computational steps.

The value of *const* is dependent on the data set and its norm. The value of σ_i is reciprocal to the preceding dimensionality $dim(U_{r+1})$ (Equation 8.79), and the computing costs are expressed by

$$cost_s \approx 1/const \cdot \left(\frac{dim(U_0)}{dim(U_1)} + \frac{dim(U_1)}{dim(U_2)} + \ldots + \frac{dim(U_{t-1})}{dim(U_t)} \right) + dim(U_t) \cdot s.$$
(8.80)

Supposing $d = dim(U_t)$ and $n = dim(U_0)$

$$cost_s \approx 1/const \cdot d \cdot \log_d(n) - d + d \cdot s.$$
(8.81)

For a dimension d, the metric index trees (for example kd-tree or R-tree) operate efficiently with a nearly logarithmic search time. For the bound with $\sigma_0 < d$, the value $1/const \ll s$

$$cost_s \approx 1/const \cdot d \cdot (\log_d(n) - 1) + d \cdot \log_d(s).$$
(8.82)

Intelligent Big Multimedia Databases

It follows that the lower bound of the computational cost is

$$\Omega(\log(n) + \log(s)). \tag{8.83}$$

8.3.7 *Requirements*

The subspace tree approach requires that the distances between the data points are Gaussian distributed[2]. It means that the histogram of distances of a randomly chosen data point out of the dataset set corresponds to a Gaussian (normal) distribution. In Figure 8.11 (a) a histogram representing 10000 random variables out of a Gaussian distribution with the mean value 17000 and the standard deviation 4000 is shown. In Figure 8.11 (b) we see the data set, and in Figure 8.11 (c) the sorted data set. Note that the sorted data set has the same shape as the characteristic (line 1) in Figure 8.8. If the distribution of distances between the data points departs to much from from the Gaussian distribution the subspace tree approach cannot be applied. For example the subspace tree cannot be applied if the distribution of the distances of the data points of a dataset set is highly skewed. In a skewed distribution the bulk of the data are at one end of the distribution.

- If the bulk of the distribution is on the left, so the tail is on the right, then the distribution is called right skewed or positively skewed, see Figure 8.12.
- If the bulk of the distribution is on the right, so the tail is on the left, then the distribution is called left skewed or negatively skewed, see Figure 8.13.

In this case either no ϵ value exists (see corollary 8.1), or no computing time can be saved (see corollary 8.2). The subspace tree cannot be applied to sparse representation, as present in the vector space model [Baeza-Yates and Ribeiro-Neto (1999a)], or for sparse normalised vectors as used in information retrieval. It seems that the distances between sparse vectors are highly positively skewed and the distances between sparse normalised vectors as used in information retrieval are highly negatively skewed.

---

[2]The following section is based on ideas of João Sacramento.

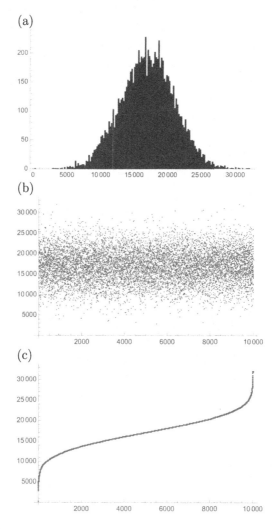

Fig. 8.11 (a) A histogram representing 10000 random variables of a Gaussian distribution with the mean value 17000 and the standard deviation 4000. (b) The data set. (c) The sorted data set. Note that the sorted data set has the same shape as the characteristic (line 1) in Figure 8.8.

8.4 Conclusion

An adaptive projection that satisfies the 1-Lipschitz property defined by the first principal component was introduced. We indicated the behavior of

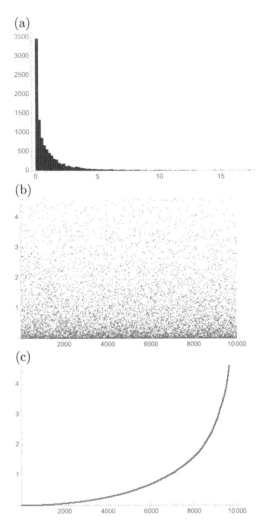

Fig. 8.12   (a) A histogram representing 10000 random variables of a right skewed or positively skewed distribution. (b) The data set. (c) The sorted data set.

the projections for the l_p norms. The Manhattan distance l_1 loses the least information, followed by Euclidean distance function. Most information is lost when using the Chebyshev distance function. Motivated by the tree structure, we indicated a family of projections that defines a mapping that satisfies the 1-Lipschitz property. It is composed of orthogonal or adaptive projections in the l_p space. Each projection is applied recursively in a low-

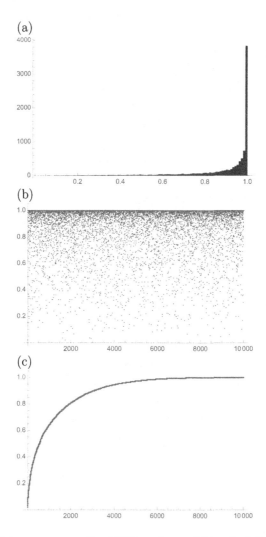

Fig. 8.13 a) A histogram representing 10000 random variables of a left skewed or negatively skewed distribution. (b) The data set. (c) The sorted data set.

dimensional space, where "the curse of dimensionality" conjecture does not apply.

Chapter 9

Dealing with Text Databases

The descriptor represents the relevant information about a text by a feature vector that indicates the presence or absence of terms. Terms are words with specific meaning in a specific context; they may deviate from the meaning the same words have in other contexts. The frequency of the occurrence of each term in a document and the information content of the term according to the entire document collection can be employed. During information retrieval, the feature vectors are used to determine the similarity between two text documents, which is represented by the cosine of the angle between the feature vectors. Because the vectors are extremely sparse (most dimensions are zero), we cannot apply the previously introduced indexing methods. The semantic gap exists because the text documents are described by feature vectors without additional semantical information. Text understanding systems are developed in the field of AI; however, they only work in a narrow domain and are computationally expensive [Winston (1992); Russell and Norvig (2003)].

9.1 Boolean Queries

Text can be described by a set of discrete words, which are also referred to as terms. The similarities among terms can be defined as a function of the terms the text has in common. Binary vectors can represent terms. A one represents a term at the corresponding position of a binary vector, whereas its absence is denoted by a zero [Manning *et al.* (2008)]. The term set

$$Caeser, Brutus, Claudius, David, Eva, Cleopatra,$$

$$Astrix, Obelix, Idefix, girl, flower$$

is represented by a binary vector of dimension 11. The presence of terms *Calpurnia* and *Eva* in a document a is represented by the binary vector a,

$$\mathbf{a} = (0\ 0\ 1\ 0\ 1\ 0\ 0\ 0\ 0\ 0\ 0)^\top.$$

Document b contains the terms *Caeser*, *Astrix* and *Obelix* and is represented by the vector b

$$\mathbf{b} = (1\ 0\ 0\ 0\ 0\ 0\ 1\ 1\ 0\ 0\ 0)^\top,$$

the document b contains the terms *Astrix* and *Obelix* and *idefix* s represented by the vector c

$$\mathbf{c} = (0\ 0\ 0\ 0\ 0\ 0\ 1\ 1\ 1\ 0\ 0)^\top$$

and so on. Usually a document collection is described by a binary matrix composed by the column vectors representing the documents. Each column represents a document, each row a term. Our example is represented by the matrix C

$$C = \begin{pmatrix} \mathbf{a} & \mathbf{b} & \mathbf{c} & \cdots \end{pmatrix}$$

with

$$C = \begin{pmatrix} 0 & 1 & 0 & \cdots \\ 0 & 0 & 0 & \cdots \\ 1 & 0 & 0 & \cdots \\ 0 & 0 & 0 & \cdots \\ 1 & 0 & 0 & \cdots \\ 0 & 0 & 0 & \cdots \\ 0 & 1 & 1 & \cdots \\ 0 & 1 & 1 & \cdots \\ 0 & 0 & 1 & \cdots \\ 0 & 0 & 0 & \cdots \\ 0 & 0 & 0 & \cdots \end{pmatrix}. \tag{9.1}$$

Each term can be represented by a vector as well, for example

$$\mathbf{Astrix} = (0\ 1\ 1\ \cdots)^\top.$$

To answer a binary query we preform logical AND, OR and NOT operations on the binary vectors that represent the terms. For example to answer the query to get all documents that contain the terms *Astrix* and *Obelix* and *NOT Ceaser* we preform the logical operations on the vectors that represent the terms

$$\mathbf{Astrix} \wedge \mathbf{Obelix} \wedge \neg\mathbf{Cesar} =$$

$$(0\ 1\ 1\ \cdots)^\top \wedge (0\ 1\ 1\ \cdots)^\top \wedge \neg (1\ 0\ 0\ \cdots)^\top =$$

$$(0\ 1\ 1\ \cdots)^\top \wedge (0\ 1\ 1\ \cdots)^\top \wedge (0\ 1\ 1\ \cdots)^\top = (0\ 1\ 1\ \cdots)^\top.$$

The Boolean queries are precise, a document matches condition or not. For each term we must store a vector of pointers or a list of all documents that contain term. We can use the inverted index in which the position indicate the documents in which certain term is present, like

$$Astrix = b, c, \ \cdots$$

For real data matrix C becomes very big, it has much, much more zeros then ones. The matrix is extremely sparse because not every term is in every document present. For a very small number of 1s of the vectors a sparse code is given, we only record the 1 positions . For binary vectors with more zeros then ones pointer coding can be used. In the pointer coding only the positions of the vector components unequal to zero are represented by a string,

$$01000110000,$$

the pointer representation of ones is given by

$$2, 6, 7.$$

9.2 Tokenization

The process of tokenization of the text corresponds to the conversion of each document into a list of terms[1]. Creating a suitable definition of a term can be challenging. Word tokenization is simple in a language that separates words by spaces. However, not every language incorporates this feature and tokenization is particularly difficult for languages without word boundaries, such as Ancient Greek, Chinese, Japanese and Thai.

9.2.1 *Low-level tokenization*

A tokenizer frequently uses a simple heuristic, such as separating terms by whitespace characters, in languages such as English. However, a heuristic cannot address some cases, such as contractions or hyphenated words. These cases are processed by low-level tokenization:

---

[1]In general, tokenization is the process of breaking a stream of text into meaningful elements named tokens

- segmenting text into tokens that represent terms,
- handling abbreviations,
- numerical and special expressions,
- handling end-of-line hyphens are used for splitting entire words into parts to justify text during typesetting,
- handling true hyphenated words, such as "forty-two", and should not be removed.

9.2.2 *High-level tokenization*

All text does not pass through an editing and spell check process. Spelling errors and unexpected characters are corrected during high-level tokenization. High-level tokenization is linguistically motivated and requires some linguistic processing. Linguistic preprocessing produces a list of normalized terms. The most standard method for normalizing is to create equivalence classes that are named after one member of the set. Multiple occurrences of the same term from the same document are then merged; for example *friend, friends, Friend, Friends* are mapped to the normalized token *friend*. The search for one term will retrieve documents that contain either one or more elements inside the class represented by the corresponding normalized token. The input to indexing is a list of normalized tokens that represents the presence of terms for each document.

9.3 Vector Model

We can rank the documents with respect to a query by the Hamming distance D. The Hamming distance is an overlap measure; it is the number on which two binary vectors differ [Baeza-Yates and Ribeiro-Neto (1999b); Manning *et al.* (2008)]. For binary vectors, it corresponds to the Taxicab or Manhattan metric d_1.

9.3.1 *Term frequency*

However, the Manhattan metric does not consider the term frequency in a document. If a document discusses a topic, then it is a better match. For each term, we can store the frequency (tf) of its occurrence in a document, which is represented as

$$tf_{t,d} \qquad (9.2)$$

where t denotes the term (the dimension in the vector) and d denotes the corresponding document (the vector that represents the document). Each document is represented by a sparse vector in each dimension that indicates the frequency of the occurrence of a term in the document. The similarity between the documents can be measured by the Euclidean distance d_2. In the case that we do not want to consider the length of the documents, we can normalize the vectors that represent the documents. By normalizing the vectors to the length one, the Euclidean distance function is constrained to the unit sphere.

$$0 \le d \left(\frac{\mathbf{a}}{\|\mathbf{a}\|}, \frac{\mathbf{b}}{\|\mathbf{b}\|} \right) = \left\| \frac{\mathbf{a}}{\|\mathbf{a}\|} - \frac{\mathbf{b}}{\|\mathbf{b}\|} \right\| \le \sqrt{2} \qquad (9.3)$$

and corresponds to the angle ω between the vectors

$$\cos \omega = \frac{\langle \mathbf{a} | \mathbf{b} \rangle}{\|\mathbf{a}\| \cdot \|\mathbf{b}\|} \qquad (9.4)$$

with a similarity function

$$0 \le sim(\mathbf{a}, \mathbf{b}) = \cos \omega \le 1. \qquad (9.5)$$

The similarity function is a popular measure in the information retrieval (IR) community.

The term frequency (tf) can be as well scaled logarithmically to deal with a large range of quantities,

$$wf_{t,d} \begin{cases} wf_{t,d} = 0 & if \ tf_{t,d} = 0 \\ wf_{t,d} = 1 + \log(tf_{t,d}) \ else \end{cases} \qquad (9.6)$$

with $wf_{t,d}$ being the "word" frequency.

9.3.2 *Information*

Document frequency is the number of documents in the collection containing a certain term

$$df_t, \qquad (9.7)$$

if s is the number of documents in the collection, then surprise of a $term_t$ is defined as

$$s_t = \frac{s}{df_t}. \qquad (9.8)$$

The bigger the probability $p(term_t)$

$$p(term_t) = \frac{df_t}{s}. \qquad (9.9)$$

that a term is present in a document collection, the less surprised we are. Information of a term is defined as

$$I_t = log_2(s_t) = -log_2(p(term_t)).$$ (9.10)

With n being the number of different terms $term_i$ and $p(terem_i)$ the probability of of occurrence of the term, then the theoretical minimum average number of bits of a document is computed using the Shannon's formula of entropy

$$H = -\sum_i^n p(term_i) \cdot \log_2 p(term_i).$$ (9.11)

9.3.3 Vector representation

Each document is represented by sparse vector in each dimension indicates the frequency of the occurrence of a term in the document either by the term or word frequency. In the information retrieval community information of each term is also called inverse document frequency

$$idf_t := I_t = log_2(s_t) = -log_2(p(term_t)) = \log_2\left(\frac{s}{df_t}\right) \approx \log\left(\frac{s}{df_t}\right)$$ (9.12)

and the combination of information and the frequency of occurrence of each term in a document is called the $tf.idf$ measure

$$w_{t,d} = tf_{t,d} \times \log\left(\frac{s}{df_t}\right) = tf_{t,d} \cdot I_t$$ (9.13)

or

$$w'_{t,d} = wf_{t,d} \times \log\left(\frac{s}{df_t}\right) = wf_{t,d} \cdot I_t.$$ (9.14)

Each document d is represented by sparse vector in each dimension t indicates $w_{t,d}$ or $w'_{t,d}$.

9.3.4 Random projection

For a query vector $\mathbf{q}$ and a document collection represented by s vectors of the dimension n we want to find documents that are close together using the similarity function

$$sim(\mathbf{q}, \mathbf{x}) = \cos\omega$$

The dimension of the space that is defined by the terms can be huge. The dimension n can be quite huge, for example the Oxford English Dictionary contains full entries for 171476 words in current use. Because the vectors are extremely sparse (most dimension are zero), we cannot use the previously introduced indexing methods to sped up the computation. Usually random projection is used to speed up the computation for approximate-NN computation [Manning *et al.* (2008)].

A random projection from n to m with

$$m \ll n$$

is given by this simple algorithm:

- choose a random direction $\mathbf{a}_1$ in the vector space;
- for $i = 2$ to m
- choose a random direction a_i that is orthogonal to $\mathbf{a}_1, \mathbf{a}_2, \cdots \mathbf{a}_{i-1}$;
- project each document vector of dimension n into the subspace spanned by $\{\mathbf{a}_1, \mathbf{a}_2, \cdots, \mathbf{a}_m\}$.

The subspace spanned by $\{\mathbf{a}_1, \mathbf{a}_2, \cdots, \mathbf{a}_m\}$ defines a projection matrix of the dimension $m \times n$

$$A = \begin{pmatrix} \mathbf{a}_1^T \\ \mathbf{a}_2^T \\ \vdots \\ \mathbf{a}_m^T \end{pmatrix} = \begin{pmatrix} a_{11} & a_{12} & \cdots & a_{1n} \\ a_{21} & a_{22} & \cdots & a_{2n} \\ \vdots & \vdots & \ddots & \vdots \\ a_{m1} & a_{m2} & \cdots & a_{mn} \end{pmatrix}. \tag{9.15}$$

The vectors that represent the document collection and the query vector are projected with the projection matrix A into m dimensional space. Relative distances are preserved by projection A with high probability according to the The Johnson-Lindenstrauss lemma, see section 7.4. An alternative formulation of the lemma states that for any $0 < \epsilon, \delta < 1/2$ and a positive integer n there exists a distribution over $R^{m \times n}$, from which the matrix A is drawn such that such that for

$$m = O\left(\epsilon^{-2} \cdot \log\left(\frac{1}{\delta}\right)\right) \tag{9.16}$$

and for any unit-length vector

$$\mathbf{x} \in R^n, \quad \|\mathbf{x}\|_2 = 1,$$

$$P(|\|A \cdot \mathbf{x}\|_2^2 - 1| > \epsilon) < \delta, \tag{9.17}$$

with the length of the vector after the projection nearly one. Hecht-Nielsen also observed that in high dimensional spaces a random projection matrix over a distribution is close to be orthogonal [Hecht-Nielsen (1994)].

9.4 Probabilistic Model

In a probabilistic model the IR problem is captured using a probabilistic framework. For example, if we know that some documents are relevant and some irrelevant then we can build a probabilistic classifier, for example a Naïve Bayes classifier.

9.4.1 *Probability theory*

Probability theory is built around Kolmogorov's axioms (first published in 1933, [Kolmogorov (1933)]). All probabilities are between 0 and 1. For any proposition a,

$$0 \leq P(a) \leq 1$$

and

$$P(true) = 1, \quad P(false) = 0.$$

To each sentence, a numerical degree of belief between 0 and 1 is assigned, which provides a way of summarizing the uncertainty. The last axiom expresses the probability of disjunction and is given by

$$P(a \vee b) = P(a) + P(b) - P(a \wedge b)$$

The degree of belief $P(a)$ is attached to a sentence a before any evidence about the nature of the sentence is obtained; we call this probability the prior (before) probability. Arising from the frequentist approach, one can determine the probability of an event a by counting. If Ω is the set of all possible events, $P(\Omega) = 1$, then $a \in \Omega$. The cardinality determines the number of elements of a set, $card(\Omega)$ is the number of elements of the set Ω, $card(a)$ is the number of elements of the set a and

$$P(a) = \frac{card(a)}{card(\Omega)}. \tag{9.18}$$

Now we can define the posterior probability, the probability of a after the evidence b is obtained

$$P(a|b) = \frac{card(a \wedge b)}{card(b)}. \tag{9.19}$$

The posterior probability is also called the conditional probability. From

$$P(a \wedge b) = \frac{card(a \wedge b)}{card(\Omega)} \tag{9.20}$$

and

$$P(b) = \frac{card(b)}{card(\Omega)} \tag{9.21}$$

we get

$$P(a|b) = \frac{P(a \wedge b)}{P(b)} \tag{9.22}$$

and

$$P(b|a) = \frac{P(a \wedge b)}{P(a)}. \tag{9.23}$$

9.4.2 *Bayes's rule*

The Bayes's rule follows from both equations

$$P(b|a) = \frac{P(a|b) \cdot P(b)}{P(a)}. \tag{9.24}$$

For mutually exclusive events $b_1, ..., b_n$ with

$$\sum_{i=1}^{n} P(b_i) = 1 \tag{9.25}$$

the law of total probability is represented by

$$P(a) = \sum_{i=1}^{n} P(a) \wedge P(b_i), \tag{9.26}$$

$$P(a) = \sum_{i=1}^{n} P(a|b_i) \cdot P(b_i). \tag{9.27}$$

Bayes rule can be used to determine the prior total probability $P(h)$ of hypothesis h to given data D.

- $P(D|h)$ is the probability that a hypothesis h generates the data D. $P(D|h)$ can be easily estimated. For example, what is the probability that some illness generates some symptoms?
- The probability that an illness is present given certain symptoms, can be then determined by the Bayes rule

$$P(h|D) = \frac{P(D|h) \cdot P(h)}{P(D)}. \tag{9.28}$$

The most probable hypothesis h_i out of a set of possible hypothesis $h_1, h_2, \cdots$ given some present data is according to the Bayes rule

$$P(h_i|D) = \frac{P(D|h_i) \cdot P(h_i)}{P(D)}. \tag{9.29}$$

To determine the maximum posteriori hypothesis h_{MAP} we maximize

$$h_{map} = argmax_{h_i} \frac{P(D|h_i) \cdot P(h_i)}{P(D)}. \tag{9.30}$$

The maximization is independent of $P(D)$, it follows

$$h_{map} = argmax_{h_i} P(D|h_i) \cdot P(h_i). \tag{9.31}$$

Given the scores x and y

$$x = P(D|h) \cdot P(h), \quad z = P(D|\neg h) \cdot P(\neg h)$$

the probabilities $P(h|D)$ and $P(\neg h|D)$ can be determined by normalization, talking into account $1 = P(h|D) + P(\neg h|D)$.

9.4.3 Joint distribution

The joint distribution for n possible variables is described by 2^n possible combinations. The probability distribution $d_1 \times d_2 \times \cdots \times d_n$ corresponds to a vector of length 2^n. For a joint distribution of n possible variables, the exponential growth of combinations being true or false becomes an intractable problem for large n. For

$$P(h_i|d_1, d_2, d_3, .., d_n) = \frac{P(d_1, d_2, d_3, ..., d_n|h_i) \cdot P(h_i)}{P(d_1, d_2, d_3, ..., d_n)} \tag{9.32}$$

all $2^n - 1$ possible combinations must be known. There are two possible solutions to this problem. A simple solution is the decomposition of large probabilistic domains into weakly connected subsets via conditional independence,

$$P(d_1, d_2, d_3, ..., d_n|h_i) = \prod_{j=1}^{n} P(d_j|h_i). \tag{9.33}$$

This approach is known as the Naïve Bayes assumption and is one of the most important developments in the recent history of Artificial Intelligence. It assumes that a single cause directly influences a number of events, all of which are conditionally independent,

$$h_{map} = argmax_{h_i} \prod_{j=1}^{n} P(d_j|h_i) \cdot P(h_i). \tag{9.34}$$

However, this conditional independence is very restrictive. Often, it is not present in real life events.The Naïve Bayes approach is related to simple counting if we follow the frequentist approach [Wichert (2013a)]. For maximum a posteriori hypothesis h_{map}

$$h_{map} = argmax_{h_i} \prod_{j=1}^{n} P(d_j|h_i) \cdot P(h_i) \tag{9.35}$$

Ω is a set of all possible events

$$P(h_i) = \frac{card(h_i)}{card(\Omega)} \tag{9.36}$$

and

$$P(d_j|h_i) = \frac{card(d_j \wedge h_i)}{card(h_i)}, \tag{9.37}$$

$$h_{map} = argmax_{h_i} \prod_{j=1}^{n} \frac{card(d_j \wedge h_i)}{card(h_i)} \cdot \frac{card(h_i)}{card(\Omega)}. \tag{9.38}$$

Because Ω is a set of all possible events it does not play a role in the process maximization of h_{map}

$$h_{map} = argmax_{h_i} \prod_{j=1}^{n} card(d_j \wedge h_i) \tag{9.39}$$

we can apply *log*

$$h_{map} = argmax_{h_i} \log \left(\prod_{j=1}^{n} card(d_j \wedge h_i) \right), \tag{9.40}$$

$$h_{map} = argmax_{h_i} \sum_{j=1}^{n} \log \left(card(d_j \wedge h_i) \right). \tag{9.41}$$

For the process of maximization h_{map} we can simply write

$$h_{map} = argmax_{h_i} \sum_{j=1}^{n} card(d_j \wedge h_i). \tag{9.42}$$

9.4.4 Probability ranking principle

Let R represent relevance of a document d of a collection for a fixed query and let NR represent the non-relevance [Manning *et al.* (2008)]. With $p(R)$ and $p(NR) = p(\neg R)$ prior probability of retrieving a relevant non-relevant document. With the known probability $p(x|R)$ that a relevant document that is retrieved is x and the probability $p(x|\neg R)$ and $p(x)$ we get according to the Bayes's rule

$$P(R|x) = \frac{P(x|R) \cdot P(R)}{P(x)}.$$ (9.43)

and

$$P(\neg R|x) = \frac{P(x|\neg R) \cdot P(\neg R)}{P(x)}$$ (9.44)

with

$$P(R|x) + P(\neg R|x) = 1.$$ (9.45)

d is relevant if

$$P(R|x) > P(\neg R|x).$$

For given documents and a query we order documents by decreasing probability.

9.4.5 Binary independence model

Binary models the documents are represented as binary incidence vectors of terms as in the binary query model [Manning *et al.* (2008)]. A one represents a term at the corresponding position of a binary vector, its absence is denoted by a zero.

$$\mathbf{x} = (x_1, x_2, x_3, \cdots, x_n)$$ (9.46)

with $x_i = 1$ if *term$_i$* is present in document otherwise 0 and $\mathbf{x}_k$ being a document from the collection of s documents. It is also supposed that the terms occur in documents independently. For a query y represented by the binary vector

$$\mathbf{y} = (y_1, y_2, y_3, \cdots, y_n)$$ (9.47)

we could compute the Hamming distance to the document $\mathbf{x}$. Instead we define the similarity using odds and Bayes' rule

$$sim(\mathbf{x}, \mathbf{y}) = \frac{p(R|\mathbf{y}, \mathbf{x})}{p(\neg R|\mathbf{y}, \mathbf{x})} = \frac{\frac{p(R|\mathbf{y}) \cdot p(\mathbf{x}|R, \mathbf{y})}{p(\mathbf{x}|\mathbf{y})}}{\frac{p(\neg R|\mathbf{y}) \cdot p(\mathbf{x}|\neg R, \mathbf{y})}{p(\mathbf{x}|\mathbf{y})}}$$ (9.48)

it follows

$$sim(\mathbf{x}, \mathbf{y}) = \frac{p(R|\mathbf{y})}{p(\neg R|\mathbf{y})} \cdot \frac{p(\mathbf{x}|R, \mathbf{y})}{p(\mathbf{x}|\neg R, \mathbf{y})}. \tag{9.49}$$

For a given query $\mathbf{y}$

$$\frac{p(R|\mathbf{y})}{p(\neg R|\mathbf{y})}$$

is constant, it is independent of $\mathbf{x}$. We need to estimate

$$\frac{p(\mathbf{x}|R, \mathbf{y})}{p(\mathbf{x}|\neg R, \mathbf{y})}.$$

With the independence assumption we get

$$\frac{p(\mathbf{x}|R, \mathbf{y})}{p(\mathbf{x}|\neg R, \mathbf{y})} = \prod_{i=1}^{n} \frac{p(x_i|R, y_i)}{p(x_i|\neg R, y_i)} \tag{9.50}$$

and

$$\prod_{i=1}^{n} \frac{p(x_i|R, y_i)}{p(x_i|\neg R, y_i)} = \prod_{x_i=1} \frac{p(x_i|R, y_i)}{p(x_i|\neg R, y_i)} \cdot \prod_{x_i=0} \frac{p(x_i|R, y_i)}{p(x_i|\neg R, y_i)}. \tag{9.51}$$

With

$$p_i = p(x_i = 1|R, y_i = 1), \quad r_i = p(x_i = 1|\neg R, y_i = 1) \tag{9.52}$$

we get

$$\prod_{x_i=1} \frac{p(x_i|R, y_i)}{p(x_i|\neg R, y_i)} \cdot \prod_{x_i=0} \frac{p(x_i|R, y_i)}{p(x_i|\neg R, y_i)} = \prod_{x_i=y_i=1} \frac{p_i}{r_i} \cdot \prod_{(x_i=0) \wedge (y_i=1)} \frac{1 - p_i}{1 - r_i} \tag{9.53}$$

$(x_i = 0) \wedge (y_i = 1)$ takes into account non matching query terms, $y_i = 1$ without the x_i condition takes into account all query terms,

$$\prod_{x_i=y_i=1} \frac{p_i}{r_i} \cdot \prod_{x_i=0, y_i=1} \frac{1 - p_i}{1 - r_i} = \prod_{x_i=y_i=1} \frac{p_i \cdot (1 - r_i)}{r_i \cdot (1 - p_i)} \cdot \prod_{y_i=1} \frac{1 - p_i}{1 - r_i}. \tag{9.54}$$

For a given query $\mathbf{y}$

$$\prod_{y_i=1} \frac{1 - p_i}{1 - r_i}$$

is constant because it takes into account all query terms. We need to estimate

$$\prod_{x_i=y_i=1} \frac{p_i \cdot (1 - r_i)}{r_i \cdot (1 - p_i)}, \tag{9.55}$$

of which the logarithmic value is called the retrieval status RSV and is given by

$$RSV = \log\left(\prod_{x_i=y_i=1} \frac{p_i \cdot (1-r_i)}{r_i \cdot (1-p_i)}\right) = \sum_{x_i=y_i=1} \log\left(\frac{p_i \cdot (1-r_i)}{r_i \cdot (1-p_i)}\right). \quad (9.56)$$

With

$$c_i = \log\left(\frac{p_i \cdot (1-r_i)}{r_i \cdot (1-p_i)}\right) \quad (9.57)$$

we rewrite RSV as

$$RSV = \sum_{x_i=y_i=1} c_i. \quad (9.58)$$

We can estimate c_i. For the whole document collection of s documents count the number of documents with

- α_i: the number of all documents with $x_i = 1, R, y_i = 1$.
- β_i: the number of all documents with $x_i = 0, R, y_i = 1$.
- γ_i: the number of all documents with $x_i = 1, \neg R, y_i = 1$.
- δ_i: the number of all documents with $x_i = 0, \neg R, y_i = 1$.

We can then estimate

$$p_i = \frac{\alpha_i}{\alpha_i + \beta_i}, \quad (1-p_i) = \frac{\beta_i}{\alpha_i + \beta_i}, \quad (9.59)$$

$$r_i = \frac{\gamma_i}{\gamma_i + \delta_i}, \quad (1-r_i) = \frac{\delta_i}{\gamma_i + \delta_i}, \quad (9.60)$$

and c_i

$$c_i = \log\left(\frac{p_i \cdot (1-r_i)}{r_i \cdot (1-p_i)}\right) = \log\left(\frac{\alpha_i \cdot \delta_i}{\beta_i \cdot \gamma_i}\right) = \log\left(\frac{\alpha_i/\beta_i}{\gamma_i/\delta_i}\right), \quad (9.61)$$

and we get the relation

$$c_i = \log\left(\alpha_i/\beta_i\right) - \log\left(\gamma_i/\delta_i\right). \quad (9.62)$$

In the next step we indicate the relation to idf_t. With

$$c_i = \log\left(\frac{(1-r_i) \cdot p_i}{r_i \cdot (1-p_i)}\right) = \log\left(\frac{(1-r_i)}{r_i}\right) + \log\left(\frac{p_i}{(1-p_i)}\right) \quad (9.63)$$

if we assume that

$$\log\left(\frac{p_i}{(1-p_i)}\right) = 0,$$

it means that only non-relevant documents are approximated by the whole collection, then

$$\log\left(\frac{(1-r_i)}{r_i}\right) = \log\left(\frac{\beta_i + \delta_i}{\alpha_i + \gamma_i}\right) \tag{9.64}$$

and

$$s \approx \beta_i + \delta_i. \tag{9.65}$$

The documents that contain the trem df_t represented by the position at the at x_i are

$$df_t \approx \alpha_i + \gamma_i \tag{9.66}$$

and

$$p(term_t) = \frac{df_t}{s} \approx \frac{\alpha_i + \gamma_i}{s} \tag{9.67}$$

and

$$idf_t = -log_2(p(term_t)) = \log_2\left(\frac{s}{df_t}\right) \approx \log\left(\frac{(1-r_i)}{r_i}\right). \tag{9.68}$$

The probability of occurrence in relevant documents p_i can be estimated from relevant documents. If relevant documents are unknown, we can assume that p_i is constant over all x_i in query and interact with the user to refine the description of p_i. The user will indicated whether the retrieved document is important or not. The interaction will be repeated several times thus generating a succession of approximations of p_i and r_i.

9.4.5.1 *Conclusion*

The binary Independence model is based on a firm theoretical foundation, like for example the optimal ranking scheme. However the model is less popular then the vector model due its disadvantages:

- the term independence,
- boolean representation of document queries and relevance,
- document relevance values are independent and if unknown difficult to determine.

9.4.6 *Stochastic language models*

The the Naïve Bayes classifier is based on the Naïve Bayes assumption to determine the maximum posteriori hypothesis. It is supposed that a document $document_k$ causes terms $term_i$ that are conditionally independent. For terms the maximum posteriori hypothesis for the document is

$$document_{map} = argmax_{document_k} \prod_{i=1}^{n} P(term_i|document_k) \cdot P(document_k).$$
$$(9.69)$$

For mutually exclusive events I_1, I_2 with

$$\sum_{k=1}^{2} P(I_k) = 1 \qquad (9.70)$$

the law of total probability is represented by

$$P(term) = \sum_{r=1}^{2} P(term|I_r) \cdot P(I_r) \qquad (9.71)$$

and

$$P(term_i) = \sum_{r=1}^{2} P(term_i|I_{i,r}) \cdot P(I_{i,r}). \qquad (9.72)$$

with $P(I_{i,1})$ indicating the importance and $P(I_{i,2})$ the unimportance of the ith query term with I being a binary variable. Then we can reformulate the maximum posteriori hypothesis for the document taken into account the mutually exclusive events $I_{i,1}, I_{i,2}$ that the document $document_k$ causes terms $term_i$ that are conditionally independent. For terms the maximum posteriori hypothesis for the document is

$$document_{map} =$$

$$\prod_{i=1}^{n} \left(\sum_{r=1}^{2} P(term_i|I_{i,r}, document_k) \cdot P(I_{i,r}) \right) \cdot P(document_k). \qquad (9.73)$$

The method is called the stochastic language model and was proposed by Djoerd Hiemstra [Hiemstra (2001)]. The language query terms can be determined as follows:

- $P(document_k)$ can be assumed to be equal for all documents. For a collection of s documents the value is

$$P(document_k) = \frac{1}{s}$$

and corresponds to a normalisation factor.

- $P(term_i|I_{i,1}, document_k)$ important term is defined by the term frequency of a term in a document divided by the length of the document.
- $P(term_i|I_{i,2}, document_k) = P(term_i|I_{i,2})$ an unimportant term is defined by the number occurrences of the term in the collection divided by the total length of the collection. It is related to the inverse suprise of the term.
- $P(I_{i,1})$ and $P(I_{i,2})$ have to be learned or estimated. We have to interact with the user to estimate the values.

9.5 Associative Memory

The Lernmatrix, also simply called "associative memory", was developed by Steinbuch in 1958 as a biologically inspired model from the effort to explain the psychological phenomenon of conditioning [Steinbuch (1961, 1971)]. Later this model was studied under biological and mathematical aspects by G. Palm [Palm (1982, 1990); Fransén (1996); Wennekers (1999)]. It was shown that Donald Hebb's hypothesis of cell assemblies as a biological model of internal representation of events and situations in the cerebral cortex corresponds to the formal associative memory model. We call the Lernmatrix simply "associative memory" if no confusion with other models is possible. Associative memory models human memory [Palm (1990); Churchland and Sejnowski (1994); Fuster (1995); Squire and Kandel (1999)]. *"Human memory is based on associations with the memories it contains. Just a snatch of well-known tune is enough to bring the whole thing back to mind. A forgotten joke is suddenly completely remembered when the next-door neighbor starts to tell it again. This type of memory has previously been termed content-addressable, which means that one small part of the particular memory is linked - associated -with the rest."* Cited from [Brunak and Lautrup (1990)]. Associative memory is an ideal model for the information retrieval task. It is composed of a cluster of units which represent a simple model of a real biological neuron (see fig. 9.1).

The unit is composed of weights which correspond to the synapses and dentrides in the real neuron. They are described by w_{ij} in fig. 9.2. T is the threshold of the unit.

The patterns are represented by binary vectors. The presence of a feature is indicated by a "one" component of the vector, its absence through a "zero" component of the vector. Two pairs of these vectors are always associated and this process of association is called learning. The first of

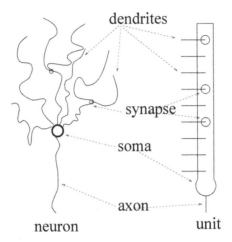

Fig. 9.1   A unit is an abstract model of a biological neuron [McClelland and Kawamoto (1986); Palm (1990); Hertz *et al.* (1991); OFTA (1991); Schwenker (1996)].

the two vectors is called the question vector and the second, the answer vector. After learning, the question vector is presented to the associative memory and the answer vector difference is determined. This process is called association.[2]

9.5.1   *Learning and forgetting*

In the initialization phase of the associative memory no information is stored. Because the information is represented in the weights, they are all initially set to zero. In the learning phase, binary vector pairs are associated. Let $\mathbf{x}$ be the question vector and $\mathbf{y}$ the answer vector, so that the learning rule is:

$$w_{ij}^{new} = w_{ij}^{old} + y_i x_j.$$

This rule is called the binary unclipped Hebb rule [Palm (1982)]. Every time a pair of binary vectors is stored this rule is used. Therefore, in each weight of the associative memory the frequency of the correlation between the components of the vectors is stored. This is done to ensure the capability to "forget" vectors which were once learned. In this case, the following

---

[2]In the literature often a distinction between heteroassociation and association is made. An association is present when the answer vector represents the reconstruction of the faulty question vector. An heteroassociation is present if both vectors are different.

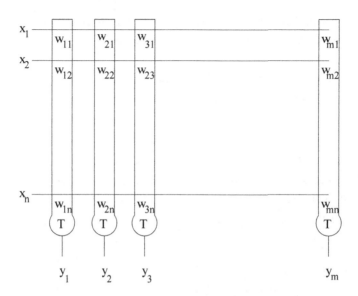

Fig. 9.2   The associative memory is composed of a cluster of units [Palm (1990); Palm *et al.* (1992)].

binary anti-Hebb rule [van Hemmen (1990)] is used:

$$w_{ij}^{new} = \begin{cases} w_{ij}^{old} - y_i x_j & \text{if } w_{ij}^{old} > 0 \\ w_{ij}^{old} & \text{if } w_{ij}^{old} = 0 \end{cases}$$

There is also the possibility to delete information described by two vectors:

$$w_{ij}^{new} = \begin{cases} 0 & \text{if } y_i x_j = 1 \\ w_{ij}^{old} & \text{if } y_i x_j = 0 \end{cases}$$

9.5.2   *Retrieval*

In the retrieval phase of the associative memory, a fault tolerant answering mechanism recalls the appropriate answer vector for a question vector $\mathbf{x}$. To the presented question vector $\mathbf{x}$ the most similar learned $\mathbf{x}^l$ question vector regarding the hamming distance is determined and the appropriate answer vector $\mathbf{y}$ is identified. For the retrieval rule the knowledge about the correlation of the components is sufficient, and the knowledge about the frequency of the correlation is not used. The retrieval rule for the determination of the answer vector y is:

$$y_i = \begin{cases} 1 & \sum_{j=1}^{n} \delta(w_{ij}x_j) \geq T \\ 0 & \text{otherwise.} \end{cases}$$

with

$$\delta(x) = \begin{cases} 1 & \text{if } x > 0 \\ 0 & \text{if } x = 0 \end{cases}$$

T_i is the threshold of the unit. There are many possibilities for its determination. For the two described strategies $\geq$ in retrieval equation can be replaced with $=$.

9.5.2.1 The hard threshold strategy

In the hard threshold strategy, the threshold T is set to the number of "one" components in the question vector. If one uses this strategy it is quite possible that no answer vector is determined. This happens when the question vector has a subset of components which were not correlated with the answer vector. This means that only the subset of the learned question vector is recognized, provided that the overlapping of learned patterns is not considered.

9.5.2.2 The soft threshold strategy

In this strategy, the threshold is set to the maximum sum $\sum_{j=1}^{n} \delta(w_{ij}x_j)$:

$$T :=_{max\ i} \sum_{j=1}^{n} \delta(w_{ij}x_j)$$

In this strategy, there is no answer in the case that all components of the question vector are not correlated, or, in other words, if the maximum sum is zero.

9.5.3 Analysis

Storage capacity   For an estimation of the asymptotic number of vector-pairs $(\vec{x}, \vec{y})$ which can be stored in an associative memory before it begins to make mistakes in retrieval phase, it is assumed that both vectors have the same dimension n. It is also assumed that both vectors are composed of M 1s, which are likely to be in any coordinate of the vector. In this case it was shown [Palm (1982); Hecht-Nielsen (1989); Sommer (1993)] that the optimum value for M is approximately

$$M \doteq \log_2(n/4)$$

and that approximately [Palm (1982); Hecht-Nielsen (1989)]

$$L \doteq (\ln 2)(n^2/M^2)$$

of vector pairs can be stored in the associative memory. This value is much greater then n if the optimal value for M is used. In this case, the asymptotic storage capacity of the Lernmatrix model is far better than those of other associative memory models, namely 69.31%. This capacity can be reached with the use of sparse coding, which is produced when very small number of 1s is equally distributed over the coordinates of the vectors [Palm (1982); Stellmann (1992)]. For example, in the vector of the dimension n=1000000 M=18, ones should be used to code a pattern. The real storage capacity value is lower when patterns are used which are not sparse or are strongly correlated to other stored patterns.

9.5.4 *Implementation*

The associative memory can be implemented using digital [Palm and Bon-hoeffer (1984); Palm (1993); Palm *et al.* (1997)] or optical hardware [Will-shaw *et al.* (1969); Kohonen (1989); Gniadek (1992); Lee *et al.* (1995)]. On a serial computer a pointer representation can save memory space if the weight matrix is not overloaded [Bentz *et al.* (1989)]. This fact is important when the weight matrix becomes very large. In the pointer format only the positions of the vector components unequal to zero are represented. This is done, because most synaptic weights are zero. For example, the binary vector [0 1 0 0 1 1 0] is represented as the pointer vector (2 5 6), which represents the positions of "ones". For a matrix each row is represented as a vector. The pointer matrix does not consider the information of frequency, it represents only the positions of components unequal to zero in the corresponding row.

For an unclipped weight matrix the frequencies are represented additionally by the shadow matrix. For each position in the pointer matrix, a corresponding number in the shadow matrix represents the frequency. For example, the vector [0 1 0 0 7 3 0] is represented by the pointer vector (2 5 6) as before, and by the additional shadow vector (1 7 3). This representation can still save memory space if the weight matrix is not overloaded.

An example of the representation of an unclipped weight matrix by the pointer matrix representing positions of components unequal to zero, and the shadow matrix representing for each position in the pointer matrix the corresponding frequency:

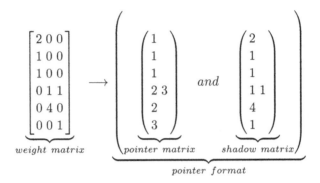

$$
\underbrace{\begin{bmatrix} 2\,0\,0 \\ 1\,0\,0 \\ 1\,0\,0 \\ 0\,1\,1 \\ 0\,4\,0 \\ 0\,0\,1 \end{bmatrix}}_{\textit{weight matrix}} \longrightarrow \underbrace{\left(\underbrace{\begin{pmatrix} 1 \\ 1 \\ 1 \\ 2\,3 \\ 2 \\ 3 \end{pmatrix}}_{\textit{pointer matrix}} \textit{and} \underbrace{\begin{pmatrix} 2 \\ 1 \\ 1 \\ 1\,1 \\ 4 \\ 1 \end{pmatrix}}_{\textit{shadow matrix}} \right)}_{\textit{pointer format}}
$$

9.6   Applications

A set of features can be represented by a binary vector and represent a category. A position in the corresponding vector corresponds to a feature. To be sparse, the set of features that describes a category compared to the dimension of the vector has to be sufficiently small. This is because, of all possible features, only some should define categories, a category corresponds to a document or document class.

9.6.1   *Inverted index*

Inverted index for IR can be represented directly by an associative memory. For real data the matrix that represents the inverted list becomes very big and is extremely sparse. The input of a query vector represents the present terms, the determined address is assigned to the corresponding documents. he ability to correct faults if false information is given. By the ability to correct faults if false information is given and complete information if some parts are missing the most similar documents can be determined. We can use the hard threshold strategy to determine only the documents that have exactly the query terms or the soft threshold strategy to determine the most similar documents.

9.6.2 *Spell checker*

In this application, with the aid of the associative memory, an unambiguous address is assigned to each word with possible type errors. The ideas for the used robust mechanism come from psychology and biology [Wickelgren (1969, 1977); Rumelhart and McClelland (1986); Bentz *et al.* (1989)]. Words are represented as sequences of context-sensitive letter units. Each letter in a word is represented as a triple, which consists of the letter itself, its predecessor, and its successor. For example, the word *desert* is encoded by six context-sensitive letters, namely: _de, des, ese, ser, ert, rt_. The character "_" marks the word beginning and ending. Because the alphabet is composed of 26+1 characters, 27^3 different context-sensitive letters exist. In the 27^3 dimensional binary vector each position corresponds to a possible context-sensitive letter, and a word is represented by indication of the actually present context-sensitive letters. Similarly written words are represented by similarly coded binary vectors, so that type errors can be tolerated. A context-sensitive letter does not need to be a triple. It can also be a tupel consisting of the letter itself and its predecessor. Tupel representation of the context-sensitive letters is more ambiguous than the representation with the triples, but it does not require as much storage space. There are only 27^2 possible tupels. In an implementation, one must find a balance between the use of storage space and the ambiguity of the word representation. In general, a context-sensitive letter can consist of any number of letters, but only the numbers two, three (Wickelfeature) and four letters seem useful. Each word and address is represented by a unit [McClelland and Kawamoto (1986); Bentz *et al.* (1989)]. The stored binary weights represent the presence or absence of a context-sensitive letter, and the unit indicates the corresponding address. Each time a new word is entered, it is tested tp see if it was already stored. The coded vector which describes this word is posed at the corresponding positions and for each unit, the sum of the product of the corresponding ones of this vector and weights is calculated. The observer is then notified about each name whose feature sum is maximal (see fig. 9.3). In the case that the word was not recognized, it is learned through the extension of the associative memory by a new unit which represents the new word [Steinbuch (1971)].

When an associative word interface (short *awi*) is integrated in bigger systems, two operation modes are needed. In the first mode, a word is entered and the address is determined. In the second, the address is given and the word that belongs to it is identified. A word could be reconstructed

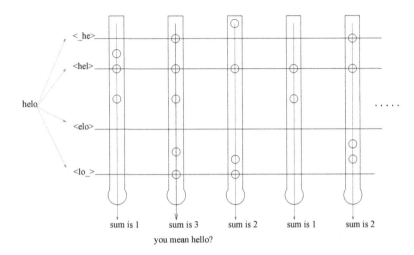

sum is 1   sum is 3   sum is 2   sum is 1   sum is 2

you mean hello?

Fig. 9.3   Assignment of an address to a misspelled word.

unambiguously with a set of given Wickelfeatures [Rumelhart and Mc-Clelland (1986)], but not with a set of given tupel representations. In our approach, each word is represented through context-sensitive letters and additionally as strings of characters. The first representation is used when a word is entered and an address is determined as stated earlier; the second representation is used to display a word when an address is given. In string representation [Anderson (1995)], each symbol of the alphabet has an unequivocal number, for example as with the ASCII code. This number is represented as a one-of-N code (the position of the one represents the number). The whole string is represented as a one behind the other representation of the symbols.

Chapter 10

Statistical Supervised Machine Learning

Several parallels between human learning and machine learning exist. Some of the techniques are inspired from the efforts of psychologists and biologists to simulate human learning via computational models. In addition to statistical machine learning, other forms of machine learning, such as inductive learning, knowledge learning, analogical learning and reinforcement learning, exist but will not be addressed in this chapter.

10.1 Statistical Machine Learning

In unsupervised learning, the algorithm groups input information that is primarily represented by vectors into groups without additional information. The algorithm attempts to find the hidden structure of unlabelled data; k-means clustering is an example of this algorithm. In supervised learning, the algorithm is presented with example inputs and their desired outputs and the goal is to learn a general rule that maps inputs to outputs. Supervised learning is frequently referred to as learning with teacher because the desired outputs are indicated by a specific type of teacher. Consequently, unsupervised learning is referred to learning without a teacher.

10.1.1 *Supervised learning*

In supervised learning, which is important in feature description, categories can be learned and labeled by known examples. Labels include as faces, nonfaces, man-made objects and nonman-made objects. Images can be labeled by classifiers using keywords that enable searching for text descriptions. In information retrieval, a classifier can be trained by labeled examples to distinguish between relevant documents and irrelevant documents.

In statistical supervised machine learning we try to learn a function $f : R^n \to R^m$,

$$\mathbf{y} = f(\mathbf{x}) \tag{10.1}$$

that is described by a sample of training data D_t of the data set D

$$D_t = \{(\mathbf{x}_1, \mathbf{y}_1), (\mathbf{x}_2, \mathbf{y}_2), \cdots ,, (\mathbf{x}_N, \mathbf{y}_N)\} \tag{10.2}$$

called training data set. The learned hypothesis h representing the function f can be then used for mapping new examples. The hypothesis h representing the function f has to generalize from the training data set to unseen data points. It is validated on unseen validation data set D_v of the data set D

$$D_v = \{(\mathbf{x}_1', \mathbf{y}_1'), (\mathbf{x}_2', \mathbf{y}_2'), \cdots ,, (\mathbf{x}_M', \mathbf{y}_M')\} \tag{10.3}$$

with

$$\emptyset = D_t \cap D_v, \quad D \supset D_t, \quad D \supset D_v.$$

The validated is done by comparing the hypothesis h outputs

$$\mathbf{o}_k = h(\mathbf{x}_k') \tag{10.4}$$

with correct values $\mathbf{y}_k'$ of the validation data set D_v by the mean squared error

$$MSE_{Dv}(h) = \sum_{k=1}^{M} \|\mathbf{y}_k' - \mathbf{o}_k\|^2. \tag{10.5}$$

10.1.2 *Overfitting*

The smaller the $MSE(D_v)$ the better the hypothesis h describing the function f. We can define the mean squared error for the training data set D_t

$$MSE_{Dt}(h) = \sum_{k=1}^{M} \|\mathbf{y}_k - \mathbf{o}_k\|^2, \tag{10.6}$$

usually

$$MSE_{Dv}(h) > MSE_{Dt}(h).$$

If we have two hypothesis h_1 and h_2 with

$$MSE_{Dt}(h_1) < MSE_{Dt}(h_2), \quad MSE_{Dv}(h_1) > MSE_{Dv}(h_2). \tag{10.7}$$

then we say that the hypothesis h_1 overfits the training data set D_t, h_1 fits better the training examples than h_2, but performs more poorly over examples it didn't learn. It seems as h_1 learned by heart D_t and not the topological structure that describe the function f, on the other hand h_2 learned the corresponding structure and can generalise [Mitchell (1997)].

Based on perceptrons, we introduce the back-propagation algorithm and the radial-basis function networks, where both may be constructed by the support-vector-learning algorithm. Because the models are inspired by the human brain (see Figure 10.1). We describe first the artificial neuron model that is more complex then unit that was introduced during the introduction of the associative memory.

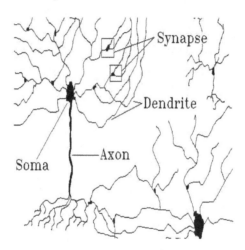

Fig. 10.1 The supervised learning models are inspired by the neurons of the human brain.

10.2 Artificial Neuron

Having two vectors of the same dimension n, the vector $\mathbf{x}$ representing a pattern and the vector $\mathbf{w}$ representing some stored pattern (weights) we can define the similarity between them by the cosine similarity

$$\cos \omega = \frac{\langle \mathbf{x} | \mathbf{w} \rangle}{\|\mathbf{x}\| \cdot \|\mathbf{w}\|} \tag{10.8}$$

with a similarity function

$$0 \leq sim(\mathbf{x}, \mathbf{w}) = \cos \omega \leq 1, \qquad (10.9)$$

similarity function as used in information retrieval (IR). If we do not normalise the vectors, then we get the simple scalar product also called the dot product

$$\langle \mathbf{x} | \mathbf{w} \rangle = \cos \omega \cdot \|\mathbf{x}\| \cdot \|\mathbf{w}\|, \qquad (10.10)$$

it is measure of the projection of one vector onto another. The dot product of a vector with a unit vector is the projection of that vector in the direction given by the unit vector. The dot product is a linear representation represented by the value *net*, see Figure 10.2.

$$y = net := \langle \mathbf{x} | \mathbf{w} \rangle = \sum_{i=1}^{n} w_i \cdot x_i, \qquad (10.11)$$

Non linearity can be achieved be a non liner transfer function $\phi()$ with

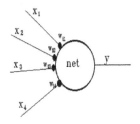

Fig. 10.2 A model of an artificial neuron (unit).

$$o = \phi(net) = \phi(\langle \mathbf{x} | \mathbf{w} \rangle) = \phi\left(\sum_{i=1}^{n} w_i \cdot x_i\right). \qquad (10.12)$$

Examples of nonlinear transfer functions are the *sgn* function

$$\phi(net) := sgn(net) = \begin{cases} 1 & \text{if} \quad net \geq 0 \\ -1 & \text{if} \quad net < 0 \end{cases}, \qquad (10.13)$$

it gives -1 or 1 depending on whether *net* is negative, or positive with zero, see Figure 10.3. The *sgn(net)* operation is related to the threshold

(a)   (b)

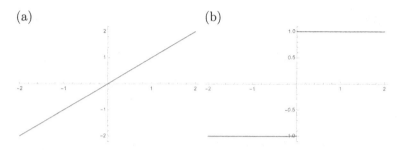

Fig. 10.3   (a) Linear transfer function. (b) Nonlinear *sgn* function gives −1 or 1 depending on whether *net* is negative, or positive with zero.

operation of a real biological neuron with −1 not firing and 1 firing, see Figure 10.3. Because of that an artificial neuron is a mathematical function $\phi(net)$ conceived as a model of biological neuron. The transfer function is also called the activation function. The *sgn* activation function can be scaled to the two values 0 or 1 for not firing and firing,

$$\phi(net) := sgn_0(net) = \begin{cases} 1 \text{ if } net \geq 0 \\ 0 \text{ if } net < 0 \end{cases} \tag{10.14}$$

Both non linear function $sgn(net)$ and $sgn_0(net)$ are non continuous. The activation function $sgn_0(net)$ can be approximated by the non linear continuous function $\sigma(net)$

$$\phi(net) := \sigma(net) = \frac{1}{e^{(-\alpha \cdot net)}} \tag{10.15}$$

in which the value α determines its steepness, see Figure 10.4. For *s* artificial neurons an index *k* is used with

$$k \in \{1, 2, \cdots, s\}$$

to identify the wight vector $\mathbf{w}_k$ and the *k*the outputt o_k of the neuron.

$$o_k = \phi(net_k) = \phi(\langle \mathbf{x} | \mathbf{w}_k \rangle) = \phi \left(\sum_{i=1}^{n} w_{k,i} \cdot x_i \right). \tag{10.16}$$

10.3   Perceptron

The perceptron algorithm was invented in 1957 by Frank Rosenblatt [Rosenblatt (1962)], it is represented by the McCulloch-Pitts model of a neuron. The model of the neuron is represented by the linear threshold unit (LTU)

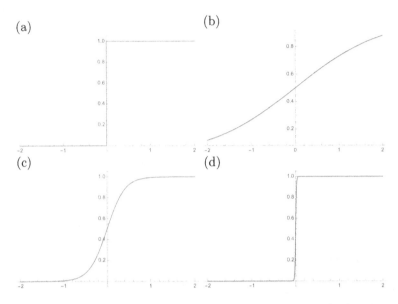

Fig. 10.4   (a) The activation function $sgn_0(net)$. (b) The function $\sigma(net)$ with $\alpha = 1$. (c) The function $\sigma(net)$ with $\alpha = 5$. (d) The function $\sigma(net)$ with $\alpha = 10$ is very similar to $sgn_0(net)$, bigger α make it even more similar.

described by the mathematical function $sgn_0(net_0)$ with $x_0 = 1$ [Hecht-Nielsen (1989); Hertz *et al.* (1991)],

$$net_0 := \sum_{i=0}^{n} w_i \cdot x_i = \sum_{i=1}^{n} w_i \cdot x_i + w_0 = \langle \mathbf{x}|\mathbf{w}\rangle + w_0 \cdot x_0 \qquad (10.17)$$

and

$$o = sgn_0(net_0) = \phi(net_0). \qquad (10.18)$$

The value x_0 is called the "bias", it is a constant value that does not depend on any input value. The goal of the perceptions is to correctly classify the set of pattern into one of the classes $C_0 = 0$ and $C_1 = 1$

$$D = \{(\mathbf{x}_1, y_1), (\mathbf{x}_2, y_2), \cdots, , (\mathbf{x}_N, y_N)\} \qquad (10.19)$$

with

$$y_k \in \{0, 1\},$$

the output for class C_0 is $o = 0$ and for C_1 is $o = 1$ with

$$o = sgn_0\left(\sum_{i=0}^{n} w_i \cdot x_i\right) = sgn_0\left(\langle \mathbf{x}|\mathbf{w}\rangle + w_0 \cdot x_0\right) \qquad (10.20)$$

and $x_0 = 1$. Simplified, the perceptron is an algorithm for learning of a function $f(\mathbf{x})$

$$f(\mathbf{x}) = \begin{cases} 1 \text{ if } & \langle \mathbf{x} | \mathbf{w} \rangle + b \geq 0 \\ 0 & \text{otherwise,} \end{cases} \tag{10.21}$$

with

$$b := w_0$$

that describes a hyperplane in n dimensional space with

$$-b = \langle \mathbf{x} | \mathbf{w} \rangle \tag{10.22}$$

or

$$0 = \langle \mathbf{x} | \mathbf{w} \rangle + b. \tag{10.23}$$

The hyperplane is described by $\mathbf{w}$ and b. The perceptron considers only linearly separable problems. It determines the correct weights by supervised learning. Perceptron learning algorithm verifies, if for the input $\mathbf{x}_k$ the output value o_k belongs to the desired class represented by y_k and modifies the weights if required with the learning rule

$$w_i^{new} = w_i^{old} + \Delta w_i \tag{10.24}$$

and

$$\Delta w_i = \eta \cdot (y_k - o_k) \cdot x_i, \tag{10.25}$$

$(y_k - o_k)$ plays the role of the error signal with being either zero, 1 or -1 and η is called the learning rate with

$$0 < \eta \leq 1.$$

The algorithm converges to the correct classification, if the training data is linearly separable and η is sufficiently small.

10.3.1 *Gradient descent*

If the training data is not linearly separable, the perceptron learning algorithm can fail to converge. However the delta rule that is based on the gradient descent overcomes these difficulties. To understand, consider simpler linear unit with a linear activation function

$$o = \sum_{i=0}^{n} w_i \cdot x_i = net_0. \tag{10.26}$$

We can define the training error for a training data set D_t of N elements with

$$E(\mathbf{w}) = \frac{1}{2} \cdot \sum_{k=1}^{N} (y_k - o_k)^2 = \frac{1}{2} \cdot \sum_{k=1}^{N} \left(y_k - \sum_{i=0}^{n} w_i \cdot x_{k,i} \right)^2 . \qquad (10.27)$$

The training error is function of $\mathbf{w}$, with $\mathbf{w} = (w_0, w_1)$ we can represent all possible values as a two dimensional function, see Figure 10.5. The function corresponds to the error surface with a minimum. The task of the learning algorithm is to determine the corresponding minimum. We can find the

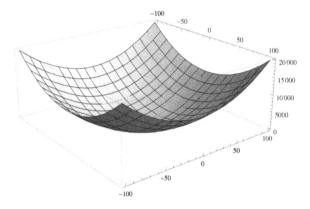

Fig. 10.5 The training error is function of $\mathbf{w}$, with $\mathbf{w} = (w_0, w_1)$ we can represent all possible values as a two dimensional function The x-axis represents w_0, the y-axis represents w_1 and the z-axis the value $E(\mathbf{w}) = E((w_0, w_1))$. The function corresponds to the error surface with a minimum. The task of the learning algorithm is to determine the corresponding minimum. The error surface as defined by $E(\mathbf{w})$ contains only one global minimum.

solution without the need to determine all possible $\mathbf{w}$ value combinations by an optimization algorithm, namely the gradient descent [Mitchell (1997)]. To find a local minimum of a function $E(\mathbf{w})$ using gradient descent, one takes steps proportional to the negative of the gradient

$$-\nabla E(\mathbf{w}) = - \left(\frac{\partial E}{\partial w_0}, \frac{\partial E}{\partial w_1}, \cdots, \frac{\partial E}{\partial w_n} \right) \qquad (10.28)$$

of the function at the current point. One starts the process at some randomly chosen point $\mathbf{w}^{initial}$ and modifies the weights if required with the learning rule

$$\mathbf{w}^{new} = \mathbf{w}^{old} + \Delta \mathbf{w} \qquad (10.29)$$

with

$$w_i^{new} = w_i^{old} + \Delta w_i \qquad (10.30)$$

and

$$\Delta \mathbf{w} = -\eta \cdot -\nabla E(\mathbf{w}) \qquad (10.31)$$

with

$$\Delta w_i = -\eta \cdot \frac{\partial E}{\partial w_i}. \qquad (10.32)$$

The weight vector is moved by η within the direction that decrease $E(\mathbf{w})$, η is called the learning rate. For a sufficiently small η the algorithm will converge to a solution, because the error surface defined by $E(\mathbf{w})$ contains only one global minimum. For to large η the search could overstep the minimum in the error surface. The value

$$\frac{\partial E}{\partial w_i} = \frac{\partial}{\partial w_i} \frac{1}{2} \cdot \sum_{k=1}^{N} (y_k - o_k)^2 = \frac{1}{2} \cdot \sum_{k=1}^{N} \frac{\partial}{\partial w_i} (y_k - o_k)^2 \qquad (10.33)$$

is given by

$$\frac{\partial E}{\partial w_i} = \frac{1}{2} \cdot \sum_{k=1}^{N} 2 \cdot (y_k - o_k) \cdot \frac{\partial}{\partial w_i} (y_k - o_k) \qquad (10.34)$$

$$\frac{\partial E}{\partial w_i} = \sum_{k=1}^{N} (y_k - o_k) \cdot \frac{\partial}{\partial w_i} \left(y_k - \sum_{i=0}^{n} w_i \cdot x_{k,i} \right) \qquad (10.35)$$

$$\frac{\partial E}{\partial w_i} = \sum_{k=1}^{N} (y_k - o_k) \cdot (-x_{k,i}) \qquad (10.36)$$

$$\frac{\partial E}{\partial w_i} = -\sum_{k=1}^{N} (y_k - o_k) \cdot x_{k,i}. \qquad (10.37)$$

The update rule for gradient decent is given by

$$\Delta w_i = \eta \cdot \sum_{k=1}^{N} (y_k - o_k) \cdot x_{k,i}. \qquad (10.38)$$

10.3.2 *Stochastic gradient descent*

The gradient decent training rule updates summing over all N training examples. Stochastic gradient approximates gradient decent by updating weights incrementally and calculating the error for each example according to the update rule by

$$\Delta w_i = \eta \cdot (y_k - o_k) \cdot x_{k,i}. \tag{10.39}$$

This rule is known as delta-rule or LMS (last mean-square) weight update This rule is used in Adaline (Adaptive Linear Element) for adaptive filters and was developed by Widroff and Hoff [Widrow and Hoff (1960)], [Widrow and Hoff (1962)].

10.3.3 *Continuous activation functions*

For continuous activation function $\phi()$

$$o_k = \phi\left(\sum_{i=0}^{n} w_i \cdot x_{ik,}\right). \tag{10.40}$$

we can define as well the update rule for gradient decent with the differential

$$\frac{\partial E}{\partial w_i} = \sum_{k=1}^{N} (y_k - o_k) \cdot \frac{\partial}{\partial w_i}\left(y_k - \phi\left(\sum_{i=0}^{n} w_i \cdot x_{k,i}\right)\right) \tag{10.41}$$

$$\frac{\partial E}{\partial w_i} = \sum_{k=1}^{N} (y_k - o_k) \cdot \left(-\phi'\left(\sum_{i=0}^{n} w_i \cdot x_{k,i}\right) \cdot x_{k,i}\right) \tag{10.42}$$

$$\frac{\partial E}{\partial w_i} = -\sum_{k=1}^{N} (y_k - o_k) \cdot \phi'\left(\sum_{i=0}^{n} w_i \cdot x_{k,i}\right) \cdot x_{k,i}. \tag{10.43}$$

For the non linear continuous activation function $\sigma()$

$$o_k = \sigma\left(\sum_{i=0}^{n} w_i \cdot x_{k,i}\right) \tag{10.44}$$

we can define as well the update rule for gradient decent with the differential

$$\sigma(x)' = \alpha \cdot \sigma(x) \cdot (1 - \sigma(x)) \tag{10.45}$$

we get

$$\frac{\partial E}{\partial w_i} = \sum_{k=1}^{N} (y_k - o_k) \cdot \frac{\partial}{\partial w_i}\left(y_k - \sigma\left(\sum_{i=0}^{n} w_i \cdot x_{k,i}\right)\right) \tag{10.46}$$

$$\frac{\partial E}{\partial w_i} = -\alpha \cdot \sum_{k=1}^{N} (y_k - o_k) \cdot \sigma \left(\sum_{i=0}^{n} w_i \cdot x_{k,i} \right) \cdot \left(1 - \sigma \left(\sum_{i=0}^{n} w_i \cdot x_{k,i} \right) \right) \cdot x_{k,i}.$$

(10.47)

$$\frac{\partial E}{\partial w_i} = -\alpha \cdot \sum_{k=1}^{N} (y_k - o_k) \cdot \sigma \left(net_{k,i} \right) \cdot \left(1 - \sigma \left(net_{k,i} \right) \right) \cdot x_{k,i}.$$

(10.48)

10.4 Networks with Hidden Nonlinear Layers

The limitations of a simple perceptron do not apply to feed-forward networks with hidden nonlinear units. An example of a feed-forward network with one hidden layer is shown in Figure 10.6. The input pattern is represented by the five-dimensional vector $\mathbf{x}$; nonlinear hidden units compute the output V_1, V_2, V_3 and two output units compute the output o_1 and o_2. The units V_1, V_2, V_3 are referred to as hidden units because we cannot see their outputs and cannot directly perform error correction [Hertz *et al.* (1991)]. Feed-forward networks with hidden nonlinear units are universal approximators; they can approximate every bounded continuous function

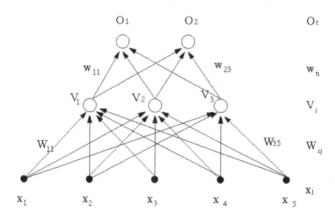

Fig. 10.6 The input pattern is represented by the five-dimensional vector $\mathbf{x}$; nonlinear hidden units compute the output V_1, V_2, V_3 and two output units compute the output o_1 and o_2. The units V_1, V_2, V_3 are referred to as hidden units because we cannot see their outputs and cannot directly perform error correction.

with an arbitrarily small error. Each Boolean function can be represented by a network with a single hidden layer. However, the representation may require an exponential number of hidden units. The hidden units should be nonlinear because multiple layers of linear units can only produce linear functions. The output layer of a feed-forward network can be trained by the perceptron rule. For simplification, we employ the notation in Figure 10.6,

$$\Delta w_{ti} = \eta \cdot (y_{k,t} - o_{k,t}) \cdot V_{k,i}. \tag{10.49}$$

For continuous activation function $\phi()$

$$o_{k,t} = \phi\left(\sum_{i=0}^{3} w_{ti} \cdot V_{k,i}\right). \tag{10.50}$$

and

$$E(\mathbf{w}) = \frac{1}{2} \cdot \sum_{t=1}^{2}\sum_{k=1}^{N}(y_{kt} - o_{kt})^2 = \frac{1}{2} \cdot \sum_{t=1}^{2}\sum_{k=1}^{N}\left(y_{kt} - \phi\left(\sum_{i=0}^{3} w_{ti} \cdot V_{k,i}\right)\right)^2. \tag{10.51}$$

we get

$$\frac{\partial E}{\partial w_{ti}} = -\sum_{k=1}^{N}(y_{kt} - o_{kt}) \cdot \phi'\left(\sum_{i=0}^{n} w_{ti} \cdot V_{k,i}\right) \cdot V_{k,i}. \tag{10.52}$$

For the nonlinear continuous function $\sigma()$

$$\frac{\partial E}{\partial w_{ti}} = -\alpha \cdot \sum_{k=1}^{N}(y_{kt} - o_{kt}) \cdot \sigma(net_{k,t}) \cdot (1 - \sigma(net_{k,t})) \cdot V_{k,i} \tag{10.53}$$

and

$$\Delta w_{ti} = \eta \cdot \alpha \cdot \sum_{k=1}^{N}(y_{kt} - o_{kt}) \cdot \sigma(net_{k,t}) \cdot (1 - \sigma(net_{k,t})) \cdot V_{k,i}. \tag{10.54}$$

10.4.1   *Backpropagation*

We can determine the Δw_{ti} for the output units, but how can we determine ΔW_{ij} for the hidden units? If the hidden units use a continuous non linear activation function $\phi()$

$$V_{k,i} = \phi\left(\sum_{j=0}^{5} W_{ij} \cdot x_{k,j}\right). \tag{10.55}$$

we can define the training error for a training data set D_t of N elements with

$$E(\mathbf{w}, \mathbf{W}) = \frac{1}{2} \cdot \sum_{k=1}^{N} \sum_{t=1}^{2} (y_{kt} - o_{kt})^2 \tag{10.56}$$

$$E(\mathbf{w}, \mathbf{W}) = \frac{1}{2} \cdot \sum_{k=1}^{N} \sum_{t=1}^{2} \left(y_{kt} - \phi \left(\sum_{i=0}^{3} w_{ti} \cdot V_{k,i} \right) \right)^2 \tag{10.57}$$

$$E(\mathbf{w}, \mathbf{W}) = \frac{1}{2} \cdot \sum_{k=1}^{N} \sum_{t=1}^{2} \left(y_{kt} - \phi \left(\sum_{i=0}^{3} w_{ti} \cdot \phi \left(\sum_{j=0}^{5} W_{ij} \cdot x_{k,j} \right) \right) \right)^2 . \tag{10.58}$$

We already know

$$\frac{\partial E}{\partial w_{ti}} = - \sum_{k=1}^{N} (y_{kt} - o_{kt}) \cdot \phi'(net_{k,t}) \cdot V_{k,i}. \tag{10.59}$$

For $\frac{\partial E}{\partial W_{ij}}$ we can use the chain rule and we obtain

$$\frac{\partial E}{\partial W_{ij}} = \sum_{k=1}^{N} \frac{\partial E}{\partial V_{ki}} \cdot \frac{\partial V_{ki}}{\partial W_{ij}}. \tag{10.60}$$

with

$$\frac{\partial E}{\partial V_{ki}} = - \sum_{k=1}^{N} \sum_{t=1}^{2} (y_{kt} - o_{kt}) \cdot \phi'(net_{k,t}) \cdot w_{t,i}. \tag{10.61}$$

and

$$\frac{\partial V_{ki}}{\partial W_{ij}} = \phi'(net_{k,i}) \cdot x_{k,j} \tag{10.62}$$

it follows

$$\frac{\partial E}{\partial W_{ij}} = - \sum_{k=1}^{N} \sum_{t=1}^{2} (y_{kt} - o_{kt}) \cdot \phi'(net_{k,t}) \cdot w_{t,i} \cdot \phi'(net_{k,i}) \cdot x_{k,j}. \tag{10.63}$$

The algorithm is called back propagation because we can reuse the computation that was used to determine Δw_{ti},

$$\Delta w_{ti} = \eta \cdot \sum_{k=1}^{N} (y_{kt} - o_{kt}) \cdot \phi'(net_{k,t}) \cdot V_{k,i}. \tag{10.64}$$

and with

$$\delta_{kt} = (y_{kt} - o_{kt}) \cdot \phi'(net_{k,t}) \tag{10.65}$$

we can write

$$\Delta w_{ti} = \eta \cdot \sum_{k=1}^{N} \delta_{kt} \cdot V_{k,i}. \tag{10.66}$$

and

$$\Delta W_{ij} = \eta \sum_{k=1}^{N} \sum_{t=1}^{2} (y_{kt} - o_{kt}) \cdot \phi'(net_{k,t}) \cdot w_{t,i} \cdot \phi'(net_{k,i}) \cdot x_{k,j} \tag{10.67}$$

we can simplify (reuse the computation) to

$$\Delta W_{ij} = \eta \sum_{k=1}^{N} \sum_{t=1}^{2} \delta_{kt} \cdot w_{t,i} \cdot \phi'(net_{k,i}) \cdot x_{k,j}. \tag{10.68}$$

With

$$\delta_{ki} = \phi'(net_{k,i}) \cdot \sum_{t=1}^{2} \delta_{kt} \cdot w_{t,i} \tag{10.69}$$

we can simply to

$$\Delta W_{ij} = \eta \sum_{k=1}^{N} \delta_{ki} \cdot x_{k,j}. \tag{10.70}$$

This approach can be extended to any numbers of layers [Hertz *et al.* (1991)]. The coefficient are usual forward, but the errors represented by δ are propagated backward. Backpropagation algorithm will find a local, not necessarily global error minimum. This is because the error surface defined by $E(\mathbf{w}, \mathbf{W})$ can have many local minima beside the global minimum. The found minima depends on the initial start of the gradient decent that is defined by random values of the initial weights. Stochastic gradient descent can some times over come this problem. Additionally multiple nets can be trained with different initial weights preforming a blind search for the possible global minimum. The gradient descent can be very slow if η is to small, and can oscillate widely if η is to large. Training can take thousands of iterations and is slow, however the classification after training is very fast.

10.4.2   *Radial basis function network*

Feed-forward networks with hidden nonlinear units are universal approximators, this is as well true for the radial basis function network (RBF) [Haykin (2008)]. It shares this property with feed forward networks with hidden layer of nonlinear units. For simplification we will use the notation of the Figure 10.6. We can determine the Δw_{ti} for the output units as before. In the radial basis function network the hidden units represent the radial basis function

$$V_{k,i} = e^{\frac{-\|\mathbf{W}_i - \mathbf{x}_k\|^2}{2 \cdot \sigma^2}} = e^{\frac{-(\mathbf{W}_i - \mathbf{x}_k)^T \cdot (\mathbf{W}_i - \mathbf{x}_k)}{2 \cdot \sigma^2}} \qquad (10.71)$$

which is related to the Gaussian. Every hidden unit has a receptive field defined by the basis-function

$$\mathbf{W}_i = \mathbf{x}_k$$

with maximum output $V_{k,i}$. The output $V_{k,i}$ for other values drops as $\mathbf{x}_k$ deviates from $\mathbf{W}_i$. The output has a significant response to the input $\mathbf{x}_k$ only over a range of values called receptive field, The size of the receptive field is defined by σ, $\mathbf{W}_i$ may be called mean and σ standard deviation and the function

$$e^{\frac{-\|\mathbf{W}_i - \mathbf{x}_k\|^2}{2 \cdot \sigma^2}}$$

is radially symmetric around the mean $\mathbf{W}_i$.

10.4.2.1 *Training*

The values $\mathbf{W}_i$ can be determined by k-means clustering over the training set, $\mathbf{W}_i$ represent the k centroids

$$\mathbf{W}_i := \mathbf{c}_i.$$

In the example of Figure 10.6, $k = 3$. Each determined centroid corresponds the centre $\mathbf{W}_i$ of a receptive field of a hidden unit. The aim is to cover the input space with receptive fields of the size σ. If the spacing is not uniform, it may be necessary for each hidden unit to have its own σ_i with

$$V_{k,i} = e^{\frac{-(\mathbf{W}_i - \mathbf{x}_k)^T \cdot (\mathbf{W}_i - \mathbf{x}_k)}{2 \cdot \sigma_i^2}}. \qquad (10.72)$$

Each cluster C_i contains the points that are closest to the centroid $\mathbf{c}_i = \mathbf{W}_i$, it is defined as the set of points with

$$C_i = \{\mathbf{x} | d_2(\mathbf{x}, \mathbf{W}_i) = \min_t d_2(\mathbf{x}, \mathbf{W}_t)\}. \qquad (10.73)$$

For each hidden unit σ_i can be chosen as the root mean square (RMS) between the centroid and the the the set of points inside the cluster

$$\sigma_i = \sum_{x \in C_i} \sqrt{\frac{1}{|C_i|} \|\mathbf{x} - \mathbf{W}_i)\|^2}. \qquad (10.74)$$

10.4.3   *Why does a feed-forward networks with hidden non-linear units work?*

The hidden layer applies a nonlinear transformation from the input space to the hidden space. In the hidden space a linear discrimination can be performed, for example by a perceptron. The transformation of the hidden space is actually a mapping into a higher dimensional space in which the separation by a hyperplane into two classes C_0 and C_1 is possible. The higher dimensional space is hidden in the non linear operation of the hidden units. This operation can be seen as a kernel function that computes the inner product between the two vectors $\mathbf{W}_i$ and $\mathbf{x}_k$ of dimension n in in a higher dimensional space h,

$$n < h.$$

Kernel methods owe their name to the use of kernel functions, which enable them to operate in a high-dimensional, implicit feature space without ever computing the coordinates of the data in that space, but rather by simply computing the inner products between the images of all pairs of data in the feature space. For example the polynomial kernel function computes the inner product between the two vectors $\mathbf{x}$ and $\mathbf{y}$ of dimension two

$$K(\mathbf{x}, \mathbf{y}) = (1 + x_1 \cdot y_1 + x_2 \cdot y_2)^2 \tag{10.75}$$

and corresponds to the scalar product of the five dimensional feature space described by the mapping $\vartheta()$

$$\vartheta(\mathbf{x}) = \left(1, \sqrt{2} \cdot x_1, \sqrt{2} \cdot x_2, x_1^2 \cdot x_2^2, \sqrt{2} \cdot x_1 \cdot x_2\right) \tag{10.76}$$

and

$$\vartheta(\mathbf{y}) = \left(1, \sqrt{2} \cdot y_1, \sqrt{2} \cdot y_2, y_1^2 \cdot y_2^2, \sqrt{2} \cdot y_1 \cdot y_2\right) \tag{10.77}$$

given by

$$\langle \vartheta(\mathbf{x}) | \vartheta(\mathbf{y}) \rangle = K(\mathbf{x}, \mathbf{y}) = (1 + x_1 \cdot y_1 + x_2 \cdot y_2)^2 \tag{10.78}$$

The inner product can be computed by $K(\mathbf{x}, \mathbf{y})$ without going through the map $\vartheta(\mathbf{x})$ and $\vartheta(\mathbf{y})$ [Haykin (2008)]. This relation is also known as the kernel trick. By specifying the kernel function $K(\mathbf{x}, \mathbf{y})$ we specify as well the mapping $\vartheta(\mathbf{x})$ and $\vartheta(\mathbf{y})$. Examples of kernel functions are the radial basis function as used by the RBF networks and the sigmoid kernel function which is related to the sigmoid function that is used in the back propagation algorithm.

10.5   Cross-Validation

In supervised machine learning, the introduced algorithms have the two hypotheses h_1 and h_2, which represent two architectures with different parameters

$$MSE_{Dt}(h_1) < MSE_{Dt}(h_2), \quad MSE_{Dv}(h_1) > MSE_{Dv}(h_2), \qquad (10.79)$$

We suggest that the hypothesis h_1 overfits the training data set D_t and h_1 achieves a better fit with the training examples compared with h_2 but performs poorly with examples that it did not learn. How can we prevent overfitting? We can measure performance over training data and stop the learning procedure once the performance worsens [Haykin (2008)]. To determine the correct parameters, such as the number of hidden units or the number of layers, we can measure the performance over separate validation data sets. Cross-validation enables us to estimate the accuracy of a hypothesis induced by a supervised learning algorithm. It enables us to predict the accuracy of a hypothesis over future unseen instances and to select the optimal hypothesis from a given set of alternative hypotheses (best architecture). The partition of the data set D into a training data set D_t and the validation data set D_v can cause an insufficient use of data and both sets may be correlated. The k-fold cross-validation splits the data set D into k mutually exclusive subsets $D_1, D_2, \cdots, D_k$ The algorithm is trained and tested k times; each time, it is trained on $D - D_i$ and tested on D_i. For $k = 4$, we divide the dataset D into four subsets

$$D = D_1 \cup D_2 \cup D_3 \cup D_4. \qquad (10.80)$$

A complete k-fold cross-validation, splits the dataset of size s in all s/k possible ways (selecting s/k instances out of s), whereas the folds are stratified in stratified cross-validation to ensure that they contain approximately the same proportion of labels as the original data set. For $k = 4$ the algorithm is trained and validated 4 times;

- trained on $D_2 \cup D_3 \cup D_4$ and validated on D_1,
- trained on $D_1 \cup D_3 \cup D_4$ and validated on D_2,
- trained on $D_1 \cup D_2 \cup D_4$ and validated on D_3,
- trained on $D_1 \cup D_2 \cup D_3$ and validated on D_4.

10.6   Support Vector Machine

Support vector machine (SVM) is a useful alternative to neural networks, the algorithm has no biological motivation. The SVM algorithm represents a constrained optimization problem, it may construct polynomial learning machines, radial-basis functions networks and two-layer perceptrons [Haykin (2008)].

10.6.1   *Linear support vector machine*

Simplified, the perceptron is an algorithm for learning of a function $f(\mathbf{x})$ that describes a hyperplane in n dimensional space with

$$0 = \langle \mathbf{x}|\mathbf{w}\rangle + b. \qquad (10.81)$$

For linearly separable data we can select two hyperplanes distance

$$1 = \langle \mathbf{x}|\mathbf{w}\rangle + b \qquad (10.82)$$

$$-1 = \langle \mathbf{x}|\mathbf{w}\rangle + b \qquad (10.83)$$

in a way that they separate the data and there are no points between them. We then try to maximize the distance m

$$m = \frac{2}{\|\mathbf{w}\|} \qquad (10.84)$$

between them. To maximize the distance m we have to minimizing $\|\mathbf{w}\|$. The SVM classifies the set of pattern into one of the classes $C_0 = -1$ and $C_1 = 1$

$$D = \{(\mathbf{x}_1, y_1), (\mathbf{x}_2, y_2), \cdots, , (\mathbf{x}_N, y_N)\} \qquad (10.85)$$

with

$$y_k \in \{-1, 1\},$$

and with the decision boundary

$$y_k \cdot (\langle \mathbf{x}|\mathbf{w}\rangle + b) \geq 1 \qquad (10.86)$$

This can be expressed as a constrained optimization problem

$$Minimize \; \frac{1}{2} \cdot \|\mathbf{w}\|^2 \qquad (10.87)$$

subject to

$$y_k \cdot (\langle \mathbf{x}|\mathbf{w}\rangle + b) \geq 1$$

The problem can be transformed with Lagrange multipliers to its dual without changing the solution, In this form it is a quadratic programming optimization problem and can be solved by standard quadratic programming techniques.

10.6.2 *Soft margin*

The soft margin method permits mislabeled examples by allowing an error ξ_k in the classification of $\mathbf{x}_k$ ($\xi_k = 0$ if there is no error in the classification). The algorithm chooses a hyperplane that splits the examples as cleanly as possible, while still maximizing the distance to the nearest cleanly split examples. In the optimization theory ξ_k are celled the slack variables with

$$\xi_k \geq 0$$

$$\langle \mathbf{x}|\mathbf{w}\rangle + b \geq 1 - \xi_k \quad if \quad y_k = 1$$

$$\langle \mathbf{x}|\mathbf{w}\rangle + b \leq -1 + \xi_k \quad if \quad y_k = -1.$$

The constraint optimization problemis with C being a tradeoff parameter between error and margin

$$Minimize \quad \frac{1}{2} \cdot \|\mathbf{w}\|^2 + C \cdot \sum_{k=0}^{N} \xi_k \tag{10.88}$$

subject to

$$y_k \cdot (\langle \mathbf{x}|\mathbf{w}\rangle + b) \geq 1 - \xi_k, \quad \xi_k \geq 0.$$

Again the problem can be transformed with Lagrange multipliers to its dual without changing the solution, In this form it is a quadratic programming optimization problem and can be solved by standard quadratic programming techniques.

10.6.3 *Kernel machine*

Kernel machine is a name for a nonlinear support vector machine. The difference between a linear support vector machine and a kernel machine is that the scalar product is replaced by a nonlinear kernel function

$$0 = K(\mathbf{x},\mathbf{y}) + b = \langle \vartheta(\mathbf{x})|\vartheta(\mathbf{y})\rangle + b. \tag{10.89}$$

This allows the algorithm to fit the maximum-margin hyperplane in a transformed feature space [Haykin (2008)].

10.7   Deep Learning

Deep learning enables high-level abstractions in data by architectures composed of multiple nonlinear transformations. It offers a natural progression from low-level structures to high-level structure, as demonstrated by natural complexity [LeCun and Bengio (1998); Riesenhuber *et al.* (1999); Riesenhuber and Poggio (2000, 2002)]. Hubel and Wiesel's discoveries have inspired several models for pattern recognition [Hubel (1988)]. In these models, the neural units have a local view unlike the common fully connected networks. Neocognitron [Fukushima (1980, 1988, 2001)] was the first model of pattern recognition. It has local receptive fields, which indicates the existence of a local view in the network elements. It gradually reduces the information from the input layer to the output layer by integrating local features into more global features in sequential transformations. Its purpose is to classify topological data by gradually reducing the information from the input layer to the output layer. Each of these transformations is composed of two different steps. The first step reduces the information by representing it with previously learned templates, which are represented by S-cells (resemble simple cells). The second step blurs the information with C-cells (resemble complex cells) to enable positional shifts and give the model some invariance using shifts and distortions.

10.7.1   *Map transformation cascade*

A less complex description of the the Neocognitron is the hierarchical neural network called map transformation cascade [Wichert; Kemke and Wichert (1993); Cardoso and Wichert (2010)]. The information is processed sequentially, each layer only processes information after the previous layer is finished. The input is tiled with a squared mask, where each sub-pattern is replaced by a number indicating a corresponding class. By doing so, we get a representation of the pattern in the class space. The mask has the same behavior in all different positions, resembling the weight-sharing mechanism in Neocognitron. In the following step, the class representation of the pattern is transformed by losing the exact positional information. The corresponding representation of the pattern in the class space is tiled with a squared mask, eliminating the positional information of each class inside the mask. The layers of a Map Transformation Cascade can be seen as filters, since they have a clear and interpretable output, which is a modification of the input information. Several filters transform and map the input pattern into a space where patterns of the same class are close. The output of the filters is then passed to a simple classifier, which produces a classification for the input pattern. The Map Transformation Cascade model is also as the Neocognitron composed of two types of cells, simple and complex. A layer is a set of cells of the same type.

10.7.1.1 *S-layer*

The S-layer corresponds to a layer of simple cells in the visual cortex. It maps the input into the class space [Cardoso and Wichert (2010)]. The input is tiled with a squared mask, where each sub-pattern is replaced by a number indicating a corresponding class. The masks that tile the pattern may overlap. The S-layer learning is performed by a clustering algorithm like k-Means, see Figure 10.7 and Figure 10.8. During mapping,

Fig. 10.7   Example of a binary input pattern .

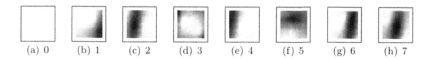

(a) 0   (b) 1   (c) 2   (d) 3   (e) 4   (f) 5   (g) 6   (h) 7

Fig. 10.8   (a) Represents the background information by the class 0. (b) to (h) represent the seven learned classes by $1, 2, 3, 4, 5, 6, 7$.

the corresponding sub-patterns of an input pattern are mapped into the corresponding classes. The binary input pattern is tiled with a squared mask M of size $j \times j$. The tiling can be generated dynamically by scanning a mask over the input pattern. In each position, a mask is applied to the input, and the sub-pattern is compared with the previously learned classes. For each position, the input is mapped into the most similar class represented by the index i (between 0 and k). The index 0 represents the background, by convention, and the indices 1 to k represent other classes. For each sub-pattern $\mathbf{x}$ the most similar class i is determined according to the Euclidean distance:

$$\{i|\min_i d(\mathbf{x}, \mathbf{c}_i), i \in \{0, 1, ..., k\}\}. \tag{10.90}$$

In Figure 10.9 we see the representation of Figure 10.7 in the class space.

0	0	0	0	0	0	0	0	0	0	0	0	0	0	0	0	0	0	0	0
0	0	0	0	0	0	0	3	3	1	1	3	3	3	0	0	0	0		
0	0	0	0	0	3	1	1	1	1	1	1	3	3	3	0	0	0		
0	0	0	0	3	1	1	1	1	5	5	1	7	2	3	3	0	0		
0	0	0	3	1	1	7	3	5	5	5	5	5	2	4	3	0	0		
0	0	3	1	1	7	5	5	5	5	5	5	5	7	2	4	0	0		
0	0	3	1	6	7	2	4	3	3	3	1	6	7	2	4	3	0		
0	0	1	6	7	2	4	3	0	0	0	3	6	7	2	4	3	0		
0	3	1	6	7	2	4	3	0	0	0	3	6	7	2	4	3	0		
0	3	1	7	2	4	3	0	0	0	0	3	6	7	2	4	3	0		
0	1	6	7	2	4	3	0	0	0	0	1	6	7	2	4	3	0		
0	1	6	7	2	4	0	0	0	0	0	1	6	7	2	4	3	0		
0	1	6	7	2	4	0	0	0	0	3	1	6	7	4	4	0	0		
0	1	6	7	2	3	0	0	0	3	1	6	7	2	4	3	0	0		
0	1	6	7	2	4	3	3	3	1	1	7	7	2	4	3	0	0		
0	1	6	7	2	4	1	1	1	1	7	7	2	4	3	0	0	0		
0	3	6	5	5	1	1	1	7	7	5	5	3	3	3	0	0	0		
0	3	3	5	5	5	5	5	5	5	5	3	3	3	0	0	0	0		
0	0	3	3	5	5	5	5	5	4	3	3	0	0	0	0	0	0		
0	0	0	3	3	3	3	3	3	3	3	0	0	0	0	0	0	0		
0	0	0	0	0	0	0	0	0	0	0	0	0	0	0	0	0	0		

Fig. 10.9   The representation of the pattern of Figure 10.7 in the class space. Only the information in the center, where the pattern is represented, is shown here. The background information is represented by 0.

10.7.1.2   C-layer

The C-layer, which corresponds to a layer of complex cells in the visual cortex, transforms the input it receives from the S-layer. The transformation performed by the C-layer is fixed and can be not modified. Its purpose is to allow positional shifts, thus giving the model shift invariance. The class representation of a pattern is tiled with a squared mask, eliminating the positional information of each class inside the mask. The class representation of a pattern is tiled m times with a squared mask M of size $l \times l$. In each position, a vector c_h, with $h \in \{1, 2, ..., m\}$, of dimensions $l \times l$, is determined. The vector c_h describes the presence of some classes inside the mask M. There are two categories of classes: The classes that describe the presence of some features, and the background class represented by zero. The transformation function in the first step eliminates zeros from the corresponding vector. After the first step, the vector represents the classes without exact positional information. In the next step, there are several possible alternatives. We could apply the mode, defined in statistics. The mode is the value that occurs most frequently. The mode is not unique, since the same maximum frequency may be attained at different values. For example the mode of $\{1, 6, 3, 6, 3, 3, 3\}$ is $\{3\}$, but the mode of $\{1, 6, 3, 6, 3\}$ is $\{3, 6\}$. However the mode eliminates too much important information; for example the vector $\{1, 6, 3, 6, 3, 3, 3\}$ indicates the presence of several classes, 1, 3 and 6. Instead of using the mode, we eliminate the frequency information for each present class. As a result the position and frequency information of the classes inside the mask are discarded. The same operation is performed by the C-cells of Neocognitron. Figure 10.10 shows the input into a C-layer mask. The output of the C-layer mask for this position will be the set of all present classes. The background and the frequency information is discarded by the C-layer [Cardoso and Wichert (2010)].

0	0	0	1	6
0	0	0	3	6
0	0	0	3	3
0	0	0	0	3
0	0	0	0	0

Fig. 10.10   C-layer mask input in a given position when scanning Figure 10.9, its output is $\{1, 6, 3\}$. It indicates the presence of these classes.

The output of a mask of a C-layer is represented by a binary vector. A 'one' represents a class at the corresponding position of a binary vector; its absence is denoted by a 'zero'. The class set $\{1, 2, 3, 4, 5, 6, 7\}$ is represented by a binary vector of dimension 7. The presence of the classes $\{1, 6, 3\}$ is represented by the binary vector $\mathbf{u} = [1\ 0\ 1\ 0\ 0\ 1\ 0]$, with ones in the corresponding positions 1, 3, and 6. We call this vector the unsharp vector. The class representation of a pattern is transformed into an unsharp class representation. For p classes, we get a unshrap vector $\mathbf{u}$ of dimension p. The more ones are present in the unsharp vector $\mathbf{u}$, the more information is lost. The result of a transformation of m squared masks M covering a class pattern is a $(m \times p)$-dimensional binary unsharp class vector $\mathbf{U}$. This binary vector is composed of m unsharp vectors

$$\mathbf{U} = (\mathbf{u}_1, \mathbf{u}_2, ..., \mathbf{u}_m).$$

10.7.1.3 *Cascade*

The two layers are highly related, since the output of the C-layer is just a blurred version of the S-layer output. There are two different categories the input layer and hidden layer, which differ in their input type. In the input layer, the input is a binary pattern; in the hidden layer, it is the representation of the pattern in the class space. The layers of a Map Transformation Cascade can be seen as filters, since they have clear and interpretable output that is a transformation of the input information. Several filters map and transform the input pattern into a space where patterns of the same class are close [Cardoso and Wichert (2010)].

10.7.1.4 *Output layer*

The output of the filters is then passed to a supervised classifier in the output layer.

10.7.1.5 *Experiments*

The Map Transformation Cascade (MTC) shows good generalization for a small number of training examples and achieved performance similar to that of Neocognitron in combination with a simple nearest neighbour in the output layer. The combination of MTC and a linear SVM achieves competitive results, greatly improves the results relatively to using a deep belief network with a linear SVM [Cardoso and Wichert (2013)]. The proposed MTC network achieved as well a higher noise tolerance than some of related models [Cardoso and Wicher (2014)].

10.7.2 *Relation between deep learning and subspace tree*

We demonstrate that deep learning is intimately related to a subspace tree. In a simplified MTC model without a C-layer, we have to distinguish between two different representations during image retrieval: the class space and the re-projection space. The class space of a layer is the representation sub-pattern in a mask by a number that indicates that a corresponding class as employed by the MTC during the classification. The dimension of a class space is dependent on the size of the mask and the hierarchy. The re-projection space, which is employed during image retrieval, is the representation of the image by the corresponding features by backward projection; it has the same dimension as the input image [Wichert (2009a)]. The re-projection space of the preceding layer as the input for the following layer forms the quantized representation, as shown in Figure 10.11. During similarity-based image retrieval, the search begins with the images that are represented by global features. In this representation, the set of all possible similar images is determined. In the next stage, additional information that corresponds to the representation of more local features is used to reduce this set, which is represented by specific triggered units. This procedure is repeated until similar images can be determined.

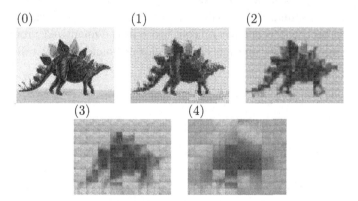

Fig. 10.11 Gray image (0) and its quantized representation (1-4) with a hierarchy of four S-layers.

10.7.2.1 *Hierarchical quantization*

We group the sub-vectors of dimension $p = dim(m/f)$ into clusters represented by the cluster centres c_j of dimension p. We assume that all sub-quantizers have the same number k of clusters and represent vectors by the corresponding cluster centres:

$$U(\;\mathbf{x}) = \underbrace{c_{i1}, c_{i2}, \cdots, c_{ip}}_{u_1(\mathbf{x})=c_{1(x)}=c_i}, \cdots, \underbrace{c_{j1}, \cdots, c_{jp}}_{u_f(\mathbf{x})=c_{f(x)}=c_j} \qquad (10.91)$$

To a query vector y we determine the most similar vector x of the database using the qunatizied codes and the Euclidean distance function d.

$$d(U(\mathbf{x}), U(\mathbf{y})) = \sqrt{\sum_{t=1}^{f} d(u_t(\mathbf{x}), (u_t(\mathbf{y}))^2} = \sqrt{\sum_{t=1}^{f} d(c_{t(x)}, c_{t(y)})^2} \qquad (10.92)$$

By using $d(U(\mathbf{x}), U(\mathbf{y}))$ instead of $d(\mathbf{x}, \mathbf{y})$ an estimation *error* is produced:

$$d(U(\mathbf{x}), U(\mathbf{y})) + error = d(\mathbf{x}, \mathbf{y}) \qquad (10.93)$$

To determine ϵ similar vectors according to the Euclidean distance to a given query y, we have to compute $d(\mathbf{x}, \mathbf{y})$ for all vectors x out of the database. If the distances computed by the quantized product $d(U(\mathbf{x}), U(\mathbf{y}))$ are smaller or equal than the distances in the original space $d(\mathbf{x}, \mathbf{y})$, a lower bound which is valid in both spaces can be determined. The distance of similar objects is smaller or equal to ϵ in the original space and, consequently, it is smaller or equal to ϵ in the quantized product as well. Because of the estimation error the lower bound is only valid for a certain ω value:

$$d(U(\mathbf{x}), U(\mathbf{y})) - \omega \leq d(\mathbf{x}, \mathbf{y}) \qquad (10.94)$$

and

$$d(U(\mathbf{x}), U(\mathbf{y})) \leq d(\mathbf{x}, \mathbf{y}) + \omega \leq \epsilon + \omega. \qquad (10.95)$$

We apply the product quantizier recursively. The vector $\mathbf{x}$ of dimension m is split into f distinct subvectors of dimension $p = dim(m/f)$. The subvectors are quantized using f quantiziers, the resulting quantized vectror are quantized using e quantiziers with $g = dim(m/e)$ and $f > e$

$$\mathbf{x} = \underbrace{x_1, x_2, \cdots, x_p}_{u1_1(\mathbf{x})}, \cdots, \cdots, \cdots, \underbrace{x_{m-p+1}, \cdots, x_m}_{u1_f(\mathbf{x})} \qquad (10.96)$$
$$\underbrace{}_{u2_1(U(\mathbf{x}))} \qquad \underbrace{\phantom{x_{m-p+1}, \cdots, x_m}}_{u2_e(U(\mathbf{x}))}$$

with following hierarchical representation,

$$U_1(\ \mathbf{x}) = U(\ \mathbf{x}) = c_{i1}, c_{i2}, \cdots, c_{ip}, \cdots, c_{j1}, \cdots, c_{jp}$$
$$U_2(\ \mathbf{x}) = U(U_1(\ \mathbf{x})) = c_{i1}, c_{i2}, \cdots, c_{ig}, \cdots, c_{j1}, \cdots, c_{jg} \qquad (10.97)$$
$$\cdots$$
$$U_r(\ \mathbf{x}) = U(U_{(r-1)}(\ \mathbf{x})) = c_{i1}, c_{i2}, \cdots, c_{il}, \cdots, c_{j1}, \cdots, c_{jl}$$

and

$$d^*(U_r(\mathbf{x}), U_r(\mathbf{y}) = d(U_r(\mathbf{x}), U_r(\mathbf{y})) - \omega_k \le d(\mathbf{x}, \mathbf{y}), \qquad (10.98)$$

The set of similar multimedia objects in correspondence to $U_r(\mathbf{y})$, $U_r(DB[\mathbf{y}])_\epsilon$ is the subset of $U_r(DB)$,

$$U_r(DB[\mathbf{y}])_\epsilon := \{U_r(\mathbf{x}_k) \in U_r(DB) \mid d^*(U_r(\mathbf{x}_k), U_r(\mathbf{y})) \le \epsilon\}.$$

for each quantified space U_r, the number of points below the bound ϵ is indicated by the value σ_r

$$\sigma_r := |U_r(DB[\mathbf{y}])_\epsilon,$$

it follows that

$$\sigma_0 < \sigma_1 < \ldots < \sigma_t < s \qquad (10.99)$$

where s is the size of the data set. Note that we need to use $d^*(U_r(\mathbf{x}), U_r(\mathbf{y})$ for exact search. $d(U_r(\mathbf{x}), U_r(\mathbf{y})$ would give us some approximate results.

10.7.2.2 *Costs*

To speed up the computation of $d(U(\mathbf{x}), U(\mathbf{y}))$ all the possible $d(c_{j(x)}, c_{j(y)})^2$ are pre-computed and stored in a look-up table. For simplicity we assume that the the cost for a look-up operation is a constant $c = 1$. This is the case given the size of the look-up tables for each hierarchy is constant. Consequently the computational dimensions of the quantized vector $\mathbf{x}$ is $dim(U_r) = m/f$, where $dim(U_r)$ is the number of distinct subv-ectors of dimension f of the vector $\mathbf{x}$. It follows, that $dim(U_r)$ is the number of quantiziers. The higher the hierarchy, the lower the number of the used quantiziers. Given that $dim(U_0) =: m$ (the dimension of the vector $\mathbf{x}$), the computational cost of a hierarchy on t is

$$cost_s = \sum_{i=1}^{t} \sigma_i \cdot dim(U_{i-1}) + s \cdot dim(U_t). \qquad (10.100)$$

10.7.2.3 *Experiments*

Experiments on image retrieval on one thousand ($s = 1000$) grey images of the size 128×96 resulting in vectors of dimension 12288. Each grey level is represented by 8 bits, leading to 256 different grey values. We use a hierarchy of four $n = 4$, which is 12.4 times less complex than a list matching [Wichert (2012)]. Further optimization of our results could be achieved by better quantization training (clustering algorithms). The improvement is worse then that of the subspace-tree, because we have to use $d^*(U_r(\mathbf{x}), U_r(\mathbf{y}))$ for exact search. $d(U_r(\mathbf{x}), U_r(\mathbf{y}))$ has equivalent cost to the subspace-tree, but the results are not exact.

10.7.2.4 *Deep belief network and subspace tree*

A restricted Boltzmann machine (RBM) is a stochastic artificial neural network that can learn a probability distribution over its set of inputs. It has binary-valued hidden h_j and visible units v_i and associated connections that are described by the weight matrix W, as shown in Figure 10.12. RBM are trained to maximize the product of probabilities assigned to some

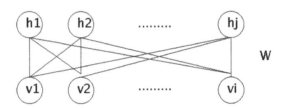

Fig. 10.12   A restricted Boltzmann machine.

training set as a visible vector of the visible units. Restricted Boltzmann machines can be used in deep learning networks called deep belief networks, see Figure 10.13. The goal is to reach a high level of abstraction. Deep belief networks are composed of multiple stacked RBMs. Learning consists of greedy training each level in a sequential manner from the bottom with fine-tuning by the back-propagation algorithm. A possible explanation of the success of deep belief networks is related to the subspace tree; each layer of the deep belief network represents a more abstract representation of the data, which corresponds to a lower resolution of the data by orthogonal projection [Mehta and Schwab (2014)]. The deep belief network learns to

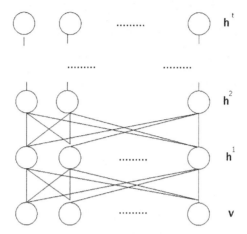

Fig. 10.13   A deep belief network.

disregard irrelevant features while simultaneously learning relevant features.

Chapter 11

Multimodal Fusion

A multimodal search enables an information search using search queries in multiple data types, including text and other multimedia formats. The information is described by some feature vectors and categories that were determined by indexing structures or supervised learning algorithms. A feature vector or category can belong to different modalities, such as word, shape, and color.

11.1 Constrained Hierarchies

The easiest way to handle multimodal fusion is to employ hierarchies of modalities instead of fusion. From the most important modality to the least important modality

$$keyword \subseteq shape \subseteq color.$$

First, search for specific keywords and determine the subset that contains these keywords. From this subset, determine another subset with a certain shape. From this subset, determine which multimedia objects exhibit a certain color distribution. Generally,

$$modal_1 \subseteq modal_2 \subseteq \cdots \subseteq modal_n,$$

the first $modal_1$ search determines a solution set_1 in the set_1 and the second $modal_2$ search determines a solution set_2. A unimodal search for each modal is performed; the search continues until all modals are satisfied or a solution set is empty.

11.2   Early Fusion

One can perform either late fusion or early fusion. During early fusion, the information is performed prior to the beginning of the search. An example is the scaled RGB image representation that contains the color distribution and the shape representation, as shown in Figure 11.1. A feature vector

Fig. 11.1   A scaled RGB image representation that contains both the color distribution and the shape representation.

can be formed by concatenation. Assume that we extract l, v, q features from the visual, audio, and caption tracks of videos. We can treat these features as one modality and form a feature vector of $l + v + q$ dimensions.

11.3   Late Fusion

Our brain performs a unimodal search with late fusion. For example, the visual system recognizes objects in an image. Researchers have suggested [Gross and Mishkin (1977)] that the brain includes two mechanisms for visual categorization [Posner and Raichle (1994)]: a mechanisms for the representation of the object and a mechanism for the representation of the localization [Kosslyn (1994)]. The first mechanism is referred to as the *what* pathway and is located in the temporal lobe. The second mechanism is referred to as the *where* pathway and is located in the parietal lobe.

11.3.1 *Multimodal fusion and images*

For image retrieval, we prefer a unimodal search for each modality and then combine the results of the unimodal search; for example, by a simple weighted-sum rule. The signature for the image can be extracted by segmenting the image into regions based on color. Each region is associated with the following information:

- color information,
- texture information,
- shape information.

The signature contains this region-based information and global color, texture, and shape information to represent these attributes for the entire image. The similarity measure for each visual attribute (modality) is calculated as the score or distance between the two images with respect to the attribute. The score is normalized to a certain range (for example, between 0 and 1) and then weights for each modality are determined between 0 and 1. Each weight represents the percentage of the contribution of each modality to the score. During the process, the values can be normalized to yield a total maximal score of 1. Instead of summing the values, we can perform multiplication and interpret the score and the weights as probabilities. This approach is related to the Naïve Bayes model. The the Naïve Bayes classifier is based on the Naïve Bayes assumption for determining the maximum posteriori hypothesis, which assumes the modality independence.

11.3.2 *Stochastic language model approach*

We can use the product combination rule to multiply the probabilities of the modality by the stochastic language model for features and categories [Hiemstra (2001); Westerveld *et al.* (2003)]

$$document_{map} =$$

$$\prod_{i=1}^{n} \left(\sum_{r=1}^{2} P(term_i | I_{i,r}, document_k) \cdot P(I_{i,r}) \right) \cdot P(document_k). \quad (11.1)$$

The feature query terms can be determined as follows:

- $P(document_k)$ can be assumed to be equivalent for all documents. For a collection of s documents, the value in this case is
$$P(document_k) = \frac{1}{s}$$
and corresponds to a normalization factor.

- The $P(term_i|I_{i,1}, document_k)$, which is an important term, is defined by the term frequency of a term in a document divided by the length of the document. In the case in which the $term_i$ is a feature vector, it is defined by the correlation to the feature vector that describes the document. For example, if the feature vector represents a scaled RGB image, the important image $(=term_i)$ is defined by the correlation of this image to the image in the document.

- The $P(term_i|I_{i,2}, document_k) = P(term_i|I_{i,2})$, which is an unimportant term, is defined by the number occurrences of the term in the collection divided by the total length of the collection. For a feature vector, it is defined as the correlation to the mean feature vector, which is composed of all feature vectors in the multimedia database.

- $P(I_{i,1})$ and $P(I_{i,2})$ have to be learned or estimated. We have to interact with the user to estimate the values.

Using this approach, we can combine the information retrieval results (text) with feature based indexing (images and videos).

11.3.3 *Dempster-Shafer theory*

Imagine a robot with two sensors, one tells the robot to go right the other to go left. How do we preform sensor fusion, do we add both values and compute the mean value? Does the robot go straight? Or do we assume that one sensor gives us wrong information and chose the information of the other one? In the Dempster-Shafer theory it is possible to associate measures of uncertainty with sets of hypotheses and to distinguish between uncertainty and ignorance [Lucas and van der Gaag (1991)]. The Dempster's rule of combination derives common shared belief between multiple sources and ignores all the conflicting (non-shared) beliefs [Shafer (1976)]. Let θ be the set representing all possible states of a system, then the power set is given by 2^θ, the set of all subsets of θ. The elements of the power set can be taken to represent propositions concerning the actual state of the system. The theory of evidence assigns a belief mass to each element of the power set and has three requirements:

- the mass function has to be a value between 0 and 1, $m : 2^\theta \to [0, 1]$,
- the mass of the empty set is zero, $m(\emptyset) = 0$,
- the sum of the masses of the remaining elements is 1,

$$\sum_{A \in 2^\theta} m(A) = 1. \tag{11.2}$$

The belief is the lower bound of the confidence interval and is defined as being the total evidence that supports the hypothesis, that is, it is the sum of all the masses of the subsets associated to set A.

$$Belief(A) = \sum_{B | B \subseteq A} m(B). \tag{11.3}$$

With

$$\theta = \{a, b, c\},$$

$$Belief(\theta) = m(a) + m(b) + m(c) + m(\{a, b\}) + m(\{a, c\}) +$$

$$+ m(\{b, c\}) + m(\{a, b, c\})$$

and

$$Belief(b, c) = m(b) + m(c) + m(\{b, c\}).$$

In the same way, the plausibility corresponds to the upper bound of the confidence interval and is defined as being the sum of all the masses of the set B that intersect the set of interest A,

$$Plausibility(A) = \sum_{B | B \cap A \neq \emptyset} m(B). \tag{11.4}$$

Again, with

$$\theta = \{a, b, c\},$$

$$Plausibility(b, c) = m(b) + m(c) + m(\{a, b\}) + m(\{a, c\}) +$$

$$+ m(\{b, c\}) + m(\{a, b, c\})$$

It follows

$$Belief(A) \leq P(A) \leq Plausibility(A). \tag{11.5}$$

To combine the evidences detected by modalities the Dempster-Shafer theory provides a combination rule which is given by Equation 11.7.

$$m_{1,2}(\emptyset) = 0 \tag{11.6}$$

$$(m_1 \oplus m_2)(A) = \frac{1}{1-K} \cdot \sum_{B \cap C = A \neq \emptyset} m_1(B) \cdot m_2(C). \qquad (11.7)$$

In the above formula, K measures the amount of conflict between the two modalities (or sensors) and is given by Equation 11.8.

$$K = \sum_{B \cap C = \emptyset} m_1(B) \cdot m_2(C), \qquad (11.8)$$

and is part of normalization factor $1 - K$. It has the effect of ignoring conflict by attributing any mass associated with conflict to the null set. Suppose that two friends, want to go to a restaurant one evening, and that there are only three restaurants in town: Italian, Indian and Chinese. The first friend express his preference for Italian restaurant with probability 0.99 and for Indian restaurant probability of 0.01. The second friend prefers the Chinese restaurant with probability 0.99 and the Indian restaurant with probability of 0.01. Thus

$$m_1(Italian) = 0.99, \quad m_1(Indian) = 0.01,$$

$$m_2(Chinese) = 0.99, \quad m_2(Indian) = 0.01.$$

Then

$$K = m_1(Italian) \cdot m_2(Chinese) + m_1(Indian) \cdot m_2(Chinese) +$$

$$+ m_1(Italian) \cdot m_2(Indian) = 0.9999,$$

$$1 - K = 0.001,$$

and

$$(m_1 \oplus m_2)(Italian) = 0,$$

$$(m_1 \oplus m_2)(Indian) = \frac{1}{0.001} \cdot m_1(Indian) \cdot m_2(Indian) = 1,$$

$$(m_1 \oplus m_2)(Chinese) = 0.$$

When combining the preferences with Dempster's rule of combination it turns out that their combined preference results in probability 1.0 for Indian restaurant, because it is the only restaurant that both friends agree at. Instead of restaurants we can imagine different multimedia objects, and instead of friends different modalities.

Chapter 12

Software Architecture

We highlight some basic architecture issues related to multimedia databases and big data. Big data is a large collection of unstructured data that cannot be processed with traditional methods, such as standard database management systems.

12.1 Database Architecture

Formal database architecture separates a user viewpoint from a system viewpoing. In a three-layer architecture, the external level provides the user's viewpoint of the database. The conceptual level comprises the community viewpoint of the database, as observed by the system administrator of the database [Dunckley (2003)]. The internal level indicates how the data is physically stored and includes the indexing structure that is implemented in a programming language. The architecture of the database system is influenced by the underlying computer and network system.

12.1.1 *Client-server system*

A centralized database system runs on a single computer system that does not interact with other computer systems. In a client-server system, networking computers enable the division of work. Tasks that are related to a database structure are executed on a server and presented on a client computer. Problems frequently arise when server selection is primarily based on system defaults or user choice. The super server concept prevents local load problems that are caused by dynamic server selection by alternatively mapping the servers in a local cluster.

12.1.2   *A peer-to-peer*

A peer-to-peer (P2P) application differs from a traditional client-server model. It is a network in which each workstation has equivalent capabilities and responsibilities, the applications serve as both client and server, and no central server is present. A P2P network is simpler then a client-server system but performs poorly under heavy loads.

12.2   Big Data

Big data is a large collection of unstructured data that cannot be processed with traditional methods, such as standard database management systems. Big data cannot be processed by one server but requires the processing power of hundreds to thousands of servers. The definition of big data changes with time and computer development. Currently, (2015) the size of big data corresponds to the size of a few dozen terabytes (1000^4) to many petabytes (1000^5) and may correspond to yottabytes ($1000^8 = 1$ trillion terabytes) in the future.

12.2.1   *Divide and conquer*

For the fast access of big data, divide and conquer methods, which are based on hierarchical structures that can be parallelized, can be employed. Data can be distributed and processed by multiple processing units. After processing, the results are integrated and presented to the user on a front end application server. The subspace tree can be easily parallelized for big high-dimensional multimedia data to perform a rapid and exact search. Different parts of the database may be individually processed by different processors or servers.

12.2.2   *MapReduce*

Big data is usually processed by a distributed file-sharing framework for data storage and querying. An example is the MapReduce framework [Lämmel (2008)]. MapReduce provides a parallel processing model and associated implementation to process an immense amount of data. Queries are split and distributed across parallel nodes (servers) and processed in parallel (the Map step). The nodes are referred to as a cluster if all nodes are located in the same local network and use similar hardware. They are referred to as a grid if they are not located in the same local network and use heterogenous hardware. The processing occurs on data stored in a file system, such as unstructured multimedia data or a relational database. The results are subsequently collected and delivered (the Reduce step). MapReduce is a model for distributed computing that functions as a pipeline

$$Input \rightarrow Map \rightarrow (Shuffle \wedge Sort) \rightarrow Reduce \rightarrow Output.$$

Assume that we wish to perform a word count for a set of documents. The input to the mapper are the lines of the input text, whereas the output is each word with the value 1. The input to the reducer is the set of words with the value 1; the set is represented by repetition of the count of the words. The output is a list of words with the values that represent the count, as shown in Figure 12.1. Usually there are as many maps as the number of distributed file system blocks being processed.

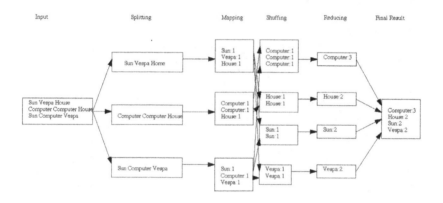

Fig. 12.1   MapReduce is a model for distributed computing, it works like a pipeline with Input → Map → (Shuffle ∧ Sort) → Reduce → Output. For a word count the input to the mapper are the lines of the input text, the output is each word with the value 1. The input to the reducer is the set of words with the value 1, the set is representing by repetition the count of the words. The output is a list of words with the values representing the count.

12.2.2.1   *Hadoop*

Hadoop is an open-source implementation from MapReduce; its framework consists of two main layers[1]:

---
[1] http://hadoop.apache.org

- distributed file system (HDFS),
- execution engine (MapReduce).

It enables the use of a large number of low-end inexpensive machines that operate in parallel to solve a computing problem. A HDFS instance may consist of thousands of server machines, in which each machine stores part of the file system's data. Hadoop automatically handles failures by restarting tasks if a server fails; it runs multiples copies of the same task to prevent a slow task from slowing down the entire job. Figure 12.2 shows the map reduce data flow in Hadoop with a single reduce task. Figure 12.3 shows the map reduce data flow in Hadoop with multiple reduce tasks.

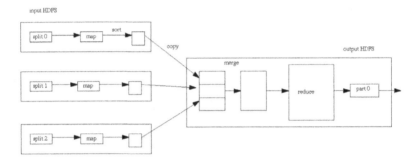

Fig. 12.2   Mapreduce data flow in Hadoop with a single reduce task.

12.3   Evaluation

We can specify our system by some objective values for example the speed and size, like

- how fast does the system index,
- how fast does he system search,
- and what is the space requirement.

All this criteria are objective and measurable, we can quantify speed and size.

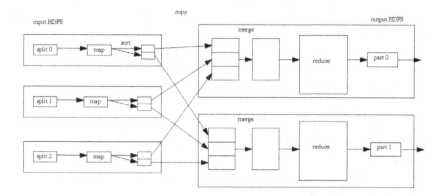

Fig. 12.3 Mapreduce data flow in Hadoop with multiple reduce tasks.

12.3.1 *Precision and recall*

Some measures are subjective; for example, does the user find what he was looking for? Is the corresponding document relevant to the needs of the user? We evaluate whether the obtained document addresses the information needs of the user. Similarity to the feature vector that represents the query is not sufficient. We define precision and recall as:

- Precision: fraction of retrieved documents that are relevant with
$$p(relevant \mid retrieved),$$
- Recall: fraction of relevant documents that are retrieved with
$$p(retrieved \mid relevant).$$

Using the Table 12.1, we get

Table 12.1 Relevant and not relevant versus retrieved and not retrieved.

	Relevant	Not Relevant
Retrieved	true positive	false positive
Not Retrieved	false negative	true negative

$$Precision = \frac{true\ positive}{true\ positive + false\ positive} \tag{12.1}$$

and

$$Recall = \frac{true\ positive}{true\ positive + false\ negative}. \tag{12.2}$$

A high recall value without a high precision value does not address the information needs of the user [Manning *et al.* (2008); Powers (2011)]. We can obtain a high recall value by retrieving all documents (the entire database) for a given query. We do not miss any relevant documents and the recall value will be one; however, the precision value will be low. By retrieving one important document, we obtain the maximal precision value of one

$$Precision = 1 = \frac{1}{1 + 0}$$

but a low recall value. Both values have to be simultaneously interpreted and should represent an average that was determined over a large number of different queries. Both values can be combined by the harmonic mean of precision and recall,

$$F = 2 \cdot \frac{Precision \cdot Recall}{Precision + Recall} \qquad (12.3)$$

in which both values are evenly weighted. This measure is also called the balanced measure. If we want to weigh the values not evenly we use the F_β measure

$$F_\beta = (1 + \beta^2) \cdot \frac{Precision \cdot Recall}{\beta^2 \cdot Precision + Recall} \qquad (12.4)$$

with F_2 measure, which weights recall higher than precision, and the $F_{0.5}$ measure, which puts more emphasis on precision than recall. With $\beta = 1$ we get the balanced measure $F = F_1$ [Powers (2011)]. The quality of the measure is dependent on the relevance values. The relevance value is a binary value that needs to be set by human experts of the domain. The relevance cannot be translated from one domain to another domain and its quality is dependent on the quality of the human expert.

Chapter 13

Multimedia Databases in Medicine

We present multimedia examples of database applications in medicine. A hospital information system (HIS) is a comprehensive and integrated information system that is designed to manage the administrative, financial and clinical aspects of a hospital. A clinical information system (CIS) is frequently separated from a HIS due to its focus on patient-state- and clinical-state-related data. A clinical information system can be composed of a variety of subsystems in medical specialties. An example of a clinical information system is the electronic patient record (EHR). It includes information related to the current and historical health, medical conditions and medical imaging.

13.1 Medical Standards

In the following subsections, we present some important medical standards.

13.1.1 *Health Level Seven*

Health Level Seven (HL7) refers to Health Level Seven, Inc., which is a not-for-profit organization involved in the development of international health-care standards for hospital information systems[1]. Without data standards, healthcare organizations cannot readily share clinical information. Hospitals typically maintain many different computer systems, which must communicate with each other. HL7 enables the exchange and interoperability of different electronic health record applications.

---

[1]http://*www.hl7.org*

13.1.2　*DICOM*

Digital Imaging and Communications in Medicine (DICOM) is a set of standards for handling, storing, printing, and transmitting information in medical imaging[2]. It includes a file format definition and a network communications protocol. DICOM files can be exchanged between different entities, such as scanners, servers, workstations, and printers, which are capable of processing and storing image and patient data in DICOM format. DICOM groups information into a data set. For example, an X-ray image contains the patient ID; thus, the image is never mistakenly separated from the ID information. A DICOM data object consists of a number of attributes including the image pixel data, such as the patent ID, the modality work list and the modality performed procedure step. The modality work list enables the imaging equipment (a modality) to introduce the details and schedules of patients. The modality performed procedure step enables the transmission of a report about a performed examination, which includes data about the acquired images.

13.1.3　*PACS*

The picture archiving and communication systems (PACS) consist of computers or networks dedicated to the storage, retrieval, distribution and presentation of images from various modalities[3], such as ultrasonography, magnetic resonance imaging, positron emission tomography, computed tomography, endoscopy, mammography and radiography (X-rays). A PACS system should interface with existing clinical information systems.

13.2　Electronic Health Record

The electronic health record is a key element for assisting the delivery of health care to a patient. It is a dynamic informational entity that continuously monitors/the evolution of the health status of a patient. The major advantages of electronic health record over their paper-based counterparts (besides the more commonly known provided by the electronic management of data) is that all diagnostic tests, especially medical imagery, become attached to the patients profile and available on electronic format. Most of those tests consist of unstructured media formats, like the images.

---

[2]http://*dicom.nema.org*
[3]http://*www.pacshistory.org*

13.2.1 *Panoramix*

Panoramix is an example of an electronic health record [Santos *et al.* (2009)], incorporating a content-addressable multimedia database, through a fast CBIR search methods. A prototype system was successfully deployed. The system is a web based client-server (thin client) application composed by three layers (presentation, logic and data) developed in Java [Wichert and Santos (2010)]. It consists on a central server where the application is deployed, as well as the database with the patient information and the file systems where the stored medical tests are kept. The patient data masks are based on the official standard patient record forms (in paper), being used in the Portuguese Public Primary Health Care Center (see Figure 13.1). The Figure 13.2 shows part of the patient data stored in the system.

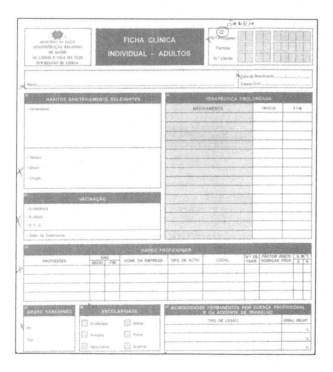

Fig. 13.1 Official form of the Portuguese Public Primary Health Care Center.

We demonstrate the CBIR by integration into an electronic health record (see Figure 13.3).

Fig. 13.2   Patient main information page based in the official form.

13.2.1.1   *CBIR in Panoramix*

In Panoramix we applied the subspace tree for medical CBIR [Santos *et al.* (2009)]. The application of the CBIR concept in medicine is relatively new, most applications depend on the imaging modalities [Zhou *et al.* (2008)]. There are some academic studies and projects including non modality-specific studies of CBIR in medicine: IRMA [Lehmann *et al.* (2004)], I2C [Orphanoudakis *et al.* (1994)], KMed [Chu *et al.* (1994)], [Muller *et al.* (2005)]. However, there still is not any integrated application fully functional in the real clinical practice.

The dataset was composed of 12,000 gray X-ray images (size 256 · 256). The images came from 116 different categories (different views of x-rayed body parts), belonging to persons of different genders, various ages and different diseases[4]. We used the subspace tree with the images with the

---

[4]We would like to thank for the permission to use the dataset for experimental tests purposes to TM Deserno, Dept. of Medical Informatics, RWTH Aachen, Germany.

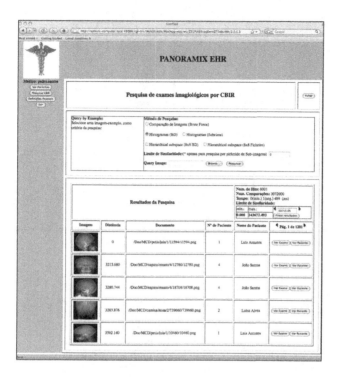

Fig. 13.3   Mask of the electronic health record with CBIR search.

resolutions as shown in the Figure 13.4. For testing purposes, a sample of 600 query images was randomly selected from the original dataset. For each image of the sample set the most similar images of the database of 12,000 images were determined using the Euclidian distance. The actual retrieval time on a computer differs from the theoretical computing cost of the subspace tree according to the Equation 8.62. In Figure 13.5, we relate the actual mean retrieval time of the most similar images on a Intel Dual Core 2.0 GHz machine measured in milliseconds [Wichert and Santos (2010)]. The actual retrieval costs depend on the implementation of the system, see as well Table 13.1.

13.2.1.2   *Subpattern matching*

In the next step, subpattern matching, which is based on the subspace tree, was introduced. The query corresponds to a template subpattern (for example, a tumor) and helps us to answer the following question: "How does

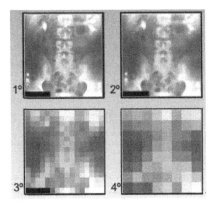

Fig. 13.4   (1) Image with the size 256 × 256. (2) Image resolution 64 × 64. (3) Image resolution 16 × 16. (4) Image resolution 8 × 8.

Table 13.1   Mean retrieval time of subspace tree of 26 most similar images compared to list matching. For each image of the sample set 26 most similar images of the database of 12, 000 images were determined using the Euclidian distance. The computing steps are indicated according to the Equation 8.62, the actual computing time on an Intel Dual Core 2 GHz is indicated seconds.

method	comparisons	time
list matching	786, 432, 000	130.1 sec
subspace tree	3, 322, 536	1.2 sec

my patient's tumor compare to similar cases?" Subpattern matching can be converted to multiple entire match queries for the same image [Ferreira (2010)]. The idea is to compare the query image with an equally sized area of the database image. Then, we shift the window to an adjacent area and compare again until we scan the entire image. Small shifts reduce the probability of missing patterns but require more comparisons, whereas large shifts may miss more patterns but require a few comparisons. Even with low shifts, we may miss a pattern if its size in both images is quite different, such as when a physician uses a zoomed image of a tumor and searches for similar tumors in X-rays of the entire chest. The solution is to use scaled-down copies of the query image (retaining the aspect ratio) and independently apply the previously described method with each copy. The tests were run on a dataset that contains 12, 000 X-ray images of 116

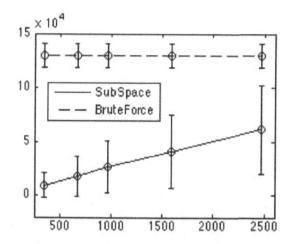

Fig. 13.5 Mean retrieval time of the sample to on an Intel Dual Core 2 GHz by hierarchical subspace method (Subspace tree) compared to list matching (Brute Force) out of 12, 000 images. For each image of the sample set the most similar images of the database of 12, 000 images were determined using the Euclidian distance. The standard deviation of the sample is indicated by error bars. The x-axis indicates the number of the most similar images which are retrieved and the y-axis, the actual retrieval time measured in milliseconds.

different views and parts of the human body [Ferreira (2010)], including X-rays of the chest, arms, hands, pelvis, spine, legs and skull, as shown in Figure 13.6.

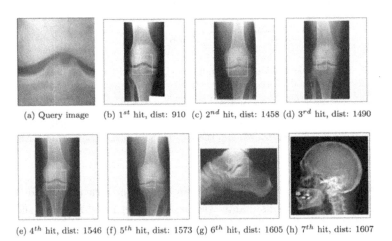

(a) Query image   (b) 1st hit, dist: 910 (c) 2nd hit, dist: 1458 (d) 3rd hit, dist: 1490

(e) 4th hit, dist: 1546 (f) 5th hit, dist: 1573 (g) 6th hit, dist: 1605 (h) 7th hit, dist: 1607

Fig. 13.6   To retrieve the 17 most similar images our system took on average 7.3 sec compared to 2.5 hours while performing the same operation using list matching on an AMD Athlon II 2.70 GHz.

13.3 Conclusion

In this book we covered the essential concepts and algorithms for intelligent big multimedia databases. We employed the idea of a hierarchical organization of information processing and representation in many areas. Based on these ideas, we introduced the subspace tree. This algorithm can be easily parallelized for big data and is promising for addressing the logarithmic retrieval complexity of extremely high-dimensional features.

Bibliography

Anderson, J. R. (1995). *Cognitive Psychology and its Implications*, 4th edn. (W. H. Freeman and Company).

Andoni, A., Dater, M., Indyk, P., Immorlica, N. and Mirrokni, V. (2006). Locality-sensitive hashing using stable distributions, in MIT-Press (ed.), *Nearest Neighbor Methods in Learning and Vision: Theory and Practice*, chap. 3 (T. Darrell and P. Indyk and G. Shakhnarovich), pp. 61–72.

Baeza-Yates, R. and Ribeiro-Neto, B. (1999a). Modeling, in R. Baeza-Yates and B. Ribeiro-Neto (eds.), *Modern Information Retrieval*, chap. 2 (Addison-Wesley), pp. 19–71.

Baeza-Yates, R. and Ribeiro-Neto, B. (1999b). *Modern Information Retrieval* (Addison-Wesley).

Bate, D. (2009). *Photography: The Key Concepts* (Bloomsbury Academic).

Bentley, J. L. (1975). Multidimensional binary search trees used for associative searching, *Communications of the ACM* **18**, 9, pp. 509–517.

Bentz, H. J., Hagstroem, M. and Palm, G. (1989). Information storage and effective data retrieval in sparse matrices, *Neural Networks* **2**, 4, pp. 289–293.

Besicovitch, A. S. (1929). On linear sets of points of fractional dimensions, *Mathematische Annalen* **101**, 1, pp. 161–193.

Biederman, I. (1987). Recognition-by-components: A theory of human image understanding, *Psychological Review* **94**, 2, pp. 115–47.

Black, H. S. (2013). *Modulation Theory* (Literary Licensing).

Blei, D. M. and Jordan, M. I. (2003). Modeling annotated data, in *Proceedings of the 26th annual international ACM SIGIR conference on Research and development in informaion retrieval*, pp. 127–134.

Böhm, C., Berchtold, S. and Kei, A. K., D. (2001). Searching in high-dimensional spaces—index structures for improving the performance of multimedia databases, *ACM Computing Surveys* **33**, 3, pp. 322–373.

Brunak, S. and Lautrup, B. (1990). *Neural Networks Computers with Intuition* (World Scientific).

Burger, W. and Burge, M. J. (2011). *Digital Image Processing: An Algorithmic Introduction using Java* (Springer).

Burt, P. J. and Adelson, E. H. (1983). The laplacian pyramidas a compact image code, *IEEE Trans. Commin* **COM-31**, 4, pp. 532–540.

Cardoso, A. and Wicher, A. (2014). Noise tolerance in a neocognitron like network, *Neural Networks* **49**, 32-38, p. 2014.

Cardoso, A. and Wichert, A. (2010). Neocognitron and the map transformation cascade, *Neural Networks* **23**, 1, pp. 74–88.

Cardoso, A. and Wichert, A. (2013). Handwritten digit recognition using biologically inspired features, *Neurocomputing* **99**, pp. 575–589.

Chen, Y. and Wang, J. Z. (2004). Image categorization by learning and reasoning with regions, *Journal of Machine Learning Research* **5**, pp. 913–939.

Chu, W., Cardenas, A. and Taira, R. (1994). Kmed: A knowledge-based multimedia distributed database system, *Information Systems* **19**, pp. 33–54.

Churchland, P. S. and Sejnowski, T. J. (1994). *The Computational Brain* (The MIT Press).

Ciaccia, P. and Patella, M. (2002). Searching in metric spaces with user-defined and approximate distances, *ACM Transactions on Database Systems* **27**, 4.

Comer, D. (1979). The ubiquitous b-tree, *Computing Surveys* **11**, 2, pp. 123–137.

Consortium, T. U. (2006). *The Unicode Standard* (Mountain View, California).

Cooley, J. W. and Tukey, J. W. (1965). An algorithm for the machine calculation of complex fourier series, *Mathematical Computation* **19**, 90, pp. 297–301.

Cormen, T. H., Leiserson, C. E., Rivest, L. R. and Stein, C. (2001a). *Introduction to Algorithms*, Second (MIT Press).

Cormen, T. H., Leiserson, C. E., Rivest, R. L. and Stein, C. (2001b). *Introduction to Algorithms, 2/e* (MIT Press).

Curtis, G. (2006). *The Cave Painters: Probing the Mysteries of the World's First Artists* (Alfred A. Knopf).

Dale, G. R. (2006). *The Nature of Prehistoric Art* (University of Chicago Press).

Daubechies, I. (1992). *Ten Lectures on Wavelets* (SIAM).

de Sá, J. P. M. (2001). *Pattern Recognition: Concepts, Methods and Applications* (Springer-Verlag).

Deller, J. R., Proakis, J. G. and Hansen, J. H. (1993). *Discrete-Time Processing of Speech Signals* (Macmillan).

Dunckley, L. (2003). *Multimedia Databases, An Object-Rational Approach* (Addison Wesley).

Edzard, D. O. (1997). *Gudea and His Dynasty* (University of Toronto Press).

Faloutsos, C. (1999). Modern information retrieval, in R. Baeza-Yates and B. Ribeiro-Neto (eds.), *Modern Information Retrieval*, chap. 12 (Addison-Wesley), pp. 345–365.

Faloutsos, C., Barber, R., Flickner, M., Hafner, J., Niblack, W., Petkovic, D. and Equitz, W. (1994). Efficient and effective querying by image content, *Journal of Intelligent Information Systems* **3**, 3/4, pp. 231–262.

Faloutsos, C. and Roseman, S. (1989). Fractals for secondary key retrieval, in *PODS '89 Proceedings of the eighth ACM SIGACT-SIGMOD-SIGART symposium on Principles of database systems* (ACM), pp. 247–252.

Ferreira, N. R. A. (2010). *Content Based Image Retrieval (CBIR) for Medical Images*, Master's thesis, Instituto Superior Técnico - Universidade de Lisboa.

Flickner, M., Sawhney, H., Niblck, W., Ashley, J., Huang, Q., Dom, B., Gorkani,

M., Hafner, J., Lee, D., Petkovic, D., Steele, D. and Yanker, P. (1995). Query by image and video content the QBIC system, *IEEE Computer* , pp. 23–32.

Fransén, E. (1996). *Biophysical Simulation of Cortical Associative Memory*, Ph.D. thesis, Stockhokms Universitet, Dept. of Numerical Analysis and Computing Science Royal Institute of Technology, S-100 44 Stockholm, Sweden.

Fukushima, K. (1980). Neocognitron: a self organizing neural network model for a mechanism of pattern recognition unaffected by shift in position. *Biol Cybern* **36**, 4, pp. 193–202.

Fukushima, K. (1988). Neocognitron: A hierarchical neural network capable of visual pattern recognition, *Neural Networks* **1**, pp. 119–130.

Fukushima, K. (2001). Recognition of partly occluded patterns: a neural network model. *Biol Cybern* **84**, 4, pp. 251–259.

Fuster, J. (1995). *Memory in the Cerebral Cortex* (The MIT Press).

Gabor, D. (1946). Theory of communication, *Journal of the IEE* **93**, pp. 429 –457.

Gniadek, K. (1992). *Optyczne przetwarzanie informacij* (Wydawnictwo Naukowe PWN, Warszawa).

Gonzales, R. C. and Woods, E. W. (2001). *Digital Image Processing*, 2nd edn. (Prentice Hall).

Gross, C. and Mishkin (1977). The neural basis of stimulus equivalence across retinal translation, in S. Harnad, R. Dorty, J. Jaynes, L. Goldstein and Krauthamer (eds.), *Lateralization in the nervous system* (Academic Press, New York), pp. 109–122.

Guttman, A. (1984). R-trees: A dynamic index structure for spatial searching, in *SIGMOD '84 Proceedings of the 1984 ACM SIGMOD international conference on Management of data* (ACM), pp. 47–57.

Haines, T. (1999). *Walking with Dinosaurs - a Natural History* (BBC Worldwide Limited).

Halsall, F. (2001). *Multimedia Communications* (Addison-Wesley).

Hausdorff, F. (1919). Dimension und ausseres mass, *Mathematische Annalen* **79**, 1-2, pp. 157–179.

Haykin, S. O. (2008). *Neural Networks and Learning Machines (3rd Edition)* (Prentice Hall).

Hecht-Nielsen, R. (1989). *Neurocomputing* (Addison-Wesley).

Hecht-Nielsen, R. (1994). Context vectors: general purpose approximate meaning representations self-organized from raw data, in J. M. Zurada and R. J. Marks (eds.), *Computational intelligence: Imitating life* (IEEE Press), pp. 43–56.

Hertz, J., Krogh, A. and Palmer, R. G. (1991). *Introduction to the Theory of Neural Computation* (Addison-Wesley).

Hiemstra, D. (2001). *Using Language Models for Information Retrieval*, Ph.D. thesis, University of Twente, Centre for Telematics and Information Technology.

Hilbert, D. (1891). Ueber die stetige abbildung einer line auf ein flächenstuck, *Mathematische Annalen* **38**, pp. 459–460.

Hove, L.-J. (2004). *Extending Image Retrieval Systems with a Thesaurus for Shapes*, Master's thesis, Institute for Information and Media Sciences - University of Bergen.

Hubbard, B. B. (1998). *The World According to Wavelets: The Story of a Mathematical Technique in the Making* (A K Peters/CRC Press).

Hubel, D. H. (1988). *Eye, Brain, and Vision* (Scientific Ammerican Library, Oxford, England).

Indyk, P. (2004). Nearest neighbours in high-dimensional spaces, in J. Goodman and J. O'Rourke (eds.), *Handbook of Discrete and Computational Geometry*, chap. 39 (Boca Raton–London–New York–Wahington), pp. 877–892.

Indyk, P. and Motwani, R. (1998). Approximate nearest neighbours: towards removing the curse of dimensionality, in *Proc. 30th ACM Symp. Theory of Computing*, pp. 604–613.

Jackson, P. (1999). *Introduction to Expert Systems*, 3rd edn. (Addison-Wesley).

Jegou, H., Douze, M. and Schmid, S. (2011). Product quantization for nearest neighbor search, *IEEE Transactions on Pattern Analysis and Machine Intelligence* **33**, 1, pp. 117–128.

Jelinek, F. (1998). *Statistical Methods for Speech Recognition* (The MIT Press).

Jeon, J., Lavrenko, V. and Manmatha, R. (2003). Automatic image annotation and retrieval using cross-media relevance models, in *Proceedings of the 26th annual international ACM SIGIR conference on Research and development in informaion retrieval*, pp. 119–126.

Kemke, C. and Wichert, A. (1993). Hierarchical self-organizing feature maps for speech recognition, in *Proceedings World Congres on Neural Networks* (Lawrence Erlbaum), pp. 45–47.

Kim, H.-G., Moreau, N. and Sikora, T. (2005). *MPEG-7 Audio and Beyond: Audio Content Indexing and Retrieval* (Wiley and Sons).

Kohonen, T. (1989). *Self-Organization and Associative Memory*, 3rd edn. (Springer-Verlag).

Kolmogorov, A. (1933). *Grundbegriffe der Wahrscheinlichkeitsrechnung* (Springer-Verlag).

Kosslyn, S. M. (1994). *Image and Brain, The Resolution of the Imagery Debate* (The MIT Press).

Kurzweil, R. (1990). *The Age of Intelligent Machines* (The MIT Press).

Lambert, D. (1983). *Collins Guide to Dinosaurs* (Diagram Visual Information Ltd).

Lambert, D. (1993). *The Ultimate Dinosaur Book* (Dorling Kindersley).

Lämmel, R. (2008). Google's map reduce programming model - revisited, *Science of Computer Programming* **70**, 1, pp. 1–30.

LeCun, Y. and Bengio, Y. (1998). Convolutional networks for images, speech, and time series, in M. A. Arbib (ed.), *The handbook of brain theory and neural networks* (MIT Press, Cambridge, MA, USA), ISBN 0-262-51102-9, pp. 255–258.

Lee, D. and Wong, C. (1977). Worst-case analysis for region and partial region searches in multidimensional binary search trees and balanced quad trees, *Acta Informatica* **9**, pp. 23–29.

Lee, J. S., Yamaguchi, M. and Ohyama, N. (1995). Integrated image associative memory and its optical implementation, *Optical Review* **2**, 4, pp. 261–265.

Lehmann, T., Güld, M., Thies, C., Fischer, B., Spitzer, K., Keysers, D., Ney, H., Kohnen, M., Schubert, H. and Wein, B. (2004). Content-based image retrieval in medical applications, *Methods of information in medicine* **43**.

Li, J. and Wang, J. (2003a). Automatic linguistic indexing of pictures by a statistical modeling approach, *IEEE Transactions on Pattern Analysis and Machine Learning* **25**, 9, pp. 1075–1088.

Li, J. and Wang, J. (2003b). Studying digital imagery of ancient paintings by mixtures of stochastic models, *IEEE Transactions on Pattern Analysis and Machine Learning* , pp. 1–15.

Lieberman, P. and Blumstein, S. E. (1988). *Speech Physiology, Speech Perception, and Acoustic Phonetics* (Cambridge University Press).

Lloyd, S. P. (1982). Least squares quantization in pcm, *IEEE Transactions on Information Theory* **28**, 2, pp. 129–137.

Lowe, D. G. (2004). Distinctive image features from scale-invariant keypoints, *International Journal of Computer Vision* **60**, 2, pp. 91–110.

Lucas, P. and van der Gaag, L. (1991). *Principles of Expert Systems* (Addison Wesley).

Luger, G. F. and Stubblefield, W. A. (1993). *Artificial Intelligence: Structures and Strategies for Complex Problem Solving: Second Edition* (The Benjamin/Cummings Publishing Company, Inc, Menlo Park, CA, USA).

Luger, G. F. and Stubblefield, W. A. (1998). *Artificial Intelligence, Structures and Strategies for Complex Problem Solving*, 3rd edn. (Addison-Wesley).

Lv, Q., Josephson, W., Wang, Z., Charikar, M. and Li, K. (2007). Multi-probe lsh: Efficient indexing for high-dimensional similarity search, in *Proceedings of the 33rd international conference on Very large data bases*, pp. 950–961.

Mandelbrot, B. (1983). *The Fractal Geometry of Nature* (W. H. Freeman and Co.).

Manjunath, B., Salembier, P. and Sikora, T. (2002). *Introduction to MPEG-7: Multimedia Content Description Interface* (Wiley and Sons).

Manning, C. D., Raghavan, P. and Schütze, H. (2008). *Introduction to Information Retrieval* (Cambridge University Press).

McClelland, J. and Kawamoto, A. (1986). Mechanisms of sentence processing: Assigning roles to constituents of sentences, in J. McClelland and D. Rumelhart (eds.), *Parallel Distributed Processing* (The MIT Press), pp. 272–325.

Mehta, P. and Schwab, D. J. (2014). An exact mapping between the variational renormalization group and deep learning, *arXiv preprint arXiv:1410.3831* .

Minsky, M. (1975). A framework for representing knowledge, in P. Winston (ed.), *The Psychology of Computer Vision* (McGraw-Hill, New York), pp. 211–77.

Minsky, M. (1986). *The Society of Mind* (Simon and Schuster, New York).

Mirmehdi, M. and Periasamy, R. (2001). Cbir with perceptual region features, in T. Cootes and C. Taylor (eds.), *Proceedings of the 12th British Machine Vision Conference* (BMVA Press), pp. 511 – 520.

Mitchell, T. (1997). *Machine Learning* (McGraw-Hill).

Moon, B., Jagadish, H., Faloutsos, C. and Saltz, J. H. (2001). Analysis of the clustering properties of the hilbert space-filling curve, *IEEE TRANSACTIONS ON KNOWLEDGE AND DATA ENGINEERING* **13**, 1, pp. 124–141.

Muller, H., Rosset, A., Garcia, A., Vallee, J. and Geissbuhler, A. (2005). Benefits of content-based visual data access in radio graphics, *Informatics in radiology* **19**, pp. 33–54.

Neuenschwander, E. (1996). *Felix Hausdorffs letzte Lebensjahre nach Dokumenten aus dem Bessel-Hagen-Nachlaß* (Brieskorn).

Niblack, W., Barber, R., Equitz, W., Flickner, M., Glasman, E. H., Petkovic, D., Yanker, P., Faloutsos, C. and Taubin, G. (1993). The qbic project: Querying images by content, using color,texture, and shape, in *Storage and Retrieval for Image and Video Databases (SPIE)*, pp. 173–187.

Nilsson, N. J. (1982). *Principles of Artificial Intelligence* (Springer-Verlag).

OFTA (1991). *Les Réseaux de Neurones* (Masson).

Olafsson, A., Jonsson, B. and Amsaleg, L. (2008). Dynamic behavior of balanced nv-trees, in *International Workshop on Content-Based Multimedia Indexing Conference Proceedings, IEEE*, pp. 174–183.

Oliva, A. and Torralba, A. (2001). Modeling the shape of the scene: a holistic representation of the spatial envelope, *nternational Journal of Computer Vision* **42**, 3, pp. 145–175.

Orphanoudakis, S., Chronaki, C. and Kostomanolakis, S. (1994). I2cnet: A system for the indexing. storage and retrieval of medical images by conten, *Medical Informatics* **19**, pp. 109–122.

Palm, G. (1982). *Neural Assemblies, an Alternative Approach to Artificial Intelligence* (Springer-Verlag).

Palm, G. (1990). Assoziatives Gedächtnis und Gehirntheorie, in *Gehirn und Kognition* (Spektrum der Wissenschaft), pp. 164–174.

Palm, G. (1993). The PAN system and the WINA project, in P. Spies (ed.), *Euro-Arch'93* (Springer-Verlag), pp. 142–156.

Palm, G. and Bonhoeffer, T. (1984). Parallel processing for associative and neural networks, *Biological Cybernetics* **51**, 201-204.

Palm, G., Schwenker, F. and Bibbig, A. (1992). Theorie Neuronaler Netze 1, Skript zur Vorlesung, university of Ulm, Department of Neural Information Processing.

Palm, G., Schwenker, F., Sommer, F. and Strey, A. (1997). Neural associative memories, in A. Krikelis and C. Weems (eds.), *Associative Processing and Processors* (IEEE Press), pp. 307–325.

Paulus, D. and Hornegger, J. (2003). *Applied Pattern Recognition, Fourth Edition: Algorithms and Implementation in C++* (GWV-Vieweg;).

Peano, G. (1890). Sur une courbe, qui remplit toute une aire plane, *Mathematische Annalen* **31**, 1, pp. 157–160.

Pestov, V. (2011). Lower bounds on performance of metric tree indexing schemes for exact similarity search in high dimensions, in A. Ferro (ed.), *Proceedings of the 4th International Conference on Similarity Search and Applications*, pp. 25–32.

Pestov, V. (2012). Indexability, concentration, and vc theory, *Journal of Discrete Algorithms* **13**, pp. 2–18.

Polikar, R. (1996). The wavelet tutorial, URL http://engineering.rowan.edu/polikar/WAVELETS/WTtutorial.html.

Pöppel, E. (2009). Pre-semantically defined temporal windows for cognitive processing, *Philos. Trans. R. Soc. Lond. B Biol. Sci.* .

Posner, M. I. and Raichle, M. E. (1994). *Images of Mind* (Scientific American Library, New York).

Powers, D. M. W. (2011). Evaluation: From precision, recall and f-factor to roc, informedness, markedness & correlation, *Journal of Machine Learning Technologies* **2**, 1, pp. 37–63.

Quack, T., Mönich, U., Thiele, L. and Manjunath, B. S. (2004). Cortina: a system for large-scale, content-based web image retrieval, in *Proceedings of the 12th annual ACM international conference on Multimedia*, pp. 508–511.

Resnikoff, H. L. (1989). *The Illusion of Reality* (Springer-Verlag).

Riesenhuber, M. and Poggio, T. (2000). Models of object recognition, *Nat Neuroscience* **3**, pp. 1199–1204.

Riesenhuber, M. and Poggio, T. (2002). Neural mechanisms of object recognition, *Current Opinion in Neurobiology* **12**, pp. 162–168.

Riesenhuber, M., Poggio, T. and models of object recognition in cortex, H. (1999). Hierarchical models of object recognition in cortex, *Nature Neuroscience* **2**, pp. 1019–1025.

Robinson, A. (2000). *Writing and Script: A Very Short Introduction* (Oxford University Press).

Rosenblatt, F. (1962). *Principles of neurodynamics: Perceptrons and the theory of brain mechanisms* (Spartan Books).

Rudgley, R. (2000). *The Lost Civilizations of the Stone Age* (Simon & Schuster.).

Rumelhart, D. and McClelland (1986). On learning the past tense of english verbs, in J. McClelland and D. Rumelhart (eds.), *Parallel Distributed Processing* (MIT Press), pp. 216–271.

Russell, S. and Norvig, P. (2010). *Artificial intelligence: a modern approach*, Prentice Hall series in artificial intelligence (Prentice Hall), ISBN 9780136042594, URL http://books.google.pt/books?id=8jZBksh-bUMC.

Russell, S. J. and Norvig, P. (1995). *Artificial intelligemce: a modern approach* (Prentice-Hall).

Russell, S. J. and Norvig, P. (2003). *Artificial intelligemce: a modern approach*, 2nd edn. (Prentice-Hall).

Sakurai, Y., Yoshikawa, M., Uemura, S. and Kojima, H. (2002). Spatial indexing of high-dimensional data based on relative approximation, *VLDB Journal* **11**, 2, pp. 93–108.

Sandars, N. K. (Penguin). *The Epic of Gilgamesh (Penguin Epics)* (2006).

Santos, P., Galhardas, H. and Wichert, A. (2009). Panoramix: A content-based health record system, *Internal Journal of Computer Assisted Radiology and Surgery* **4**, p. 152.

Schwenker, F. (1996). Küntliche Neuronale Netze: Ein Überblick über die theoretischen Grundlagen, in G. Bol, G. Nakhaeizadeh and K. Vollmer (eds.), *Finanzmarktanalyse und -prognose mit innovativen und quantitativen Verfahren* (Physica-Verlag), pp. 1–14.

Shafer, G. (1976). *A Mathematical Theory of Evidence* (Princeton University Press, Princeton, NJ).

Shapiro, L. G. and Stockman, G. C. (2001). *Computer Vision* (Prentice Hall).

Smeulders, A., Worring, M., Santini, S., Gupta, A. and Jain, R. (2000). Content-based image retrieval at the end of the early years, *IEEE Transactions on Pattern Analysis and Machine Intelligence* **22**, 12, pp. 1349–1380.

Sommer, F. T. (1993). *Theorie neuronaler Assoziativspeicher*, Ph.D. thesis, Heinrich-Heine-Universität Düsseldorf, Düsseldorf.

Sommer, F. T. and Wichert, A. (eds.) (2002). *Exploratory analysis and data modeling in functional neuroimaging* (MIT Press, Boston MA).

Squire, L. R. and Kandel, E. R. (1999). *Memory. From Mind to Moleculus* (Scientific American Library).

Steinbuch, K. (1961). Die Lernmatrix, *Kybernetik* **1**, pp. 36–45.

Steinbuch, K. (1971). *Automat und Mensch*, 4th edn. (Springer-Verlag).

Stellmann, U. (1992). *Ähnlichkeitserhaltende Codierung*, Ph.D. thesis, Universität Ulm, Ulm.

Tarski, A. (1944). The semantic conception of truth and foundations of semantics, *Philos. and Phenom. Res.* **4**, pp. 241–376.

Tarski, A. (1956). *Logic, Semantics,Metamathematics* (Oxford University Press, London).

Tarski, A. (1995). *Pisma logiczno-filozoficzne. Prawda*, Vol. 1 (Wydawnictwo Naukowe PWN, Warszawa).

Topsoe, F. (1974). *Informationstheorie* (Teubner Sudienbucher).

van Hemmen, J. (1990). Hebbian learning and unlearning, in W. Theumann (ed.), *Neural Networks and Spin Glasses* (World Scientific), pp. 91–114.

W. Johnson, J. L. (1984). Extensions of lipschitz mappings into a hilbert space, in A. M. Society (ed.), *Contemp. Math*, Vol. 26, pp. 189–206.

Wang, J., Li, J. and Wiederhold, G. (2001). Simplicity: Semantics-sensitive integrated matching for picture libraries, *IEEE Transactions on Pattern Analysis and Machine Intelligence* **23**, 9, pp. 947–963.

Wang, J. Z., Wiederhold, G., Firschein, O. and Wei, S. X. (1997). Content-based image indexing and searching using daubechies wavelets, *International Journal on Digital Libraries* .

Wells, H. (1922). *A Short History Of The World* (Cassell & Co).

Wennekers, T. (1999). *Synchronisation und Assoziation in Neuronalen Netzen* (Shaker Verlag, Aachen).

Westerveld, T., Ianeva, T., Boldareva, L., de Vries, A. and Hiemstra, D. (2003). Combining information sources for video retrieval: The lowlands team at trecvid 2003, in *Proceedings of the 12th Text Retrieval Conference (TREC-12) Video Evaluation Workshop*.

Wichert, A. (1993). MTCn-nets, in *Proceedings World Congres on Neural Networks* (Lawrence Erlbaum), pp. 59–62.

Wichert, A. (2000). A categorical expert system "jurassic", *Expert Systems with Application* **19**, 3, pp. 149–158.

Wichert, A. (2008). Content-based image retrieval by hierarchical linear subspace method, *Journal of Intelligent Information Systems* **31**, 1, pp. 85–107.

Wichert, A. (2009a). Image categorization and retrieval, in J. Mayor, N. Ruh and K. Plunkett (eds.), *Proceedings of the 11th Neural Computation and Psychology Workshop* (World Scientific), pp. 117–128.

Wichert, A. (2009b). Sub-symbols and icons, *Cognitive Computation* **1**, 4, pp. 342–347.

Wichert, A. (2012). Product quantization for vector retrieval with no error, in ICEIS (ed.), *Proceeedings of International Conference on Enterprise Information Systems*, Vol. 1, pp. 87–92.

Wichert, A. (2013a). *Principles of Quantum Artificial Intelligence* (World Scientific).

Wichert, A. (2013b). Proto logic and neural subsymbolic reasoning, *Journal of Logic and Computation* **23**, 3, pp. 627–643.

Wichert, A., Abler, B., Grothe, J., Walter, H. and Sommer, F. T. (2002). Exploratory analysis of event-related fmri demonstrated in a working memory study, in F. Sommer and A. Wichert (eds.), *Exploratory analysis and data modeling in functional neuroimaging*, chap. 5 (MIT Press, Boston, MA), pp. 77–108.

Wichert, A. and Moreira, C. (2015). Projection based operators in lp space for exact similarity search, *Fundamenta Informaticae* **136**, 4, pp. 461–474.

Wichert, A. and Santos, P. (2010). Fast multimedia querying for medical applications, in C. Plant and C. Bohm (eds.), *Database Technology for Life Sciences and Medicine* (World Scientific), pp. 203–218.

Wichert, A., Teixeira, P., Santos, P. and Galhardas, H. (2010). Subspace tree: High dimensional multimedia indexing with logarithmic temporal complexity, *Journal of Intelligent Information Systems* **35**, 3, pp. 495–516.

Wichert, A. and Verissimo, A. (2012). Cbir with a subspacee-tree: Principal component analysis versus averaging, *Multimedia Systems* **18**, 4, pp. 283–293.

Wickelgren, W. A. (1969). Context-sensitive coding, associative memory, and serial order in (speech)behavior, *Psychological Review* **76**, pp. 1–15.

Wickelgren, W. A. (1977). *Cognitive Psychology* (Prentice-Hall).

Widrow, B. and Hoff, M. (1960). Adaptive switching circuits, *IRE WESCON Convention Record* **4**, pp. 96–104.

Widrow, B. and Hoff, M. (1962). Associative storage and retrieval of digital information in networks of adaptive 'neurons', *Biological Prototypes and Synthetic Systems* **1**, p. 160.

Willshaw, D., Buneman, O. and Longuet-Higgins, H. (1969). Nonholgraphic associative memory, *Nature* **222**, pp. 960–962.

Winston, P. H. (1992). *Artificial Intelligence*, 3rd edn. (Addison-Wesley).

Zhou, X., Zillner, S., Moeller, M., Sintek, M., Zhan, Y., Krishnan, A. and Gupta, A. (2008). Semantics and cbir: A medical imaging perspective, in *CIVR'08*, pp. 571–580.

Index

F_β measure, 280
Z-ordering, 156
ϵ-similar, 130
$\sigma(net)$, 243
k-means, 88, 239
l_p norm, 128, 195
n ball, 172
n-orthotope, 145
$tf.df$, 220
1-Lipschitz property, 183

AC difference, 38
activation function, 243
adaptive differential, 99
administrative task, 1
AI, 3
Alfred Tarski, 14
algebra of sets, 14
American Standard Code for
   Information Interchange (ASCII),
   19
approximate nearest neighbor, 173
artificial neuron (unit), 242
association, 232
associative memory, 231
auditory receptors (hair cells), 101

B-tree, 140
backpropagation, 250
Bag-of-Descriptors, 122
Bayes's rule, 223
belief, 272

BFILE, 27
bias, 244
big data, 276
binary search, 140
biological neuron, 243
bit rate (BR), 26
bit-shuffling, 158
BLOB, 27
Boolean logic, 15
Boolean queries, 215
brain, 3, 270
branching factor, 138

cave painting, 1
CBIR in medicine, 284
centered spectrum, 47
centroid, 88, 153
cerebral cortex, 231
chain rule, 251
children, 138
client-server system, 275
clinical information system (CIS), 281
CLOB, 27
clustering, 87
cochlea, 101
color histogram, 107
cons, 26
consonant, 126
content-based image retrieval
   (CBIR), 5, 28
content-based image retrieval by
   image pyramid, 200

content-based music retrieval, 28
content-based video retrieval, 28
context-sensitive letter units, 237
continuous activation function, 248
continuous walvelet transform
 (CWT), 57
contour, 112, 127
convolution, 71
cosine similarity, 129, 219, 241
covariance, 79
covariance matrix, 80
critical band, 101
cross-validation, 255
curse of dimensionality, 154, 171, 181

data link, 27
database architecture, 275
database management systems
 (DBMS), 13
Daubechies wavelet, 68
decibels (dB), 100
decoupled search tree, 139
deep belief networks, 266
deep learning, 258
Dempster-Shafer theory, 272
DFT matrix, 41
DICOM, 282
differential encoding, 92
discrete wavelet transformation
 (DWT), 62
Discrete cosine transform (DCT), 44
discrete Fourier transform (DFT), 37
distance, 128
divide and conquer, 276
document frequency, 219
dot product, 242
Dublin core, 32
dynamic programming, 132
dynamic time warping, 131

early fusion, 270
edge, 138
edge detection, 109
eigenvalue, 83
eigenvector, 83
electronic health record, 282

electronic patient record (EHR), 281
error surface, 246
Euclidean distance, 129
Euclidean metric, 129
Euclidean norm, 129
exact indexing, 181
EXIF, 32
expert system, 17

Faloutsos, Christos, 182
fast Fourier transform (FFT), 40
fast wavelet transform (FWT), 70
features, 28, 105
feed-forward network, 249
filter, 40
firing, 243
first-order logic, 14
format frequencies, 125
Fourier transform, 36
fractal dimension, 167
fractals, 158
frame, 101
frames, 16
frames per second (FPS), 26
frequency masking, 101
fundamental frequency, 125

Gauss, Carl Friedrich, 40
Gaussian (normal) distribution , 210
Gaussian blur, 113
Gaussian filter, 113
generic multimedia indexing
 (GEMINI), 182
geons, 123
GIST, 123
gradient descent, 245
Gray code, 163
group of pictures (GOP), 102

H.261, 103
Haar transformation matrix, 65
Haar's mother wavelet, 62
Hadoop, 277
harmonic mean, 280
Hausdorff dimension, 167
Hausdorff, Felix, 168

Health Level Seven (HL7), 281
hertz (Hz), 23
Hessian matrix, 120
heteroassociation, 232
hidden units, 249
hierarchical quantization, 264
Hilbert curve, 161
Hilbert, David, 167
histogram, 105
hospital information system (HIS),
 281
Huffman code, 96
human ear, 100
human learning, 239

I-frame, 102
ID3, 32
image pyramid, 113
image signature, 29
inference engine, 17
information, 94
instantiationed, 18
inverse document frequency (idf), 220
inverse Fourier transform, 37
inverted index, 92

Johnson-Lindenstrauss lemma, 177,
 221
JPEG, 96

Karhunen-Loève transform, 83, 203
kd-tree, 142
kernel machine, 257
kernel trick, 254
keypoint, 121
knowledge base, 17
knowledge base management system,
 18
Kolmogorov's axioms, 222

Laplace operator, 118
late fusion, 270
law of total probability, 223, 230
leaf, 138
learning teacher, 239
learning without a teacher, 239

left skewed, 210
Lempel-Ziv (LZ), 93
Lempel-Ziv-Welsh (LZW), 93
Lernmatrix, 231
linear threshold unit (LTU), 243
linearly separable, 245
local minima, 252
locality-sensitive hash, 173
locality-sensitive hashing (LSH), 171
lossless compression, 91
lossy compression, 96
lower bounding lemma, 183

machine learning , 239
map transformation cascade (MTC),
 258
MapReduce, 276
matadata, 32
maximum posteriori hypothesis, 224
mean squared error, 240
memoization, 132
Mesopotamia, 1
message alphabet, 93
metric, 128
metric index, 147
Mexican hat wavelet, 59
min-max normalization, 130
minimum bounding rectangles
 (MBR), 147
Minsky, Marvin, 17
modality, 269
Morlet hat wavelet, 59
Morse code, 93
mother wavelet, 58
moving JPEG, 102
MP3, 103
MPEG-1, 103
MPEG-2, 103
MPEG-21, 33, 104
MPEG-3, 104
MPEG-4, 104
MPEG-7, 32, 104
multimedia extender, 27
multimodal search, 269

Naïve Bayes classifier, 222

negatively skewed, 210
Neocognitron, 258
NN-similar, 130
node, 138
non linear continuous function, 243
non liner transfer function, 242
nonlinear units, 249
Nyquist theorem, 23

object database, 17
orthogonal complement, 188
orthogonal projection, 189
overfitting, 240

P-frame, 102
PACS, 282
Panoramix, 283
parallel nodes, 276
parent, 138
PCA, 203
Peano, Giuseppe, 167
peer-to-peer (P2P), 276
Perceptron, 243
perceptual encoders, 100
perceptual features, 96
phoneme, 125
pipeline, 277
pixel, 106
pixel depth, 22, 106
plain text, 19
pointer coding, 92, 217
polar coordinates, 127
positively skewed, 210
precision, 279
predicate, 14
prefix property, 96
principal component analysis (PCA), 84
product quantization, 178
projection operator, 188

QBIC, 29

R-tree, 147
radial basis function network (RBF), 252

random projection, 221
raster graphics, 21
recall, 279
relational database, 2, 14
relevance of a document, 226
restricted Boltzmann machine (RBM), 266
retina, 26
retrieval status RSV, 228
RGB, 22, 106
RGB color space, 26
right skewed, 210
rods, 26
root, 138
Rosenblatt, Frank, 243
run-length encoding (RLE), 92

sampling frequency, 23
scale function, 62
scale space, 116
scale-invariant feature transform (SIFT), 116
scaled RGB images, 108, 185
scalogram, 58
search tree, 138
semantic gap, 31
semantic nets, 16
sensitivity of the ear, 100
set of descriptor vectors, 122
Shannon's formula of entropy, 94
short-term Fourier transform (STFT), 54
Sierpinski triangle, 167
signal alphabet, 93
similarity function, 129
snake curve, 156
Sobel operator , 110
soft margin method, 257
space-filling curve, 157
sparse representation, 210
sphere, 172
SQL:1999, 17
stationary signals, 53
stochastic gradient descent, 248
stochastic language model, 230, 271

Structured Query Language (SQL), 13, 15
sub-band coding, 99
subglottal air pressure, 125
subpattern matching, 285
subspace tree, 198
subsymbolical representation, 3
supervised learning, 239
support vector machine (SVM), 256
supralaryngeal vocal tract, 124
surprise of a message, 94
symbol, 2, 14

taxonomy, 133
Taylor expansion, 119
Tedd Codd, 13
temporal masking, 101
term, 215
term frequency (tf), 218
texels, 108
texture, 108
threshold, 234
tokenization, 217
transform encoding, 91

two dimensional Haar's mother wavelet, 77
two dimensional transform, 45

Uniicode, 19
unlabelled data, 239
unsupervised learning, 89, 239
UTF-16, 19
UTF-8, 19

vector graphics, 21
VGA, 21
video, 24
vocal tract, 125
vowel, 126
voxel, 22

wavelength , 36
Wickelfeature, 237
word frequency (wf), 219

YCbCr color space, 26

Z-score normalization, 129

Printed in the United States
By Bookmasters